THE GRUBBS OF TIPPERARY

Studies in Heredity and Character

GEOFFREY WATKINS GRUBB, M.A. (Oxon.), F.R.N.S.

THE MERCIER PRESS, BRIDGE STREET, CORK, IRELAND

1972

A*

THE GRUBBS OF TIPPERARY

Nec Aspera Terrent

Motto of the Grubenhagen Line of the Dukes of Brunswick

To

My Brother

(Major Ralph Ernest Watkins Grubb, M.A. (CANTAB), F.R.I.C.S., C.C.)

and my Cousin

(Lt.-Colonel Alexander James Watkins Grubb, R.A., J.P.)

to mark their Appointments as

HER MAJESTY'S HIGH SHERIFFS

for the Counties of SUSSEX and CHESHIRE

respectively

for the Year

1972

Difficulties neither daunt nor deter them

They follow after—

Henricvs von Grubbe   EARL MARSHAL of Saxony, 1040 A.D.

    His descendants of—

The Grubenhagen Line   EARL MARSHALS of Brunswick,
1279–1496

Thomas Judkin Fitzgerald (of the Geraldine Line)
HIGH SHERIFF of County Tipperary, 1798

Samuel Thomas Grubb   HIGH SHERIFF of County Waterford, 1863

Henry Samuel Grubb   HIGH SHERIFF of County Tipperary, 1887

Louis Henry Grubb, M.A. HIGH SHERIFF of County Tipperary, 1897

Samuel Richard Grubb   HIGH SHERIFF of County Tipperary, 1914

SBN 85342 289 3

Published by
THE MERCIER PRESS, 4 BRIDGE STREET, CORK, IRELAND

and printed by
THE DEVONSHIRE PRESS, TORQUAY, ENGLAND

PREFACE

*I*T'S *a Long Way to Tipperary.* In Russia today this popular song of
World War I is often played in honour of visiting English *and*
Irish people. It is regarded as particularly representing Great Britian,
as in England the *Volga Boat Song* is thought of as representing Russia.
Thousands still thrill to hear it. Fortunate indeed are those who have
their homes in this largest, oldest, and most fertile of the 26 Counties,
often called "The Devonshire of Ireland". The Grubbs have lived and
worked there for the past three hundred years. They built mills along
the banks of the beautiful River Suir (pronounced *Shure*, never *Sewer*)
from Clonmel, one of the most flourishing towns in Munster and one of
the capitals of the County, up to Cahir and Clogheen (pronounced *Care*
and *Cloheen*) under the shadows of the Knockmealdown Mountains
(pronounced *Knock-me-down*). During the early nineteenth century 60
Grubbs could regularly be seen out hunting together in the Golden Vale
of Tipperary. If it is a long way to Tipperary, I hope these pages may
bring it nearer.

Ireland has produced saints and scholars, great soldiers and sailors,
lucid writers, brilliant orators—and devils. Wrote Sean O'Casey—
"Irish History began in a mist, and has grown into a sun, and has sent
through her children a gay green beam to the four quarters of the world."

The GRUBBS OF TIPPERARY have helped to reflect that "gay green
beam" in America and Canada, Australia and New Zealand, South
Africa, South America and Congo. Ordinary men and women for the
most part, with a strong family spirit, they are typical of the great mass of
ordinary men and women the world over, from whom occasionally the
outstandingly great man or woman is born; faithful followers of that
which they believe in, rather than among the famous whose praise is in
the history book. In County Tipperary they flourished through their
industry and multiplied through their Quaker faith, in a century and a half
when it was forbidden them to marry outside Quakerism. Large families
were the aim of Irish parents, be they Roman Catholics or Protestants.
Family planning was unknown. "When Irish eyes are smiling," stirring
is the attractive beauty of Irish women.

The history of the Grubbs illustrates a great principle of human life,
that families and peoples not content to let time pass them by, or to relapse
into decline *must choose* at some time whether to strike out a new path, or
let events overwhelm them. From Germany to England: to settle in Ireland

vii

after the Civil War in 1656: to cross the Atlantic to the American Colonies in a sailing boat, and return: to put down roots at Clonmel, and pull them up again for Clogheen and then Cahir: to leave Ireland for army and missionary lives, some to return again to the land of their fathers—so unfolds the history of my family in the following chapters. My object is not merely to interest posterity in their activities and travels, or to preserve family records from oblivion, but rather through their lives and characters to discover the foundation of rock from whence they were hewn, about which the storms of controversy, and the tempests of sorrow and misfortune rage and beat in vain. To discover that "something in their blood" which we call heredity, in the same way as men speak of "Royal Blood" which distinguishes the Royal Family from every commoner. To discover finally the varying ways and means by which the Guidance of God was made known to them.

I have tried to reclothe our ancestors with flesh and blood, to show what they owed to their German and supposedly Danish origins, to the Castles which so often formed a background to their lives, to their business and Anabaptist life in the English Midlands, to their later Quaker faith and the influence of John Wesley, Mystic writers and Hymnody upon them: to the Authorised Version of the Bible and their inherent love of reading and flair for languages, to boarding school education at Ballitore in County Kildare (after 1760), and at Wellington College in Berkshire (after 1880), Rugby and Marlborough: to an ease of speech and friendliness and an innate Irish individualism and gaiety, to a confidence and self-assurance, not always consistent with Quaker humility, which hard work and money gave them; to gynocracy and the dominant and efficient influence of their respective and respected wives, and above all to the controlling Hand of God.

Inconsistent as all Irishmen are said to be at times, and for that matter Englishmen also, and individualists, there stands out a common denominator in generation after generation of the Family, which readers of the two most recent Grubb Biographies—those of Norman Grubb, M.C., Missionary and Author [*Once Caught; No Escape* (1969)] and his brother, Sir Kenneth Grubb, K.C.M.G., LL.B., for 25 years President of the Church Missionary Society (of which their father had been a Secretary), and an expert upon ecumenical relations [*Crypts of Power* (1971)] will not fail to recognise.

The marriage of Henry VIII to Anne of Cleves; Quaker and Church weddings; the social history of Ireland; the Irish Settlements and rebellions; the Irish milling industry—in their heyday the Grubbs owned 17 mills along the River Suir, from "Anners" (famous for its trout stream) on the Waterford side of Clonmel up to Clogheen and Cahir; tours of Grubb "Public Friends" in Ireland and on the Continent; methods of travel; horseriding; and sea voyages to America, Ceylon, and up the newly opened Suez Canal—such and other formative backcloths in the lives of the Grubbs may not prove without interest to the general reader. Great Britain owes more than is often today remembered, with the constant influx of immigrants, to its old and established families. In an increasingly "permissive society", the grand heritage of strong and reliable Christian families that *both* Britain *and* Ireland possess, is the greatest contribution they can make now either to the Commonwealth or to Europe.

Because I am frequently asked for information about other branches of the Grubb stock to my own, and about the Grubbs in America and Canada where there has existed for a long time a "Grubb Family Association", I have added at the end of each chapter a Collateral Table, endeavouring to keep the typescript as free as possible of sidelines and dull family dates. I am conscious of gaps which still exist in the long family history, and in Chapter Three I have included an essay in Historical Research.

If two views are to be found of some of the characters I have depicted, or statements I have made, I can only plead that this is to be expected in Ireland, where two views are to be found on practically everything.

Wheatridge Lodge,
Torquay.   *St. Patrick's Day, 1972.*

ACKNOWLEDGEMENTS

My gratitude is abundantly due to my Cousin, S. L. Grubb, Esq., M.A., of Beechmount, Fethard, County Tipperary, for making available to me the results of much research by previous generations in the many MSS. and books which have come into his possession, forming the essential basis to this present work, and for much hospitality and information, when I have been in Ireland. Likewise to the many books on the Irish Quakers by another Cousin, Dr. Isabel Grubb, M.A. of Carrick-on-Suir and Waterford; my indebtedness is revealed on many pages. The helpfulness of the Torbay Library Service in obtaining for me many books of reference from Libraries all over the country is also gratefully acknowledged, and the kindness of very many correspondents. Among them I should especially mention Mrs. M. E. Grubb, of Ross-on-Wye; Mrs. Hunt-Grubbe of Potterne, Wiltshire; the late Col. and Mrs. Raymond Grubb of Castle Grace, Co. Tipperary; Dr. E. A. Payne, C.H., President of the Baptist Historical Society; the Rev. Thos. Shaw of St. Keverne; the Vicars of Ravensthorpe, Potterne, and Stoke-Climsland in Cornwall; Herr Klaus Jebens of Hamburg and Annaghs Castle, Co. Kilkenny; W. Hubert Poole, Esq., of Cahir; John MacConville, Esq. of Clonmel and Eleanor Fairburn, whose books and broadcasts have helped to set me on the right trail. I am also indebted to the Keepers or Curators of the Archives or Record Offices at Copenhagen; Malmo; and Northampton; the Methodist Archives and Research Dept.; the Y.M. Quaker Historical Library in Dublin and the Harleian MSS. at the British Museum. Also to Tony Durston, Esq., Geography Master of Audley Park School, Torquay, for drawing the maps, and to Messrs. Scott-Galloway of Torquay for the photographs of my coins. Above all to my wife, quick and observant, who nearly forty years ago was content to change her name from that of one of the fastest of creatures, to become a Grubb, without whose understanding and encouragement this book could never have seen daylight. I am alone responsible for any mistakes, and have provided two pages of addenda at the end of the book, on which any omissions may be recorded.

CONTENTS

CONTENTS

MAPS

REPRODUCTIONS

COLLATERAL TABLES

ILLUSTRATIONS

xvii

ILLUSTRATIONS

To face page

To face page

NOTES

upon

PLATE II

THE VON GRUBBES' CASTLE IN THE HARTZ MOUNTAINS

Burg Grubenhagen im Mittlelalter

GRUBE aus EINBECK

der Haupstadt des chemaligen Fürstentums Grubenhagen

From an original print in the possession of Robert Hunt-Grubbe, M.A. of
Eastwell, Potterne, Devizes.

CHAPTER ONE

Castles and Character

CASTLES, forts, strongholds, are the earliest form of community life and later of city life. They were fashioned by primitive man for security and protection, because he was fearful and afraid before ever he became courageous. Fearful of marauding animals, fearful of the storms and lightning, fearful of what other men or tribes might do to him; so he tried to shut himself in. To obtain what they thought was security, our earliest ancestors had to erect barricades and fences to separate themselves from others. The emotion of fear precedes the emotion of courage. Courage is the overcoming of fear.

It was natural that those inside the castle, the fort, or the stronghold, being separated from all outside, should become knit together into the closest of families. They depended upon one another; they intermarried one with another, for they had no other choice. They belonged to one another and inside their fortress they became a strong and united family. Ever after its members and descendants looked back to their castle as their place of origin. It had fashioned their characters, protected them, and given them confidence over their earliest fears.

The life of the Chosen People began in an enclosed strong ship or Ark, constructed by Divine Command to give them protection from the Flood. It was later to be continued in the " Stronghold or Castle of David " on Mount Zion.[1] The Castle of David became the City of David. An object of true religion throughout the centuries is that men should build again Jerusalem and find fellowship and peace within its walls. The Bible emphasises that King Jotham, one of David's successors, "did right, because he built much: he built cities in the mountains and in the forests he built castles and towers".[2]

Centuries passed, and the first to bear the surname Grubb or Grubbe or Von Grubbe, inspired perhaps by this Old Testament passage, copied Jotham's example. Among the forests of the Hartz Mountains of Brunswick in North Germany, he built the schloss or castle of the Grubbes, whose ruined tower still stands above the trees. (*See* Chapter Two.) Here generations of Grubbes were born. Outward and forward-looking

---

[1] II Samuel v. 7; I Chronicles xi, 7.
[2] II Chronicles xxvii, 4.

character was being formed in the building of castles and towers pointing heavenwards.

The earliest European castles were really fortresses of earth, deeply fossed and crowned with a pallisade and tower of timber; they consisted of a high flat-roofed mound, surrounded by a deep ditch or moat or fosse. Great stone castles with keep and bailey and drawbridges came with the Normans.[3] One such castle became the Grubbe's first home in Ireland.

The arms of the Grubbe family have been identified on the walls of the Castle of Malmo, across the Sound from Copenhagen, owned by Sigvardus von Grubbe (1566–1636). One of his descendants built the first European fort or citadel in Ceylon.[4]

The very name Grubb originally meant " one who grubs in the ground " whether as a miner, or to throw up ramparts and castles, or even burial mounds. The long history of the Grubbs shows their attraction to castles. John Grubbe of Ravensthorpe, an Anabaptist preacher in Puritan England, spent his earlier years seeking to draw men within the walls of salvation: he served in the Roundhead army under Oliver Cromwell at the Battle of Naseby, and as a reward for his services was offered by the Protector on his resettlement of Ireland one of its 3,000 castles. Annaghs Castle on the River Barrow in County Kilkenny, four miles from New Ross, was his first home in Ireland. When the family became Quakers, they yet chose to live under the security of the old walls and castle of Clonmel, capital of County Tipperary, for over 100 years. At the turn of the 19th century they moved some 15 miles to Clogheen under the shadow and protection of the Knockmealdown Mountains, where a branch of the family have continued to this day in the ownership of Castle Grace, once known as Castle Le Gros, with its well-preserved castle ruins.

Castle Grace was built by the Anglo-Norman knight Raymond (Le Gros) Fitzgerald of Carew, nephew of Maurice Fitzgerald and a brother-in-law of Earl Strongbow, leaders of the "Geraldine" invasion of Ireland from Wales in 1169, of which he was the popular commander. He was nicknamed "Le Gros" (the original name of the castle) on account of his excessive girth and bulk, and made up for his heaviness of body by his lightheartedness and gaity.[5] He was a grandson of the beautiful Welsh Princess Nesta of Degeubarth, descendant of the near-legendary kings of South Wales, a mistress of King Henry I, mother of Robert of Gloucester,[6] and wife of Gerald de Windsor, a Norman Knight, Castellan of Pembroke Castle. He built Castle Grace (Le Gros) to secure one of the entrances into

---

[3] *Irish Castles* by H. G. Leaske.

[4] *Dansk Biografisk Leksikon*, pt. viii., pp. 344–346 (Kobenhavn MCMXXXVI) and *Adels Aarbog*, pt. xii (1895), p. 163.

[5] *The Geraldines* by Brian FitzGerald, pp. 38–40, 58–65. *A History of Ireland*, by Professor E. Curtis, pp. 50, 58, and 122.

[6] See the charming story of the Princess Nesta and her family in the *Golden Hive* by Eleanor Fairburn (Heinemanns).

PLATE III

CASTLE GRACE, CLOGHEEN, Co. TIPPERARY

Originally known as CASTLE LE GROS

The twelfth century Anglo-Norman castle, built by Raymond Le Gros 1186 A.D.

IRISH SILVER GROATS used at the Castle in Henry VIII's reign

*The first coinage to bear the Harp of Ireland. On either side the initial of
Henry VIII (H), and of his first three wives (K: A: J)*

1	2	3	4
Obverse	H – K	H – A	H – J
The Royal Arms	Henry VIII and	Henry VIII and	Henry VIII and
of England	Katherine of Aragon	Ann Boleyn	Jane Seymour

From the Author's Collection

County Tipperary across the high mountains from the south, and modelled it on Pembroke. Wherever the mail-clad Norman knights secured a firm foothold in Ireland, they raised a castle. The rapid and general castellation of the conquered parts of the country was a chief cause of the Norman and Geraldine success. The 3,000 or more Irish castles, most of them now in ruins, cannot be over-estimated in the formation of Irish character, and the later characters of the Grubb family. No one has the desire, or money, to demolish them.

Could the walls of Castle Grace but speak to tell how frequently the castle changed hands in the constant fighting in turbulent Ireland between the Earls of Desmond and of Kildare, and the large Butler family who became Earls of Ormonde, and Lords of County Tipperary; of its gorgeous new chatelaine early in the sixteenth century; and of that famous Countess of Desmond, who lived to the ripe old age of 147 years, and whose promising career was only ended by a fall from a cherry tree she had climbed one morning before the servants were up, to pick and enjoy the finest fruit and save it from the birds; the story these walls could unfold might obviate the need for further research by the generations to come!

At Cahir Abbey, but ten miles from Castle Grace (the very name of the town means " a stronghold "), lived the senior branch of the Grubbs of Tipperary in the 19th century, within view of its outstanding Norman castle, home of the Butler family. Here their tenure of the pacifist views of the Quakers ended. From Cahir went forth the first soldier in the family since Oliver Cromwell's time, to fight in the Maori Wars, to demolish ancient citadels in Ceylon, to serve under the bastion of Malta G.C. and of the Danish castle at Wicklow, and to buy a castle in Kent overlooking the Thames on his retirement from the army. His eldest son spent many years of his army life in developing the use of balloons, the "castles of the air".

Out of date in a world of United Nations, Ecumenicism, and the Common Market, castles form a not unsuitable structure to consider the conservatism, the courage, and the constructiveness in the Grubb lineage. They explain the assurance and confidence found in every generation, the disciplines and tenacity in their lives, their strivings for social and religious reform, their intrepid missionary attacks on the powers of evil, their faithful perseverance. Castles have seemed throughout the ages to speak to the Grubbs of the constant need for watchfulness, if they would know security, of the lookout and sentry's duty, to be ever ready to meet whatever may come, and the unexpected; in a word— *of activity.*

Whatever their faults, and we have them, the Grubbs have never been characterised by idleness and *laissez-faire*; impetuosity perhaps, eagerness and enthusiasms, at times an almost crusading spirit to right the wrongs of

3

the world, in which inventiveness and ingenuity have frequently been manifest. If during the 150 years that they were Quakers, they seemed to shut themselves within the fence and castle of Quaker separateness, yet they have sallied forth as good soldiers of their Master in Heaven to undermine and break up new ground for the Kingdom of God, to serve their country in times of war as soldiers and sailors and steadily to do their duty as inheritors of great opportunities, and members of a good and long-established family to which they are proud to belong. The Grubb family owes much to its castle origins. Succeeding chapters illustrate the close connection of castles with character.

CHAPTER TWO

"In Search of Origins."

" As unknown, and yet well known."

THE origins of the Grubbs of Tipperary lay in North Germany, and earlier still, as the family have believed, in Scandinavia. They look back to Danish princes, German judges and landowners, and to Dukes of Brunswick among their ancestors on the paternal side; and to a Scottish Queen, the Princess Nesta of Wales and her legendary Welsh royal ancestors, and to the Butler family, descendants of the Irish Earls of Ormonde, as well as to the well-known Quaker families of the Shackletons, Greers, and Haughtons on their maternal side.

THE GERMAN VON GRUBBES

(i) In the Hartz Mountains in Brunswick in North Germany, near Einbeck, stood the impregnable castle or schloss of the Von Grubbe family, some 40 miles south of "Hamelin's Town in Brunswick," of which only its 258-metre-high tower (above sea-level), rising majestically above the trees, remains today. It stands 17·2 metres high, with 160 steps leading to its parapet. Largely hidden from view in the valley below by the giant conifers of the hillside, this huge stone mass of frowning towers, small windows, parapets and dungeons would have seemed from a distance to be but part of the overhanging crag. It could only be approached by a steep climb through the forests surrounding and below it. It was the headquarters for more than four centuries of the senior line of the descendants of Henricvs Von Grubbe, who in 1040 A.D. held sway as Sovereign Lord of the Principality of Brittore, and Earl Marshal to King Conrad I of Saxony. He was succeeded by his eldest son and grandson as Earl Marshals to Kings Conrad II and Henry the Lion of Saxony, an office which the head of the family continued to hold, and later to Dukes of Brunswick. They were to prove themselves wise counsellors and patient, if austere, judges in an hereditary system, comparable perhaps to that of Lord Chancellor in mediaeval England. In the fifteenth century Johanan Von Grubbe owned vast territories and villages over the mountains and surrounding valleys, known as *the Principality of Grubenhagen*. He was an intimate friend, as well as Chief Justice to Duke Otto of Brunswick with whose family the Von Grubbes had intermarried, forming the

5

GRUBENHAGEN LINE of the Brunswick Duchies (1279–1496), of which he was head. Some of the Von Grubbes are said to have become Protestants through the preaching of John Huss,[1] a disciple of John Wycliffe, and as a result of the consequent persecutions of the Hussites, to have migrated into England about 1440 and settled near Lutterworth on the Leicestershire-Northamptonshire border. Johanan himself remained a Catholic, and endowed a *Marian* Monastery, perhaps in reparation for the Protestantism of his relatives, and where he is said to have been buried. His huge properties passed gradually, whether by intermarriage or by gift or sale, into the hands of the Dukes of Brunswick. These properties included his gold and silver mines throughout the Hartz area, chief source of the wealth of his family, and later of the Dukedom of Brunswick. The very name Grube or Grubbe means " a miner " or " a possessor of mines " and owes its derivation to the Hartz Mountains, always prolific in mines. An interesting collection of some dozen Grube talers, minted at the Lauthenhals, Cronenburge, Regensbogen, and Bleyfelt mines in those mountains has been assembled by the author of this book. Little wonder is it that the present generation of Grubbs, with their German origin, have not been numbered among the opponents of the policy of the present and former English government, of going into Europe and the Common Market.

The complicated history of the Brunswick Duchies began in 1225 A.D. with the constitution of "Otto the Boy" of the Welf Family (in Italy the Guelph or Gheradini families who spread into Saxony and Poland) as first Duke of Brunswick, by the reigning King of Saxony, from whose vast domains the new Duchy was carved out. On Otto's death his two sons divided his territories into the Duchy of Brunswick, and the Duchy of Luneburg (which became extinct in 1369). Intermarriage with the Von Grubbes was a prime cause for the further sub-division of the Brunswick Duchy in 1279, on the death of their father, by his three children into the lines of GRUBENHAGEN, Gottingen, and Brunswick. The Grubenhagen line existed from 1279–1496. The Gottingen survived from 1279–1437. A grandson of the first Gottingen Duke, Magnus II "of the chain" inherited the extinct Luneburg duchy, and after a number of amalgamations and further sub-divisions, by 1635 the Brunswick-Danenburg line emerged in the new house of Brunswick-Wolfenbuttel. The Brunswick-Celle line, which included the old Grubenhagen line, added Hanover to its titles, and eventually passed to Ernst (*or Ernest*) Augustus, the first Elector of Hanover, Duke of Brunswick-Luneburg-Celle, and son-in-law of the Princess Elizabeth of England; his son George Ludwig (*Louis*) succeeded to the throne of England, Ireland,

---

[1] *The life of Edward Grubb* by James Dudley. (1946) p. 18.

and France (*sic*) in 1714 on the death of Queen Anne, but preferred to continue living in Hanover and Brunswick.[2]

The science of genealogy has shown that it is highly uncommon for any family tree to rise from a traceable ancestor much before the year 1538, when in the reign of King Henry VIII the keeping of registers of christenings, marriages and burials in every parish was ordered by the King's vicar-general Thomas Cromwell.[3]

A persistent tradition however, going back in the family more than 100 years,[4] points to the arrival in Ireland in the 16th century of a granddaughter of the Duke of Brunswick and Johanan Von Grubbe, as the link between the German and Irish Grubbs. Her name in the manuscript was given as *Annie Winthrop*. This is so un-Germanic a name that it must surely be a misreading of early faded writing for Anne Von Grubbe. Phonetically the *gr*, *kr*, and *thr* gutterals spring from the same root, and the Krupp family of Essen are also descended from the Von Grubbes of the Hartz Mountains. Who in their senses would invent such a name as Annie Winthrop as the ancestress of the Irish Grubbs?

Historical research yields many surprises. More fascinating than many mystery novels has been the investigation into the origin and output of this mysterious Annie or Anne Von Grubbe (or Winthrop). It seemed there were four clues or hypotheses that could be followed in this early Grubb tradition:

(i) The whole later history of the family shows the influence and power of gynocracy in the generations; it would take a very outstanding woman to travel from Germany into turbulent Ireland in the reign of Henry VII, and following the Wars of the Roses.

(ii) Not in a cottage or cabin, but in the home of Irish aristocracy— and this would mean a castle—would the granddaughter of the Brunswick Dukedom and Johanan Von Grubbe be likely to have lived in Ireland.

(iii) That a husband's name is not given, must mean that Annie was unmarried (or a widow) on her arrival in Ireland.

(iv) That there must have been some good purpose to account for her arrival. She would not have made this difficult journey for fun!

A pointer to the solution of the mystery, if not the answer, is to be found in a broadcast over *Radio Eireann* in 1965, although its significance escaped

[2] See further: *German Talers, 1700–1800* by J. S. Davenport (1965), p. 65ff. *Note.—* The Frequent occurrence of the Christian names Ernest and Louis among the Grubbs of Tipperary.
[3] *Shield and Crest. An Account of the science of Heraldry.* Julian Franklyn. (1960). Macgibben & Kee. London. p. 373ff.
[4] Researches of the late Seymour Grubb and others, and MSs now in possession of S. L. Grubb, Esq., of Beechmount, Fethard, Co. Tipperary.

notice at the time, on the history of Castle Grace, Clogheen, in County Tipperary, the home since 1820 of a branch of the Grubb family.[5]

The relevant part is quoted *in exteuso*:

> "Castle Grace was a typical Norman stronghold; towers that bulged at the base, so that unwelcome visitors could be put off by throwing boiling water over them; arrow slits for cross-bows, which in Norman times were the latest thing in deadly weapons; in fact every modern convenience for defence was incorporated into the building. After the initial fighting Raymond Le Gros (the castle's builder) and his fellow Normans appear to have settled down, and to have inter-married with the local people. No more is heard of them at Castle Grace until the 16th century, when the chatelaine of the Castle was a very gorgeous girl called Alice, or Elice, who was presumably a descendant of Le Gros. She married a man called Piers Butler, whose grandfather was the Earl of Ormonde, and the castle passed into the hands of the Butler family; Piers Butler was created Baron of Cahir by King Henry VIII in 1543. A hundred and eleven years later the Cromwellian Survey of 1654–56 shows the proprietor as Thomas, Lord Baron of Cahir, and the lands contained 1,420 plantation acres."

In a land of beautiful girls, the epithet " a very gorgeous girl " suggests someone very much out of the run even of Ireland's lovely girls—a fair German blonde might be so described. Her appearance as the new chatelaine of Castle Grace *at exactly the same time* as Anne Von Grubbe (or Annie Winthrop) arrived in Ireland, together with the expressive phrase "presumably a descendant of Le Gros" lends additional force to the identification of Anne with Alice (or Elice) and also provides a reason for her arrival from Germany. The Geraldine family to which Le Gros, belonged, originated in Florence as the Gherardini,[6] were very wealthy, and served as consuls of the Republic. At different times members emigrated into Poland and Saxony, and into Normandy, and thence to England and Wales, where Gerald de Windsor married the beautiful Princess Nesta, whose grandson was Raymond Le Gros. The Dukes of Brunswick (and therefore Annie Winthrop) sprang from the same family (*page 6*). John MacConville, author of the broadcast, is good enough to agree with the likelihood of the identification. It leaves three loose ends to be tied up, that Anne and Alice were the same person, and that one of these Christian names (both were to become very common among the Grubbs in succeeding generations) was a misreading of the other that had probably become quite undecipherable in the original, save for the opening capital letter A. Secondly, that in feudal Ireland, when castles quickly changed hands, were conquered and re-conquered, MacConville's qualified " presumably a descendant of Le Gros " should read "Next of kin". Thirdly, that the evidence is found conclusive (*see Burke's Landed Gentry*

---

[5] Broadcast by John MacConville, Esq., March 23rd 1965. Radio Eireann.
[6] *The Geraldines.* Brian Fitzgerald. Staples Press. pp. 15ff. See also his references to Garamurini's *Account of Ancient Families of Tuscany and Umbria* (1671).

of Ireland), as the Irish Grubbs believe it to be, that Elice or Eme Butler, the daughter of Piers Butler, and his "gorgeous" wife, and great-grand-daughter of the Earl of Ormonde, was the same Elice or Eme Butler who married a Richard Grubbe at Ravensthorpe in 1540 (*see p. 15*). She had been brought up, like so many members of the Irish aristocracy (when it was the custom for children of noble birth to be educated in great households) at the court of Henry VIII.

SCANDINAVIAN GRUBBES

(ii) The earliest derivation of the name Grubb is said to come from the Danish " NEB," which means a prince. A tradition has been current in Ireland among the " Castle Grace " branch of the Grubb family, that among the Viking princes who led the invasion of Ireland long before the time William the Conqueror came from Normandy to invade England, were a number of Danish " Nebs " (sometimes called " Nibs ") or Grubbs who settled there, and built themselves castles and homesteads. As a boy at school at Ballitore in County Kildare, Samuel Grubb, father of the Castle Grace Grubbs, and in his time a learned man and wide reader (*see Chapter Seven*), had been present at the discovery of a little sepulchre at the top of Max's Hill, a few miles from his school, which contained the skeleton of a young man. A thorough examination of the bones and surroundings was carried out by an expert, Dr. Bell, and proved the skeleton to have been that of one of the Danish prince-invaders.[7] Nicholas Mansergh, in his book " Britain and Ireland," tells of the Tipperary farmer who described to him in detail and with complete accuracy how the Danes built their elaborate burial mounds; he stated quite casually that the information had been handed down in his family, generation after generation, by a remote ancestor who had actually *seen* these Danish Vikings at work. Dramatic incidents such as this colour and thrive on the Irish temperament! It is undoubted that the name Grubbe, meaning " one who grubbed in the earth," (a " miner " in Germany), also signified " one who dug graves in the earth," and so a burial mound builder, as well as a castle builder.

From the reign of King Canute, there was continued contact across the North Sea between Denmark and mediaeval England. The late Judge Ignatius Cooper Grubb, Doctor of Laws, of the Supreme Court of Delaware, U.S.A. (1841–1926), on one of his numerous trips to Denmark and England in the late nineteenth century, discovered around 1200 A.D. an early Danish Grubbe migrated to England, named Valte (or Walter) who established a shipping fleet between Denmark and London on riverside property he acquired on the Essex bank of the Thames. The later "Grub Street " was so named after this first Grubbe owner of the property through which the street ran. The family was connected with the Danish Royal House.

The arms of the Grubbe family in Denmark have been identified (*sic*) on the east wall of the Danish castle at Malmo which lies across the Sound from Copenhagen, and is now in Sweden. The castle was owned in the sixteenth century by Sigvard or Sivert (he wrote himself Sigvordt) Grubbe (1556–1636)[8], Confidential Secretary to King Charles IV of Denmark. In 1619 his son, Commander Ericus Grubbe, was given the command of a Danish fleet of six warships, sent by King Christian IV to India and Ceylon; to guard the coast of Ceylon, Ericus built the first European forts and citadels. However wanting in final proof, the Grubbs may have every right to look back to Danish princes and sea-captains and to German Dukes and judges among their ancestors. Something of the dash and adventurous spirit of the Danes, and of the wisdom and

---

[7] *The Leadbeater Papers.* Vol. i, p. 310.
[8] *Dansk Biografisk Leksikon.* (Danish Biographical Encyclopedia), part viii, pp. 344–346. *Danmarks Adels Aarbog*, 1895, part XII, 165.

obstinacy of the Germans, lies deeply embedded in the heredity and character of the family.[9]

With the failure of the Crusades, and the experiences gained of the heat and the overcrowded and largely Mohammedan dominated Mediterranean lands, a glance at any map of mediaeval Europe demonstrates that for the hardy North Germans, *expansion* westward to England and Ireland rather than due east through Poland to the steppes of Russia, offered the best prospects, when trade or persecution seemed to make emigration desirable. For the sea-faring Danes from their Viking days, all shipping to other continents or to the south of Europe must first navigate the British Isles, which were then, as they will be again under the Common Market, very much a part of Europe.

Europe BEFORE THE Reformation.

(iii) In England before the reign of King Henry VIII there are Families of the Grubbes found settled in (*a*) Hertfordshire; (*b*) Wiltshire; (*c*) Northamptonshire (and possibly Bedfordshire). The Hertfordshire Grubbes have clearly a Danish origin; the Northamptonshire Grubbes very probably a German origin. What interconnection and intermarriages

---

[9] "I always noticed something foreign looking in the features and speech of my Grubb relations". The late Mrs. Maynard (of Tunbridge Wells), in conversation with the author in 1946.

may have taken place between these two major branches of the Grubbes in England before the commencement of parish registers in 1538, is now almost impossible to determine.

(a) The descendants of (the Danish) Walter Grubbe became a Hertfordshire County family of repute, centering around St. Albans and the neighbouring parish of North Mymms.

The name of Walter Grubbe occurs in the confirmation by the Bishop of Lincoln of the Chantry of St. Catherine, dated Kalend Decr 1328.[10]

Henry Grubbe, after the Dissolution of the Monasteries, was granted the patronage of the advowson of North Mymms by King Henry VIII for a consideration.[11]

He was supposed to have been the son of Henry Grubbe, who married Joan (one account calls her Alice), daughter and heiress of Sir Richard Radcliffe, who was killed at the Battle of Bosworth Field in 1485, and attainted.[12]

Three of his grandsons were baptised at North Mymms between 1565–1567,[13] one of whom—William Grubbe—contributed £25 to the defence of the Country at the time of the Spanish Armada attempted invasion.

There was a Richard Grubbe Mayor of St. Albans in 1562.[14]

THE WILTSHIRE GRUBBES

(b) The Wiltshire Grubbes descend from Robert and Matilda Grubbe, who came from Hertfordshire about 1450, and settled in the village of Potterne, two miles from Devizes, on the edge of the industrial belt of that County, the home of a number of textile workers. They have continued the "e" at the end of the surname to the present day, and from the eighteenth century are known as the Hunt-Grubbes, when a Grubbe heiress married a Hunt. Full records of their descent are among their archives at Eastwell, a large early sixteenth century mansion, surrounded by rolling parklands, with its own bake-house, brew-house and farm, in the parish of Potterne, where they have lived continuously for some 500 years.[15] During the reign of Queen Elizabeth Sir Henry

---

[10] Notes copied by Mrs. Sara Grubb (*nee* Watkins) wife of Col. A. Grubb, R.A., from *The Parish of South Mimms* by Rev. F. C. Cass.

[11] *Ibid.*

[12] *Ibid.* See *Dictionary of National Biography* under Radcliffe.

[13] *Viz.*: William, sonne of George Grubbe, bapt. 18 Feb. 1565; Jasper, sonne of John Grubbe, bapt. 18 Aug. 1566; Henry, sonne of George Grubbe, bapt. 18 May 1567.

[14] *Ibid.* He may be conjectured as the Richard Grubbe who married Elice or Eme Butler at Ravensthorpe in 1540.

[15] See *Victoria County History of Wiltshire*, Vol. iii, pp. 207–216, and *Burke's Landed Gentry of England* (under Hunt-Grubbe). They have given distinguished service to their Country, many of them serving in the Royal Navy, and to the church and to the law.

Grubbe served as M.P. for Devizes.[16] A branch of the family migrated to Scotland, another to Gloucestershire, and a third to Cornwall.

THE NORTHAMPTONSHIRE GRUBBES

(c) In Northamptonshire Families of the Grubbes, also spelt Grub, Grubb, and Groob, were established by the end of the fifteenth century in the village of Barby, and in the next century in the

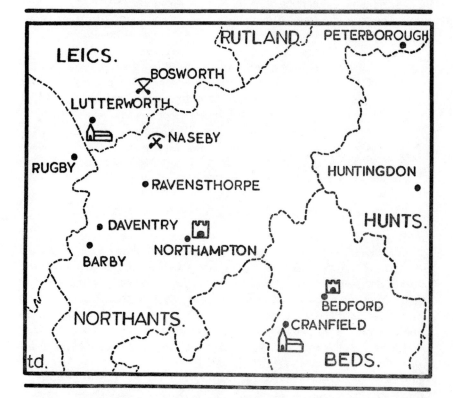

nearby villages of Ashby St. Legers and Ravensthorpe, in the north-west corner of Northamptonshire, in a triangle bounded by

[16] The late Judge Ignatius Grubb collected a great deal of data on the Grubbe family in Denmark and Germany, and traced his own descent back to John Grubb (1652–1708), born in Cornwall, a descendant of Thomas Grubbe (born in Northamptonshire or Bedfordshire), who married Frances Vane of Kent, and sailed for the New World in 1677, landing on June 16th at Marcus Hook, Pa., known as " Grubb's Landing Place". He became a Member of Assembly, and Colonial Justice. Judge Grubb's work appeared in several printed genealogical works in the U.S.A., but without the sources; correspondence with several publishing houses in New York revealed that the Judge's original manuscript had long since been lost or destroyed. (Information given the author in correspondence in 1956 with Hopkins and Hopkins, Law Officers, Cincinnati. 2. Ohio).

Rugby, Daventry, and Northampton itself, where a German community of weavers, hat-makers and linen merchants became established. Later, after the French persecutions of the Huguenots, French emigrant Protestants joined this Protestant weaving community, bringing the Christian name of Francis into the Grubbe family. Three "Francis Grubbes" are recorded in the parish registers of the village of Ravensthorpe, situated in this triangle of Northamptonshire between 1569 and 1576, and from the marriage of Francis Grubbe in 1576 to a French wife, Alis Phillippe, himself a probable descendant of Henry and Joan Grubbe, there is a likelihood that the Grubbs of Tipperary may be descended (*see Chapter Three*). Among surviving Northants wills of the sixteenth century,[17] are those of John Grubbe of Barby (will proved, October 1545), who left his best hats to his brother Thomas, and bequests to his brother Thomas' children (unnamed and torn); and of Thomas Grubbe Junior, of Barby (will proved, October 1573), who left bequests to Sawnders his son, at the age of 18, and the residue to his wife Isabel. John Grubb of Ashby St. Legers (will proved, September 15th, 1567) left his house and money to his son Edmund, and money to his daughter Margaret. Edmund, also of Ashby St. Legers, who died in 1588, left bequests to his daughter Alice and to his wife Agnes.

In the next century, William Grubb, a tailor in Barby, left 12d to his eldest son Joseph, 4d to his daughters Alice Fox, Elizabeth Wright, and Agnes Elliot, a bed to his daughters Sarah the elder, and Sarah the younger, and furniture to his sons Samuel, Nathaniel, and John Payn, alias Grubb.[18] This will was made March 3rd, 1615, and proved five years later on January 9th, 1620, Thomas Grubbe being witness and executor. This Thomas Grubbe, describing himself as a husbandman of Barby, made his own will in 1619, dividing his property between his wife Elizabeth, Thomas Grubb his eldest son, (who became the rector of the parish of Cranfield across the Bedfordshire border from 1619 until his death in 1652), and his other sons John, Richard, and Daniel, and his daughter Elizabeth. These Christian names are found in nearly every succeeding generation of the Grubb family, and point to the Bible-loving Protestant background of the family. Similar Christian names are found

---

[17] Northampton Wills. Lib. 1:52. T.97. S.17.V.345. N.135. Lib. 2. P.83.

[18] This is probably the child born three months after his mother's marriage, and for a while disowned, who sought haven in Cornwall during the Civil Wars from the Roundheads around his home, and settled at Stoke Climsland, near Bodmin, married Helen Vyvyan (Vivian) of an old Cornish County family, and was ancestor to the Cornish Grubbs. He was the recipient of a "Begging Letter" sent out on Charles I's behalf, asking for a £200 loan to help the King "to put down his enemies". It was his son, John, who sailed to America in 1677, forefather of Judge Grubb, of the Supreme Court of Delaware.

in the parish registers of Cranfield, and of Ravensthorpe, which date back to the very commencement of the keeping of parish registers in 1538.

On their first pages the Ravensthorpe church registers record:

1540. October 11. Was married Richard Grubbe and Eme Butler.

1550. 11th April. Was baptised Richard Grubbe.

The first of these entries is now so indistinct and marred by damp, that the bride's Christian name could as well be read as Anne, Alice or Elice.

Who then was this Eme Butler? Was she merely a Ravensthorpe village " beauty "? This would account for Richard Grubbe coming into the village to marry her, and settling down nearby or with his Butler " in-laws." Or was she, as for so long the Irish Grubbs have maintained, a grand-daughter of the Earl of Ormonde, and daughter of Piers Butler of Castle Grace and his " gorgeous " wife Elice or Anne, neé Von Grubbe? In such a case why the marriage in Ravensthorpe Church? The history of this period in Henry VIII's reign yields the probable answer—a period of much " coming and going " between England, France and Germany and Rome, of royal divorces and questions of royal supremacy over the Church, of the spread of Lutheran, Anabaptist and Reformed views in England by German exponents and of the suppression of the greater and lesser monasteries and abbeys. Anabaptism was first introduced into England in 1537, and January 1539–40, the same year as Richard Grubbe was to marry nine months later, saw the King's fourth marriage to a German wife, whom he had never even seen until their wedding. Anne of Cleves was sister-in-law to the powerful Protestant John Frederick, Elector of Saxony, and daughter of the former Duke of Cleves, a small State in North Germany.

With great pomp and a retinue of more than 200 middle-aged and young Germans, England's fourth Queen of Henry VIII's reign arrived from France at the recently-fortified and prepared port of Deal in Kent, to be greeted with great ceremony by Thomas Cromwell (successor to Wolsey as the King's chief minister), and as many English and Irish earls and nobles. The King's increasing difficulties with the Pope had led him to countenance and approve this " political marriage " with a German Protestant he had never seen, save for a flattering portrait by Hans Holbein, in order to create an alliance with the German Lutheran princes, known as the " Smalcaldic League." Anglo-German marriages became quite the vogue! Anne of Cleves was turned 30, tall and thin, unable to speak any other language save German, but she could beam and say " Ja, Ja ", as with her brave equipage and young German interpreters, she was welcomed at every stage of the royal procession from Deal to Canterbury, Sittingbourne, Rochester and Greenwich by Members of the Council and others, appointed to do homage to England's new Queen.[19]   Whatever the King's feelings when he first beheld her at Greenwich, the country rejoiced at the wedding, celebrated by Archbishop Cranmer on January 30th, 1539–40.   The new Queen was known to favour religious change, and to her household English and Irish known Protestants were appointed.   None could have been thought more suitable than Sir Piers Butler and his German wife from Castle Grace, whose own two children were already being brought up at the royal court.   With the invasion of County Tipperary that year by the Earl of Desmond, and his attacks on the Butler-Ormonde castles at Cahir and Castle Grace in his foolhardy attempt to make his relative, the Earl of Kildare, the king of Ireland in the place of Henry VIII, Sir Piers and Lady Butler were thankful to have this opportunity to get away from Ireland for royal service in England with the new Queen.

So the picture emerges of young Richard Grubbe, with his inherited family gift for languages, coming over from Germany in the suite of Anne of Cleves as one of her interpreters, a handsome strapping page in his court clothes, breeches of velvet and black stockings and buckled shoes, quickly catching the eye of young Elice (or Eme) Butler, one of the bridesmaids at the royal wedding.   It was exactly what her German mother had hoped for.   Her daughter could have found no young man in turbulent Ireland, among the ever-feuding Kildare, Ormonde and Desmond families, so suitable as one of her own German cousins, speaking the same language.   Their marriage was quickly arranged and given royal approval, together with a home of their own in one of the recently dissolved monastic houses, perhaps the crumbling and unimportant Pipewell Manor at Ravensthorpe, near the Grubbes settled in that corner of Northamptonshire. But, alas for the best laid plans (and conjectures!). The King quickly found he had been misled over the beauty and appeal of his new Queen, and within four months his roving eye had fallen upon a young lady in his court, Katheryn Howard.   By July a divorce by mutual consent was arranged with his fourth wife, and she was pensioned off with £4,000 p.a. and two great estates at Richmond and Bletchingly, with palatial houses, great parks, jewels, and accommodation for her retinue and households.[20]   No "court wedding", nor a wedding in troubled Tipperary was possible for Richard and Eme, and they were quietly married at Ravensthorpe among the relatives of the Bridegroom.   In its parish church of St. Denys there stands to this day a thin-steel-plated German chest of unknown origin, with six locks, dating from the early sixteenth century, which may well have arrived there after Richard's death in 1583, and been brought by him from Germany with all his belongings.

[19] *Henry VIII.* Francis Hackett. (Reprint Society.) 1956. pp. 407ff.
[20] *Henry VIII and the Reformation.* H. Maynard Smith. pp. 145, 151.

facing page 16

THE EARTH IS FULL OF THE GOODNESS OF THE LORD

Cronenburg's Fortune Mine was opened during the Quarter of Lucia 1705

The Goodness of the Lord Mine was opened in the Quarter of Reminiscere 1740

The pictures show:
DIE GRVBE
GUTE DES HERREN

Train of horses and miners at entrance to mine. Three tree-clad mountains of the Hartz. Signs of the Zodiac above under the sun.

IT SHALL NOT WITHER

Cronenburg's Fortune Mine was opened during the Quarter of Lucia 1705

DIE GRVBE
CRONENBURG'S GLUCK

Outstretched celestial arm holding wreath of Good Fortune over the Hartz Mts., and the large mine compound.

KIND GOD RETURN THE SOUND OF MUSIC ONCE CAST OUT

Lautenthal's Gluck Mine was opened in the Quarter of Reminiscere 1689

DIE GRVBE
LAUTENTHAL'S GLUCK

Lute-player or Pied Piper of Hamelin walking from church to the mine.

THERE IS MORE BEYOND

King Carl Mine was opened in the Quarter of Reminiscere 1752

DIE GRVBE
KONIG CARL

Two miners about to descend this new mine, marked by two columns, among the trees of the Hartz Mts.

PLATE IV

DIE GRVBE (MINING) TALERS

Minted from silver from the various mines in the Hartz Mountains by the two separate lines of Dukes of Brunswick–Luneburg

I THE ANGLO-HANOVERIAN LINE

II THE BRUNSWICK-WOLFENBUTTEL LINE

Obverses

ENGLAND   *QUARTERED ARMS*   FRANCE
IRELAND   BRUNSWICK

Inscription: George II. by the Grace of God, King of Great Britain, France, and Ireland, Defender of the Faith, Duke of Brunswick and Luneburg, Arch Treasurer and Elector of the Holy Roman Empire.

The two *WILD MEN OF BRUNSWICK supporting the CROWNED ARMS of this Duchy*, incorporating the eight lines (including the Grubenhagen) into which, since 1279, it has been divided

PRE-1750   From 1750
*Irregular in shape on a   Oval in shape on a V base
horizontal base*

Inscription: By the Grace of God, Carl, Duke of Brunswick and Luneburg

Reverses

An engraving of the mine from which the silver came, a surrounding latin inscription, frequently asking a blessing upon, or good luck for the mining operations (illustrative of the pious simple faith of the miners), and underneath a German inscription in four lines, advertising the mine, and the quarter of the year in which it was opened. At bottom the initials of John Benjamin Hacht, mintmaster at Zellerfield.

I

GIVE PRAISE TO GOD THE CREATOR

The Rainbow Mine was re-opened during the *Quarter of Lucia 1746*

The pictures show:
DIE GRVBE
REGENSBOGEN
Rainbow over the Hartz Mts. and the mine entrance.

THE GOLDEN TIMES RETURN

The Mine H. August Friedrich Bieyfeld was re-opened in the *Quarter of Reminiscere 1750*

DIE GRVBE
H. AUG FRIED BIEYFELD
Mining gear, and column bearing shield inscribed A.F.

THE WHITE SWAN OF THE MOUNTAINS LEADS TO THE PRIZES

The White Swan Mine was opened in the *Quarter of Lucia 1732*

DIE GRVBE
WEISSER SCHWAN
Swan on lake amid the tree-clad Hartz Mts.

KIND GOD RETURN THE SOUND OF MUSIC ONCE CAST OUT

Lautenthal's Gluck Mine was opened in the *Quarter of Reminiscere 1689*

DIE GRVBE
LAUTENTHAL'S GLUCK
Lute-player, or Pied Piper of Hamelin walking from church to the mines.

II

Chapter Three

Northamptonshire Ancestors and the Ravensthorpe Chest

An Essay in Historical Research

IN the days of merry England, of maypoles and dancing upon the village green, of poets and dramatists, William Shakespeare, Francis Bacon and the like, of English sea captains sailing the high seas to discover new worlds, and bring back captured Spanish gold and " pieces of eight," rivalling and intermingling with Scandinavian sailors, and of the spread of Puritanism and its predecessor Anabaptism across Northern Europe and England, the Ancestors of the Grubbs of Tipperary lived in the hill-top village of Ravensthorpe (once spelt " Ranstrap ") in north-west Northamptonshire in the Midlands. Their names, as given in Burke's " Landed Gentry of Ireland,"[1] with such dates as are to be found in the church registers at Ravensthorpe, are:

Richard and Eme Grubbe, married October 11th, 1540.

Richard Grubbe, baptised April 11th, 1550.

Ishmael Grubb, buried November 18th, 1680.

John Grubb. No entries at Ravensthorpe. Irish Quaker records give his dates 1620–96.

The present parish church of Ravensthorpe is dedicated to St. Denys, a French Saint. It stands in one corner of the village square, once the old village green, on the site of an old Danish church, of which its quaintly-carved Danish font only remains;[2] also part of a lovely rood screen, built in 1290 of timber obtained by Master Henry de Stokes, the rector, from the old monastic abbey of Pipewell in the parish. Surviving wills of Ravensthorpe people record in every case bequests for the maintenance of the holy lights that were kept burning in pre-Reformation days before the sacred figures above the rood screen. No wills of any Grubbes of Ravensthorpe exist, suggesting they were already Protestants when they came to the village; if they were resident there before the Reformation, they made no bequests for such purposes; this would account for their wills not having been preserved among the early church papers. From

---

[1] 1956 Edition, pp. 335ff.
[2] The Danish carving is described in the brochure on St. Denys' church.

17

1233 the patrons of the church were the Knights of St. John, or Knights Hospitallers, famous for their work in the Holy Land, Rhodes and Malta for wounded and sick pilgrims.

Large families have ever been characteristic of the Grubbs. The parish registers of Ravensthorpe record that at its Danish font were baptised Richard Grubbe in 1550, Geoffrey in 1567, John in 1568, Francis in 1569, and then after a gap of five years, another Francis in 1574, Samuel in 1576, another John in 1576, and Henry in 1583. There is no entry of the baptism of either Ishmael, or of John Grubbe, who was an Anabaptist preacher (and later went to Ireland), nor of any of the marriages of Ishmael, but five of his children were baptised there between 1627 and 1638. In 1576 Francis Grubbe was married to a certain Alis Phillippe, a woman of French descent, and probably a French Huguenot emigree (their two Christian names appear 50 years later among the five children of Ishmael Grubb), and in 1605 Henry Grubbe (Groob) married An(ne) Watles. In 1568 John Grubbe was buried; the entry could be deciphered as Joan, suggesting it was the long-lived wife of Henry Grubbe (*see Chapter Two*), and daughter of Sir Richard Radcliffe, thus explaining the frequently-found Christian name of Richard in the Grubb family. In 1583 is recorded the death of Richard Grubbe; in 1601 of Ales Grubbe, and in 1639 of Francis Grubbe. After the turn of the century baptismal entries have dropped the " e " at the end of the surname, and the parents' names of the child baptised are given, thus making identification easier.

Old armour as well as the church registers were kept for many years in Ravensthorpe's old and unique chest—perhaps the most striking feature of the present church, whose origin has hitherto defied the historian—closely banded with thin steel plates, with two lids, and six concealed locks. Some of the devices which cover the keyholes still work; for instance the second from the right is a primitive combination lock in the shape of a dice, which unless it was turned to the correct number, refuses to allow the keyhole cover to be lifted.[3] It stands where in pre-reformation days a side altar would have stood, and is of undoubted German origin and workmanship. Its wood is quite different from the timber supplied by Pipewell Abbey for the rood screen, and in all probability came from the Hartz Mountains. It may be the chest was brought by Richard Grubbe with his belongings on his arrival in England, and later, after his death, was given to the church by his heirs. Silently and enigmatically this chest continues to face his descendants, as if to say " Solve the mystery of my six locks, and stranger, and more rewarding than any Sherlock Holmes or Agatha Christie detective story, will be your discoveries of the origin of the thousand and more Grubbs, males and

---

[3] Lecture on the Church of St. Denys, Ravensthorpe, by the Rev. R. N. Serjeantson, F.S.A. given on October 9th, 1913.

females, who sprang from the owner of this repository, which dates from their ' Castle ' days in the Hartz Mountains."

Historical research before Tudor times, in the absence of wills, parchments, documents, hatchments, heraldic or archaeological discoveries, has to be built on a combination of fact, probabilities, and possibilities. It is only this combination which will open the six locks of the chest.

The sixth lock on the right opens easily on the unassailable facts that the Grubbs of Tipperary descend from John Grubb of Ravensthorpe, an Anabaptist preacher, who went to Ireland in 1656.

A clue to the discovery of the correct number on the dice which will allow the keyhole cover over *the fifth lock* to be lifted, is found in a seventeenth century Quaker document in Ireland,[4] which states that John Grubb became a Quaker in 1676, when he was 56 years of age. This puts the date of his birth at 1620. The same document states that he was the eldest son of Ishmael Grubb . . . a farmer who carried on some branches of the linen manufacture at Ranstrap (*i.e.* Ravensthorpe) in Northamptonshire where he lived. It continues: " Ishmael married three wives. By the first he had one son and two daughters, viz John, Alice, and Elizabeth, and by the second one son and one daughter, viz Richard and Sarah—The second wife proved unkind to the children of the first, but died about the 40th year of her Husband's age: wherefore he seemed inclined not to subject them to the like inconvenience again. His daughter Elizabeth became his housekeeper, & so he remained in a state of Widowhood forty years, but she (Eliza) died a maiden at the 80th year of his age. And then he married a third, a maiden between forty and 50 on whom he settled abt £150, wch two years put her in the sole Possession of. He departed this Life abt the 82 year of his age, and abt the year 1676."

Quaint as this Quaker document is in its language and descriptions, (it has often been quoted since in other papers and writings of the Grubb family[5]), its verisimilitude is questionable, when it is compared with the evidence available in the Ravensthorpe church registers. There is no entry therein of the baptism of John Grubb in or after 1620. How could there be, if he was born of Anabaptist parentage? Yet the existence at Ravensthorpe of Ishmael Grubb from 1627 onwards as a believer in infant baptism is attested by the record given of the baptism of five of his children (through two of his wives, Margaret (buried 1631), and Elizabeth (buried November 3rd, 1640). These entries record the baptisms of:

Alice, daughter of Ishmael Grubb and Margaret, his wife, in 1627.
Ishmael, sonne of Ishmael Grubb and Margaret his wife, in 1629.
Elizabeth, daughter of Ishmael Grubb and Margaret, his wife, in 1631.
Richard, sonne of Ishmael Grubb and Elizabeth his wife, in 1636.
Francis, sonne of Ishmael Grubb and Elizabeth his wife, in 1638.

[4] MS. copied by John Grubb (1766–1841) from an earlier original.
[5] *History of My Ancestors.* Elizabeth Laverick.

There is no baptism of a daughter Sarah recorded, but the burial of Ishmael in 1680.

No wonder this fifth lock does not open easily on the key number of 1620, provided by this quaint but inexact Quaker document. Blocking the keyhole are the rough and unexplained edges of conjecture—(*a*) If John was indeed the eldest son of Ishmael, who had five of his children baptised at Ravensthorpe, why was not he also baptised there? (*b*) Unless Anabaptist beliefs were already in John Grubb's family *before* his birth (thus accounting for no record of his baptism as a child having been discovered anywhere), what induced him to adopt such beliefs when grown to manhood, and where was he baptised as an adult, and trained before he became an accredited Anabaptist preacher? (*c*) How came it that *seven* years elapsed, before Ishamel had another child?

Either it must be conjectured that Ishmael Grubb was himself an Anabaptist, and since no record of Ishmael's baptism exists at Ravensthorpe, probably his parents also before him; his unusual Christian name suggests a wandering Anabaptist origin.[6] It was in 1592 (a few years before his birth on the evidence of the Quaker document that he was about 82 when he died) that Queen Elizabeth issued a proclamation ordering all Anabaptists to leave the kingdom on pain of imprisonment, and loss of goods. Many dissenters and Anabaptists withdrew to Holland, where they had liberty to profess their opinions without restraint, and formed themselves into a church at Amsterdam under the control of a Mr. Johnson as pastor.[7] They were joined in the following years by many of their countrymen, among them in 1606 the Rev. John Smyth, who resigned his benefice at Gainsborough (Lincs.) where non-conformists were numerous, with whose views and persecutions he had come to sympathise. Mr. Smythe is regarded as the father of the English General Baptists, having formed a large and flourishing Baptist church in Amsterdam, from which many of his adherents returned to England between 1615 and 1625 to spread their beliefs.[8] With their own Hussite and Puritan background it would be surprising if some of the descendants of Richard Grubbe and his sons had not linked up with the exiles in Amsterdam, and returned to England after 1615, or were converted to Anabaptist beliefs by those who returned.

The dates make it possible to conjecture that Ishmael Grubbe was

---

[6] This is the view taken in the "Biography of Edward Grubb" (1854–1939), himself a grandson of the copyist of the Quaker document above quoted (p. 19).

[7] *The History of the English General Baptists, of the 17th Century.* Adam Taylor. (1818) pp. 58–97. Two Anabaptists were burnt as Martyrs to their faith at Smithfield in 1575, and several after that date. There is no record of the baptism of any Grubbe at Ravensthorpe between 1584 and 1607.

[8] The first Baptist Church in England is regarded as that at Amersham in Bucks., where records date back to 1626. There was a Baptist church in Ravensthorpe *before* 1651, of which Benjamin Morley, a leading Northamptonshire Baptist, was Pastor.

born in Amsterdam, returned to England before 1626 with a son John, and that John's mother died before he was seven years old, or refused to return with Ishmael, being Dutch. That on Ishmael's next two marriages to Margaret (who was buried at Ravensthorpe in 1531) and to Elizabeth (his third wife therefore, who was buried also at Ravensthrope in 1540), the gynocracy found in so many succeeding generations of the Grubbs was so strong, as to compel Ishmael to compromise his former Anabaptist principles, and consent to their children being baptised. Yet " compromise " has never been found since in the Grubb descendants, and primogeniture has always been so strongly held among them, that further rough edges surround this conjecture why Ishmael left his farm and business to his third son, Richard, and not to his eldest (?) John, nor to Richard's elder step-brother, Ishmael junior? On such a conjecture Ishmael lost three wives within fifteen years.

Or it may be supposed that Ishmael's original name was Ismal, that he was of Danish birth, a son, or a natural son of Sigvard von Grubbe (1566–1636) of Malmo Castle; that he took to the sea and to a wandering life, as did his brother Commander Ericus Grubbe, who sailed to Ceylon (*see Chapter Two*); and later with a son born on his travels, that he came to settle at Ravensthorpe, never bothering to have this son, named John, baptised. Therefore that John Grubbe became a convert to Anabaptist principles as a young man. So would be explained the true basis for the long-held tradition among the Irish Grubbs of a Danish origin, but the German background through Annie Winthrop would be left unexplained. This conjecture would also explain why no record of the baptism of Ishmael Grubb is found at Ravensthorpe, and perhaps also the "unkindness" of Elizabeth Grubb to her step-children.

Both the above conjectures are possible, but afford no certain combination with fact to open the fifth lock.

If the year 1620 is to be accepted as the date of the birth of John Grubb, who was 56, according to the Quaker document, when he became a Quaker in 1676, the Church registers of Ravensthorpe provide a more probable and entirely possible explanation. That John was not the son of the perplexing Ishmael at all. That he was the second son of Henry Grubbe (baptised at Ravensthorpe in 1583) and his wife Anne Grubbe (neè Watles) who were married in their parish church in 1605. The Ravensthorpe registers record that:

An Grubb, daughter of Henry Grubb, was baptised in 1607.
Elizabeth Grubb, daughter of Henry and Anne Grubb, in 1616.
William Grubb, son of Henry and Anne Grubb, in 1618.

There are no further entries of any other children of Henry and Anne, yet large families always characterised the Grubbs, and were characteristic of the Stuart period. With the growing strength of the Anabaptists and Puritans at the end of James I's reign, much more likely it would seem that Henry and Anne became converted to such beliefs. Their subsequent children, John born in 1620, and others were therefore not baptised in infancy, but brought up as Anabaptists in a happy and undivided home, in which John so absorbed the ethos and background of the Anabaptists, as to be readily admitted by them as an accredited preacher when he came of age.

If the above combination of fact, probability and possibility has opened the fifth lock, the key to open *the fourth* is now in our hands. That it was Henry Grubbe, son of the Richard Grubbe baptised in 1550, or of Francis and Alice (neè Philippe) Grubbe who were married in 1576 through whom the Grubbs of Tipperary are descended. Richard's wife could well have been Alice Grubb, widow, of Welton, buried at Ravensthorpe in 1625, who left bequests to her son Henry and his children, in her will, dated 1622.

At the same time it must be remembered a result of Queen Elizabeth's Act of Uniformity was that many baptisms, marriages and deaths were never entered up in parish registers at all. Clergymen refusing to obey the Act had to quit their livings, and it was found impossible to fill vacancies with men of learning and character . . . "not a few mechanics altogether unlearned, were preferred to benefices". Wrote Bishop Jewel— "Great number of ministers, many deservedly in high esteem, were left destitute. All were ejected, who would not conform rigidly to the new Prayer Book and established rites and ceremonies laid down. They travelled up and down the counties from church to church, preaching where they could get leave, as if they were apostles."

When these first non-conformists could not obtain the churches to preach in, or when the weather was too cold, or the persecution too hot for them to hold forth in the streets, fields or woods, they sought the privacy of the houses or other buildings of their disciples—these were the earliest "conventicles", meeting houses, or chapels.

A diaper fabric bag of fairest linen, with small diamond patterns variegated with figures, has concealed for centuries the exquisite German ornamented key that turns *the third lock*. It may well have been made by Anne Von Grubbe herself, the Annie Winthrop of persistent Grubb tradition to have been an ancestress of the family, the grand-daughter of the Duke of Brunswick and Johanan Von Grubbe, who appeared at Castle Grace (*see Chapter Two*) as the "gorgeous new chatelaine of the castle" and wife of Piers Butler. The State Papers of Henry VIII record that Sir Piers Butler (1467–1539), who was appointed Seneschal of the Liberty of Tipperary in 1505 by his cousin, the Seventh Earl of Ormonde, and whom he succeeded in 1515 as the Eighth Earl:

> "planted great civility in the county of Tipperary to give good
> example to the people of that county, by bringing out of Flanders
> and other countreyes of Europe artificers . . . who made diaper and
> cushions and tapistreyes and turkey-carpets, and other like works."[9]

Thus is explicable the coming to Ireland of Annie Winthrop, a pseudonym for Anne Von Grubbe, and her subsequent settlement by the Eighth Earl of Ormonde in one of his castles in County Tipperary, and her marriage to one of his natural sons or grandsons.[10] The Earl had a number of natural children, one of them, Edmund Butler, becoming Archbishop of Cashel,[11] and another, Piers Butler, Baron of Cahir. This "gorgeous" German Grubbe was worthy, thought the Butlers, of a castle home in their midst. The coins she used in County Tipperary are illustrated in plate III.

If the key to *the second lock* of the huge Grubbe chest has long since perished under the cushions and tapestries—a gift from his mother-in-law to Richard Grubbe on his marriage to Eme Butler—under which it used to be hidden, it matters not. The size of the chest, and the *raison d'être* of its six locks and two lids, is now apparent. So large a chest was necessary for young Richard Grubbe to fulfil the commission he would have received from his relative in Ireland, and future mother-in-law, to bring over a further supply of diaper, and cushion materials and tapestry from Germany on his journey to England in the train of Anne of Cleves. Fresh materials also for his Grubbe relatives settled at Barby in the hat-making and drapery trades were probably included among its precious contents Ample precautions against thieves, or a young man's loss of a key from his pocket after a night's festivities, had been made.

We go back a thousand years for a clue to the remaining key for *the first lock*—to the Irish Grubb traditions that they are descended from Danish "nebs" or princes, who invaded Ireland with the Vikings, and landed at Wicklow. Such Danish "nebs" also invaded England, and some of them settled at Ravensthorpe, and built its first church and Danish font. They gave their name to a geographical feature of Northamptonshire—the small copse or wood (altogether useless for agricultural purposes, and which farmers " grub up "), near to one of which they built their first homesteads. A small copse became known as a " grub " in Northants. So in later years it was natural for other Grubbes, as they arrived in England from Denmark or Germany on account of trade or persecution, *to make for Ravensthorpe and Barby in the very centre of*

---

[9] *The State Papers of Henry VIII.* Vol. i 302; Vol. ii, 58; Vol. iii, 261.
[10] Castle Grace became one of the "Butler" manors in County Tipperary after the death of the last descendant of Raymond Le Gros, *c.* 1350 A.D.
[11] *Athenae Oxonienses*, Vol. I, p. 507. Educated at Oxford, he was Archbishop of Cashel 1527–1550, and a Privy Councillor to King Henry VIII.

England, and settle among their thriving relatives in a growing German community of linen manufacturers, weavers, dyers, hatmakers and drapers, who had made their home there. The very name of the village of Barby attracted them. It reminded them of the better known German town of Barby, not 40 miles from their earlier home in the Hartz Mountains, a great centre of hat-making.

The present age which sees a return to male long hair, may soon, perhaps, witness a return to the styles of hats made and fashioned by the Grubbes of Barby for wearing over long hair. *(See plate V)*. The fashion of wearing the hair long, for long has been prevalent in northern Europe, if only as some protection from the cold. In the "Common Market" European and German styles of male headwear may well again become popular.

If the Ravensthorpe chest is now empty, it still remains in the church, a silent witness to our ancestors, who touched, fingered and handled it. A reminder that they were real persons of flesh and blood, through whom in the succeeding four centuries more than a thousand Grubbs, males and females, have descended. It served awhile as a depository for their documents and valuables, brought home after their travels and adventures in the exciting days of Elizabethan England. It can never be supposed that, like ostriches, they buried their heads in the sands in an obscure English village. Travel, movement, activity, has been in the Grubb blood since their Viking adventures, their travels in Scandinavia and across Germany, to Ceylon and the Americas, as preachers in Anabaptist and Quaker days, as missionaries and explorers, and down to the present day. No record of travel is more exciting than that told by Sir Kenneth Grubb, K.C.M.G., in his recently published autobiography.[12] It can truly be said "It's all in the Grubb blood"—*to travel, and to explore.*

---

[12] *Crypts of Power.* (Hodder and Stoughton) Published July, 1971. Sir Kenneth Grubb spent 15 years ranging over the Latin republics of South America, from Mexico to the Argentine, from Amazonia to the Andes.

PLATE V

GENTLEMEN'S HATS OF THE TUDOR PERIOD

The product of Northamptonshire hatmakers in an age when it was fashionable
for gentlemen to grow their hair long

SIXTEENTH AND EARLY SEVENTEENTH CENTURY GRUBBES
(Variously spelt Grubbe, Grubb, Grub, Groob)

Evidence from extant Northants Wills (*W*); Ravensthorpe Church Registers (*R*);
North Mymms Register (*M*); Dictionaries (*D*); Peterborough Marriage Licences (*L*).
Abbreviations: (*b*) Baptism date; (*m*) Marriage date; (*d*) Death, or probate of will.
Dotted lines ---------- are conjectural.

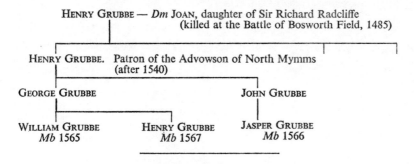

HENRY GRUBBE — *Dm* JOAN, daughter of Sir Richard Radcliffe
(killed at the Battle of Bosworth Field, 1485)

HENRY GRUBBE. Patron of the Advowson of North Mymms
(after 1540)

GEORGE GRUBBE   JOHN GRUBBE

WILLIAM GRUBBE   HENRY GRUBBE   JASPER GRUBBE
Mb 1565   *Mb* 1567   *Mb* 1566

LIVING IN N.W. NORTHAMPTONSHIRE

At RAVENSTHORPE

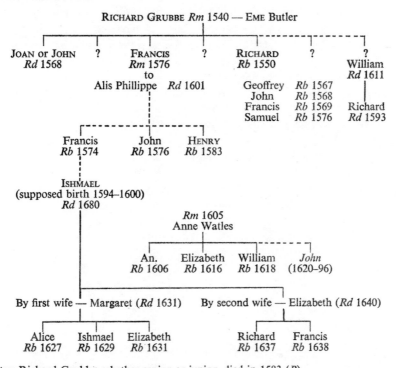

RICHARD GRUBBE *Rm* 1540 — EME Butler

JOAN or JOHN	?	FRANCIS	?	RICHARD	?	?
Rd 1568		*Rm* 1576		*Rb* 1550		William
		to				*Rd* 1611
		Alis Phillippe *Rd* 1601		Geoffrey *Rb* 1567		
				John *Rb* 1568		Richard
				Francis *Rb* 1569		*Rd* 1593
				Samuel *Rb* 1576		

Francis   John   HENRY
Rb 1574   *Rb* 1576   *Rb* 1583

ISHMAEL
(supposed birth 1594–1600)
Rd 1680

Rm 1605
Anne Watles

An.   Elizabeth   William   *John*
Rb 1606   *Rb* 1616   *Rb* 1618   (1620–96)

By first wife — Margaret (*Rd* 1631)   By second wife — Elizabeth (*Rd* 1640)

Alice   Ishmael   Elizabeth   Richard   Francis
Rb 1627   *Rb* 1629   *Rb* 1631   *Rb* 1637   *Rb* 1638

Notes: Richard Grubbe, whether senior or junior, died in 1583 (*R*).
Francis Grubbe, whether senior or junior, died in 1639 (*R*).
In 1689 the Member of Parliament for Northampton was Sir Thomas Grubb,
and in 1666 a Thomas Grubb of Daventry issued Token Money at a time in the
reign of Charles II, when royal money was non-existent.

(W. Byrne, 17th Century Tokens, p. 35)

At BARBY

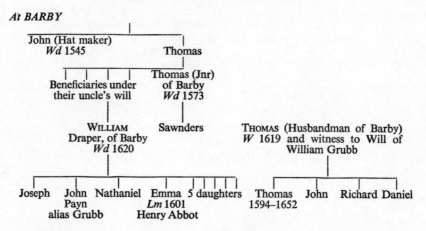

Conjectures:

1. *Francis Grubbe*, who married Alis Phillippe in 1576, could have been the son of Richard and Eme Grubbe, either father or grandfather of Ishmael Grubb, and great-grandfather of Alice and Francis Grubb, eldest and youngest children of Ishmael.

2. *Henry Grubbe*, baptised 1583, could have been a son of Francis and Alis Grubbe and the father of John Grubb (1620–1696) ancestor of the Grubbs of Tipperary.

3. Alternatively, *Alice Grubb*, widow, of Welton, whose will was made in June 1622, and left her estate to her son Edward, and to her son Henry and his children—an Alice Grubb was buried at Ravensthorpe in 1625—could have been the widow of Richard Grubb, Junior, and the mother of Henry, baptised 1583.

4. While the Richard Grubbe baptised in 1550 could be the same Richard who married Eme Butler in 1540, it is unlikely Richard and Eme waited ten years before their first son was born—the only son recorded at Ravensthorpe. It is possible that *Henry Grubbe*, *M.P.* for Devizes in 1571, died 1581, to whom the late Judge Ignatius Grubb traced back his descent (through Thomas Grubbe (d. 1617 at Devizes), a second Thomas born at Devizes 1581, who went to Northamptonshire, John Grubbe (1610–1667) his second son, who left that county during the Civil Wars, and went to Cornwall, and his son John Grubb, born in Cornwall (1652–1708) who went to America, and became a Colonial Judge), was a son of Richard and Eme. Also that other sons were John (died 1568) and Francis (married 1576).

5. Thomas Grubbe, Husbandman of Barby, whose will was made in 1619, might possibly be identified with the Thomas Grubbe born at Devizes, 1581.

PLATE VI

SILVER COIN GOBLET OF GERMAN ORIGIN

Containing "hammered" Elizabethan coins used for the popular contemporary game of Shove-Sixpences

From the Author's Collection

CHAPTER FOUR

John Grubbe.   1620—1696

Roundhead, Anabaptist, and later a Quaker, of Ravensthorpe, Northamptonshire; Annaghs (or Annis) Castle, Co. Kilkenny; Meylers (or Millers) Park, Co. Wexford

"Be faithful in this one thing—Do your utmost for the preaching of the Gospel in Ireland."—*John Owen*, preaching before Parliament at Westminster.
February 28th, 1649.

JOHN GRUBBE of Ravensthorpe was an Anabaptist preacher at a time when the pendulum of religion was swinging, during the reigns of James I and Charles I, in a Puritan direction, with an inevitable reaction against the faded colours and tawdriness and the implied materialism of the parish churches of England. He might be well described as a child of the authorised version of the Bible, produced only a few years before his birth, on the study and language of which he grew up. The English hammered silver coinage was at the height of its vogue, a sign of the prosperity of the country, following the Elizabethan age. There was no want of money among the Grubbes, and with such coins their children would play shove-six-pences on a wooden board, or upon the ground.

There were as vast differences among the Puritans as exist today among the various Christian churches. The word was used to describe all who were concerned for the purity of the Gospel and the authority of the Bible over and above that of bishops, and without " any embellishment of scripture ", who were concerned with the inward and mystical aspects of religion more than with outward ceremonies and rites. They maintained that God's free grace, mediated by the soul's faith in Christ, is the essential root of human salvation, and that God's will, revealed in His Written Word and interpreted by His Living Spirit, is the Supreme Law for human conduct, both in the sphere of the church and the world. Therefore the conscience must be free from human dictation, whether by the priest or by the monarchy. Puritanism has been described as the *Religion of the Layman*. Its influence in parliament—synods—church councils— non-conformity, and wherever responsible laymen meet in council, remains to the present day a force to be reckoned with. An increasing number in Stuart days in the established church, with the presbyterians

27

in Scotland, continental reformers, anabaptists, and many others, were included in the general name of Puritans. After the defeat of Charles I at the Battle of Naseby (1645) (fought but five miles from Ravensthorpe), in which John Grubbe took part, Puritanism dominated the established church until the Restoration of Charles II in 1660.

Anabaptism,[1] which dates back to the Biblical teachings of Wycliffe and John Huss, was an early outcome of the Protestant Reformation in Europe. Spreading from Zurich about 1523 through Switzerland and Germany before its introduction into England in 1536, it has been described as "The Spiritual Soil out of which all non-conformist sects have sprung", and "as old as the earliest movements to reform the Christian church". Truly democratic in their emphasis on the freedom and indeed necessity of *personal choice* in Jesus Christ as Lord and Saviour, and baptism as the outward sign of the adult's profession of faith, Anabaptists were highly thought of by Oliver Cromwell, in whose army thousands of them served. Many of them, being known as outstandingly honest men, and self-disciplined, were chosen and appointed by Cromwell as his officers.

Whether John Grubbe was born an Anabaptist—which would account for no entry having been discovered anywhere in a church register of his baptism as an infant—whether he was born in 1620 (as is alleged), the son of Henry (or of Ishmael) Grubbe of Ravensthorpe, or whether he was converted to this far-flung early Baptist form of religion in Stuart days, he gained renown for his itinerant ministry as an Anabaptist preacher. He was a contemporary of *Richard Baxter* (1615–1691), churchman, Puritan writer, and controversialist, whose mysticism and writings, and especially

---

[1] Anabaptists were so called, because they firmly believed, as do their successors of the Baptist Church today, that Baptism can only rightly be administered to those who ask for it, who have first professed repentance towards God and faith in the Lord Jesus Christ. They held that infant baptism is quite incompatible with the New Testament doctrine stressed by St. Paul of "Justification by Faith alone". So it followed that the true believer in Christ should separate himself from the evil customs and speech of the world aiming after holiness of life, and guarding his words and behaviour. Anabaptists further held that the Sacrament of the Lord's Supper, like the Sacrament of Baptism, should be given only to true believers, and that it should never be made a test of orthodoxy. Adult baptism should be preferably by total immersion, whether in a baptistry or a convenient river, but might be given by sprinkling. In the absence of any parent's names before 1606 being recorded in the Ravensthorpe church register, it can be supposed that the Grubbs who were baptised there were adults (and could have been Anabaptists). Continental Anabaptists in Germany suffered much persecution on account of socialistic excesses (probably falsely) charged against them, and especially because of their refusal to take an oath in their own self-defence. It follows that many Anabaptists were later well disposed to the enlightenment given to George Fox, the Founder of Quakerism, and became Friends surrendering entirely the use and practice of sacraments.

Anabaptists in England were highly thought of by Oliver Cromwell and the "Court News Book" told of swarms of them in the Roundhead armies—"sober honest men" and often put into positions of high command by Cromwell, "united to him by the point of liberty of conscience". See *The Reliquiae Baxterianae* (abridged from the folio 1696) being the autobiography of Richard Baxter. J. M. Dent. pp. 29, 49, 56, 71, 95. Also article on the Anabaptists in the *Protestant Dictionary*, and writing of Rufus M. Jones.

"The Saints Everlasting Rest" cannot but have influenced him deeply. Two of his other contemporaries were *John Bunyan* (1625–1692), of nearby Bedford, and *George Fox*, four years his junior, the Leicestershire mystic and founder of a new religious sect, called "The Friends" or "Quakers". Above all, the very times in which he lived, and the spiritual destitution of country parishes (described as follows by Richard Baxter) played a great part in developing the strong evangelical and moral character found in John Grubbe and his descendants. It is difficult to suppose the roots of such character had not been inherited from Puritan and Anabaptist parents. Wrote Baxter[2] (his description could well have been that of Ravensthorpe):

"The parson was too old for his work, about 80 years of age, that never preached, and had two churches about 20 miles distant. His eyesight failing him, he said Common Prayer without a book: but for the reading of the psalms and chapters he got a common thresher and day-labourer one year, and a tailor another year (for the parish clerk could not read well), and at last a kinsman of his own, the excellentest stage-player in all the country, and a good gamester and a good fellow, that got orders and supplied one of his places . . . and after him a neighbour's son took orders, when he had been a while an attorney's clerk, and tippled himself into so great poverty that he had no other way to live. . . . These were the schoolmasters of my youth, who read Common Prayer on Sundays and Holy Days, and taught school, and tippled on the weekdays, and whipped the boys when they were drunk, so that we changed them very oft. Within a few miles about us were near a dozen more ministers that were near eighty years of age and never preached; poor ignorant readers and most of them of scandalous lives. Only three or four competent preachers lived near us, and these were the common marks of the people's obloquy and reproach, and any that had but gone to hear them, when they had no preaching at home, were made the derision of the vulgar rabble under the odious name of Puritan.

"After the reading of the Common Prayer on Sundays, the rest of the day even until dark night almost, except eating-time, was spent in dancing under a maypole and a great tree not far from my father's door, where all the village did meet together. Though one of my father's own tenants was the piper, he could not restrain him nor break the sport. So that we could not read the Scripture in our family without the great disturbance of the tabor and pipe and noise in the street.

"Many times my mind was inclined to be among them, and sometimes I broke lose from conscience and joined with them: and the more I did it, the more I was inclined to it. But when I heard them call my father 'Puritan', it did much to cure me and alienate me from them: for I considered my father's exercise in reading the Scripture was better than theirs, and would surely be

[2] *Autobiography of Richard Baxter.* J. N. Dent (1931). pp. 94–97.

better thought on by all men at the last, and I considered what it was for that he and others were thus derided.

" . . . and about that time it pleased God that a poor pedlar came to my door that had ballads and some good books, and my father bought of him Dr. Sibbs *Bruised Reed*. This I read, and found it suited to my state, and was seasonably sent to me."

It was against such a background that the Grubbes lived at Ravensthorpe and Barby. With their ingrained Protestantism of the past 200 years since arriving in England as a result of continental (and perhaps also Huguenot) persecutions, and their Germanic and Danish fighting spirit, it would have been strange indeed if some of them had not been led to propagate the truths of the Gospel, as they understood it, as itinerant Anabaptist preachers. Baxter's description illustrates John Grubbe's boyhood experiences in a midland village, the influence of the reading of " good bookes " brought to his door by itinerants and pedlars such as John Bunyan, George Fox and many another, the religious outlook in which he was later to bring up his own family, and the type of ministry on which he himself engaged as an Anabaptist preacher. It explains the later non-conformity of the Grubbe family, their mistrust of paid ministers of the church, their avoidance of drink and dancing, even of all kinds of music for the next 200 years (*see Chapter Eleven*), their emphasis on learning and reading of the Scriptures and other books and how readily they later became Quakers. It explains also a Calvinistic belief in their calling and predestination by God for His purposes for the salvation of His world, which was deeply inbred in the Grubbe character and lineage. There are many who think of heredity as being the "*manward expression of predestination*". It helps to explain the interest and importance of historical and genealogical research.

Three other formative influences upon John Grubbe's character and outlook must be noticed:

(1) There was fairly wide-spread Baptist activity in Northamptonshire in the middle 17th century, and the word " Anabaptist " meant no more than Baptist means today, and no less. Preachers of this kind were known as " Messengers " and were authorised to cover a wide area. With the lack of competent preachers in so many of the parish churches, it is not surprising that John Grubbe, in the enthusiasms of youth, should find the call irresistible to carry the Message of the " pure Worde of God " into the villages where (he believed) it was not being preached, and to find fellowship in the small but growing communities of Northamptonshire Baptists. *Benjamin Morley* of Ravensthorpe who was about his own age, and *William Smith* of Welton, a neighbouring village, where Alice Grubbe (possibly his grandmother: *see Collateral*

Table "A") had lived, became two outstanding leaders and pastors among these Northamptonshire Baptists.[3]

(2) Constantly itinerating or riding into Northampton (and especially in his " courting " days), he would pass the battlements and keeps of its fine Norman castle, the sun often reflected upon the armour and pikes of its garrison and sentries.   The sight always enthused him with his namesake's Vision of the New Jerusalem in the last book of the Bible, when war and separation between brother and brother shall be no more, when the redeemed from every nation, the rich and the mighty, the bondman and the freeman will find their unity and equality in the Worship of the Lamb upon His Throne.   This " otherworldly " and mystic sense of the Puritans was to appear again and again in his seed after him.   (*See Chapter Six*).

(3) Across the county border in Bedfordshire lived his relative, the Reverend Thomas Grubbe, the Presbyterian-minded and Puritan rector of Cranfield.   He found peace under his ministry in that simple church when the strains and stresses of life would be removed for a while by the preaching of the pure Worde of God by its godly pastor, whose language and methods he learned to copy in his own Anabaptist preaching.   A wall plaque in the chancel of Cranfield Church thus commemorates his relative:

" Here lyeth interred the body of Thomas Grubbe
a pious and painfull (*i.e.* painstaking) Preacher
and Pastor of ye Worde of God, 33 yeares in this parish.
He was aged 58 yeares, and deceased ye 31st August 1652.

The God of Peace lent us this Man of Peace,
Who preached ye Worde of God till his decease.
　Blessings and Virtues here do lye
　Examples for Posteritye.
His charitye did all ye poore supplye.
He liued beloved, and much bewayled did dye."

While later Grubb poets may hardly acclaim the author of this epitaph, it is yet typical of the speech and spelling of the Puritan Grubbes of this period, who were striving for that mysterious relationship which exists between poetry and reality, and again it reveals the comfortable circumstances and charity of the Grubbes.

John had reached manhood when the Civil War broke across England.

[3] Information given the author by Dr. E. A. Payne, C.H., The President of the Baptist Historical Society.   See also *The History of the English General Baptists in the Seventeenth Century* (1818) by Adam Taylor, Pt. I, pp. 160, 233–234, 321.   William Smith, the Baptist Pastor at Welton is described as a "Man of excellent parts and learning, a faithful pastor, much respected, *even by* members of the Established Church.   Benjamin Morley became Baptist Pastor at Ravensthorpe after the Civil War.

He could be described as untidy by modern standards, large-boned and flaxen in colouring, a wide-brimmed hat hiding his curls for the most part, until he shaved them off on becoming a Roundhead in the army of Oliver Cromwell. He was self-reliant of necessity, somewhat abrupt and brisk in manner, able to fend for himself. The German side of his heredity was noticeable in a rather gutteral power of speech, to which in later life the soft Celtic intonations of Ireland were to add attraction to his oratory, and produced in his descendants a charm and clarity of pronunciation (the Grubbs were always great talkers!), and a facility for language and speaking. As the years passed he would describe his self-reliance as a God-given assurance of his calling and election by God. He had shared his father's concern at the action of Archbishop Laud in issuing on behalf of King Charles I in 1633 the notorious " Book of Sports " which officially authorised traditional games on Sundays up and down the land. This was too much for the Puritans. " The Archbishop must go! " —and later " The King must go! " they breathed. High regard for the office of bishop or archbishop for some 300 years found no place in the Grubb mentality. None of them has ever aspired to or received episcopal orders! So when the Parliamentary Forces congregated at near-by Northampton at the outbreak of the Civil War, John Grubbe drew his sword and joined them. He was the first soldier in the family since leaving Germany. " The Lord's Day must be kept holy "—that's what mattered to him; he needed no urging to join up and actively play his part, as he believed, for his Country, if not for his King.

It was in Northampton that John Grubbe had met Mary Towers, a bright open-faced Northampton girl, whose father had also enlisted with the Roundheads, and was imbued of the same Puritan strain as himself. Her home was close to the Castle. They saw much of each other, and shared a common faith and outlook.[4] They were married in 1643. Between the battles of the Civil War soldiers in either army came and went. John was back fighting with Oliver Cromwell's forces at the Battle of Naseby,[5] five miles north-west of Ravensthorpe (June 16, 1645), when Prince Rupert's Horse were routed, and the King fled.

" I can say this of Naseby " wrote Oliver Cromwell in his diary " that when I saw the enemy draw up and march in gallant order towards us, and we a company of poor ignorant men—the general having ordered me to command all the horse—that riding about my command, I could but smile out to God in praises and assurances of victory, because God would by things which are not, bring to nought things that are. Of which I had great assurance, and God did it."[6]

---

[4] MSS. collected by Geo. E. Wagner, Esq., Historian, and co-secretary of the "Grubb Family Association of America", of Pottsdown, Pennsylvania.
[5] *Ibid.*
[6] J. R. Green. *Short History of the English People.* p. 558.

PLATE VII

The Protector of England

Commemorative Obelisk on the site of the
Battle of Naseby (June 16, 1645)

English Silver Coins issued during the Civil War, 1640–1645
(mostly Provincial issues)

For Key see page 226.

PLATE VIII

FACSIMILE LETTER OF OLIVER CROMWELL

Written two days before the Battle of Naseby to the Speaker of the House of Commons

S^r beinge Comanded by you to this seruice, I thinke my selfe bound to acquaint you with the good hand of God towards you, and vs, Wee marched yesterday after the Kinge whoe went before vs from Dauentire to Hauerbrowe, and quartered about sixe miles from him, this dey wee marched towards him, Hee drew out to meete vs, both Armies engaged, wee, after 3. howeres fight, very doubtful att last routed his Armie, killed and tooke about 5000. very many officers

I wish this action may begett thankfull nesse, and humilitye in all that are concerned in itt, Hee that ventres his life for the libertye of his cuntrie, I wish Hee trust God for the libertye of his conscience, and you for the libertye Hee fights for, In this Hee rests whose is

your most humble seruant

Oliver Cromwell

Juno. 14th 1645.
Hauerbrowe.

From the Harleian MSS. in the British Museum.

This was the language John Grubb (in army days the " e " had disappeared from the end of his surname) knew and understood. It was the outlook and faith of many an Anabaptist, who abounded in the Roundhead army, many of them put into positions of high command by Cromwell. Dogmatic, as this assurance of victory in the good fight for liberty of conscience may sound today, the sharing of similar experiences brings men together, and strengthens their faith. A facsimile letter of Cromwell, written to the Speaker of the House of Commons two days before the Battle of Naseby (*see opposite page*), breathes the same spirit of trust and assurance that the good hand of God was with them, of thankfulness and humility, that exemplifies Puritanism at its best, and animated his soldiers—and many a soldier since.

Perhaps greatest influence upon the character of John Grubb (to be noticed in the courage of his son, John Junior in facing adversity (*see next chapter*), was that of Oliver Comwell, as prolific a diarist and writer of letters as he was an outstandingly great soldier. Some years later Cromwell offered John Grubb a castle in subjugated Ireland.

Silver Crown of Oliver Cromwell 1658 as Lord Protector; showing the Harp of Ireland with the Dragon of England. (*From the Author's collection*)

Across the sea in Ireland, while Civil War was raging in England, an attempt (was being made by the Irish sometimes called a " rebellion ") to regain the lands of which they had been dispossessed by English colonisation. Rumours told of the thousands of Protestants who were being massacred by the Roman Catholics, or perishing in the wintry weather from cold and hunger. An English army was rushed across St. George's Channel to put down the insurgents, among them a Major Grubb, who was rewarded for his services with an offer of some hundreds of Irish acres. Cromwell himself was in Ireland with a large force some years

33

later from August 15th, 1649 to May 20th, 1650, in which it may well be John Grubb served,[7] and obtained his interest in that country and its castles. Cahir Castle surrendered to Cromwell without a shot, but Clonmel Castle and town held out for two months. Athlone, Limerick and Galway were captured next year by Ireton (Cromwell's son-in-law), and after that the Irish capitulated. A great deal more force was used than by the English armies in Ulster 1969 to the present date; with the result that feelings of hatred for England and the new English settlers, mostly Roundhead soldiers to whom the conquered estates were given by Cromwell in lieu of past pay, or as a reward for their services, were engendered and lasted for the next 150 years. About two-thirds of Irish soil passed into the hands of new Protestant owners. The former Roman Catholic owners were dispossessed, and escorted over the River Shannon to the wild and barren districts of Connaught, and also into County Clare and County Kerry in the south west. Some of them were reduced to wandering the country as rapparees (lawless persons); some were sent to the West Indies. The peasant people, necessary to till the soil were left where they were, in their poor cabins and cottages, completely dependent upon their new English masters. The Cromwellian Settlement of Ireland for two centuries was to cause bitter resentment and trouble in a land that has always been divided by religion.[8]

To emigrate and start life afresh in a new country always involves a choice between present prospects and an unknown future in a strange land. An element of faith underlies a decision to emigrate, often coupled with a feeling of discontent with things as they are. Army life makes it no easier to return to settle down to the old way of living. Nowhere were castles so plentiful, or going so cheaply. But Ireland needed the Gospel. John could never forget John Owen's words, preaching before Parliament in 1649, the very year he had crossed to Ireland with Cromwell and been responsible under his command for bloodshed of the enemy in carrying

---

[7] A letter from Cromwell to a Major Grubb appeared in a book entitled *The Rose of Ireland*, now out of print and unobtainable; there is no means of certain verification whether this Major Grubb was indeed John Grubb of Ravensthorpe, or a John Grubb Esq. (no address given) who in 1642 received one of the " begging letters " sent out over the signature of King Charles I asking " of necessity from his good subjects for the loan of £200 in money or plate for the maintenance of his Army, and the defence of His Person and the Protestant Religion and the Laws of the Land." Such loan was to be handed to the bearer of the letter, on the promise " of the Word of a King to repay it with interest," and concluded—" Given at our Court at Oxford, this 17th day of Febry. 1642." The original of this letter is among the archives of the Hunt-Grubbes at Eastwell, Potterne, and a handwritten copy in the Historical Collection of the Grubb papers (Grubb Coll. S.G.A. 1), in the Friends Library, 6 Eustace Street, Dublin. How it got there is not clear: it is preceded by a moralising commentary, not in the original, and it lacks the King's autograph. There is no evidence the loan was ever made or repaid. Such silver and plate lent to the King was melted down at Provincial mints, such as Oxford and Bristol, and turned into crowns and half-crowns to pay the Cavaliers. (*See plate VII*).

[8] *The Stranger in Ireland.* C. Maxwell, formerly Lecky Professor of Modern History in the University of Dublin. 1954. p. 84ff. (Jonathan Cape.)

out his duties. " Be faithful in this one thing " emphasised John Owen. " Do your utmost for the preaching of the Gospel in Ireland ". God was clearly calling him out for this mission; the same God who had called out his forbears in Germany to suffer persecution for their Protestantism and their biblical faith. The exercise of faith was simple when assured of divine selection, and predestination to be His messenger and servant. The adventurous spirit of his ancestors was in his blood.

In August 1656, John and Mary Grubb with five young children, four girls and a boy, crossed to Waterford with two companions, Richard Draper and Frances Bambry, probably in the convoy which sailed from Bristol on August 12th, under Captain R. Hedges, who was commanded by the Navy Council to take such vessels as were ready, bound for Waterford, Youghall and Cork. There were no daily or even weekly sailings from England to Ireland in those days. Their journey took four days; it could easily have taken seven, if the winds had been contrary. The captain had indented for supplies of two weeks' provisions for his passengers and crew for the journey there and back. Frequently in succeeding centuries John's descendants made this passage, or that from Dublin to Holyhead, in as many hours. A sufficiency of currency is always necessary on any journey, never more so than on the Irish crossing in the 17th and 18th centuries, with the constant hazards of delay. John had armed his family with money bags or leather purses, containing the new Commonwealth of England silver half-pennies (issued for the last time 1649–1656), silver pennies, half-groats, sixpences, shillings, half-crowns and crowns. They were to prove thankful for this ample provision of funds on arrival in Waterford. These coins, with St. George's cross and the

COMMONWEALTH OF ENGLAND CROWN (*From the Author's collection*)
The coins struck in the Commonwealth period have inscriptions in English instead of in Latin, as hithertofore, a language which was considered by the Puritans to savour of Popery.

Irish harp taking the place of the royal arms on the reverse, often cheered them that they had done right to leave England, during the adversities of their first months in Ireland.

Landing at Waterford the new arrivals had to make a temporary home at Ballyrobin and then Old Abbey farm near that city, until they were able to take possession of the dispossessed Annaghs (or Annis) Castle and some 1,000 acres of land, running down to the River Barrow in County Kilkenny, some four miles from New Ross, which was allocated to them when its former Roman Catholic owners had at length removed across the Shannon. Came the first shock when they found this straggling hill-top castle, with its high oblong tower, stone-flagged echoing hall, its solid front door and needle gate, much too vast and cold for their habitation and sadly in need of repair. They made their home in the small castle farm, and started a linen business in an existing mill on the River Barrow close by, called Ferrybank. John's Ravensthorpe training in linens, and the German capacity in his blood for hard work, enabled him to strike out successfully with the help of a certain Thomas Bishop, in a form of business as yet little developed in Ireland. But alas, after the Restoration of Charles II to the English throne, Irish trade with Britain was to suffer from crippling import and export duties imposed by the English Parliament.

Disappointments were many. Time and time again John and Mary were driven to their knees for assurance they had done right in coming to Ireland. The slow payment or non-payment of bills owed him by his customers prevented expansion at the speed John would have liked. Labour was hard to come by. It could not be expected the new English settlers were eagerly welcomed by such of the native inhabitants as remained. Inevitably newcomers like the Grubbs could only find companionship with fellow English settlers, often living a long distance away. Very few were earnest Christians like John. Some gave up the faith they once possessed under the strain, sold out, and returned to England. As has happened to English people in the colonies, some found solace in the cheap Irish whisky, and the famous Irish poteen, leading to drunkenness, incapacity for hard work, and failure. The sale of spirits was encouraged by the Government for the sake of revenue. Living conditions and agricultural methods were primitive, and it was easy, without a living faith, for newcomers to sink to the same level as the discontented Irish labourers around them. The current rate of wages was 4d. a day, while the lowest-paid workmen in England were receiving three times as much (12d. a day). " What need had the Irish labourer to work, who could content himself with potatoes, whereof the labour of one man could feed forty? And with milk whereof one cow in summer will give meat and

PLATE IX

THE FIRST GRUBB MILL IN IRELAND

Beside the River Barrow in Co. Kilkenny, "Ferrybank Mill"

Looking up across the Park from the River near Ferrybank to—

ANNAGHS CASTLE

Photographs kindly taken for the Author 300 years later by the owner and restorer of the old Castle: Klaus Jebens, Esq., of Hamburg

drink enough for three men? . . . And why should they breed more cattle, since it was penal to import them into England? "[9]

There is no better place to test the reality of evangelical faith than the Emerald Isle, among a credulous people, surrounded by wishing wells, superstitions, the cults of St. Patrick and Celtic saints, and long memories. It needed much courage and strength of character to hold fast and persevere. John and Mary were sorely tested, but they had each other, a strong human love supported by Divine love which would not let them go. The high hopes with which they had sailed to Ireland to " do their utmost for the preaching of the Gospel " in Erin's Isle were fading. At first they had sought every opportunity to proclaim the Truth, as they knew it, but few cared to listen to them. There was no available church or chapel to use to proclaim, or to attend to listen to the proclamation of the gospel. Before long they contented themselves with expounding the scriptures to their family on Lord's Day mornings, allowing them as they grew older to attend in New Ross, four miles away, Presbyterian or Independent gatherings when a visiting preacher came to town. It was a constant fight to find new mercies each returning day, to keep fresh, and their faith alive. But man's extremity is ever God's opportunity. When they had been brought very low, their prayers were unexpectedly answered by the Almighty, as prayer so often is.

There knocked at their castle door one cold winter's day a talkative itinerant preacher, dusty, ill-clad, and hairy, (he looked to Mary Grubb rather like her mind-picture of John the Baptist) to seek hospitality and spiritual converse with them. Hospitality they gladly gave; they listened to his message of peaceful and gentle ways, of being quiet and restful before God, of listening to the Divine Voice within rather than striving to convert others. John Exham, for that was his name, was no Anabaptist but a Quaker itinerant preacher, led to tour Munster to visit home after home to expound the Truth as it had been revealed to George Fox, the Leicestershire mystic and founder of the new sect of " Friends." The year was 1676, and John himself was past middle age, 56 years old. How Exham was led to seek John out can be answered only in the same way as Philip the Deacon was sent to seek out the Ethiopian Eunuch. The Divine Spirit surely led him to those in need of his ministry, an assurance of Divine Guidance that John Grubb's missionary-hearted descendants never forgot. John and Mary Grubb's own non-conformist background made it the easier for them to change from one form of nonconformity to another. In their hour of need they accepted and adopted the new principles and truth being proclaimed by itinerants, such as W. E.

[9] *The Political Anatomy of Ireland.* (1691).

Edmundson and Exham, all over Ireland, the principles of the " Friends, the people of God, in scorn called Quakers."[10]

The Grubbs were among the early Irish Quakers, of whom the Penn family in County Cork became the most outstanding in their migration and founding of the colony of Pennsylvania in America. One of John's grandsons was to sail with Penn. Indeed many of the first Irish Quakers were led to seek new homes in the new world, or in the West Indies, particularly Barbados, and left Ireland for ever.[11] John himself remained in Ireland courageously to face his problems, but with the freshness of a new form of faith revealed to him. It is typical of his lineage that the Grubbs never ran away from difficulties. There was too much of the old German fighting spirit in their blood to give up. But as a result of their conversion to Quakerism all forms of military service were abjured by his descendants for the next 150 years, and service in local government or parliament could never be accepted which involved the taking of an oath.

By the early years of the next century it was estimated there were about 600 Quaker families in all Ireland—a number which remained pretty constant until a ' falling away ' during the 19th century. They were organised into Societies, with regular meeting-places in some 50 localities, with no professional or paid ministry, no sacraments, a very strict discipline. They were recognisable by their dark clothes, wide-brimmed hats, plainness of life, charity to the poor, their use of the second personal singular in conversation, " Thou " and " Thee " and " Thine " (never " You ' and " Yours "), their hospitality, and their " yea " and " nay." Big differences in emphasis there were soon to be among them, as among churchmen, Methodists, or Baptists. To some Christianity was a way of life rather than a Creed, and each was free, with liberty of conscience, to follow his own Inner Light. To others the light within is God the Holy Spirit in the inspired word of God, and Bible study, Lord's Day observance, and the well-tried Evangelical and Puritan doctrines of guiding and of paramount importance. But there was no falling apart between them, and what they might seem to lack in a corporate sense without sacrament or creed, was made up in individual discipline and devotion to the Society, and its monthly meetings and annual assembly. The office of Clerk of the Meeting was to become important in holding the Society together—an office frequently to be held by a Grubb.

The remainder of John Grubb's life was undistinguished. The pendulum had swung a half circle from the enthusiasms and ardour of his

[10] They preferred to be called "The Society of Friends", but when a sneering judge, before whom their founder George Fox was brought, had listened to his preaching "Tremble at the Word of the Lord", he dubbed him 'Quaker'! This nickname, given in derision, was accepted. Never was there a less suitable title.

[11] Thus there grew up a considerable trade in sugar between Quakers in Barbados and in Ireland—one source of their growing prosperity.

Anabaptist days in England to the quiet retiring life of his last 20 years, occupied in commercial and domestic interests. But here was the difference. The " Truth " as the Friends knew it could never be spread by the energy of a propagandist. John was to learn that resignation to the will of God, the acceptance of fines or even imprisonment for the non-payment of tithes, or refusal to bear arms (as at the time when Ireland was again convulsed by the fighting between James II and the Protestant Dutch King of England, William III) was the only witness he could give. Moreover within five years of his conversion, his beloved wife Mary died. With his family grown up and married he could not face the future as a widower, as his father had done for 38 or 40 years. Within a few months, his choice fell on a young Irish girl whose name was Elizabeth, less than half his age, and the next year (1682) she gave birth to a boy, John Junior, in the 62nd year of his age. To ease the situation at Annaghs Castle, where he had already taken his only son Samuel, and his son-in-law William Hughes (Quaker husband of his eldest daughter Margaret) into partnership, he went to live in New Ross, close to his second wife's family. Here they opened a shop, it is said, while they looked for a larger and more suitable home. Eighteen of his grandchildren were born at Annaghs Castle, which remained in Grubb hands until the death of his grandson (another John) in the middle of the next century.

Whether or not it was the Light Within that guided him, and without having even seen them—rather like the action of Henry VIII in taking a German wife he had never seen—John Grubb then took a lease at low rent from an absentee landlord (such absentee landlords abounded at that time) of two farms some distance away—Parkstow and Ballymooran—intending when funds allowed to purchase them. Alas for his plans; riding on his grey gelding over uncertain tracks through bogland to inspect them, he was set upon by rapparees,[12] and was robbed and stripped of all he was carrying. Naturally his wife refused to proceed with such a purchase, and removal from Ross and her kinsfolk. They were fortunate in securing a lease of the vacant Meylers or " Millers Park," an estate on the opposite side of New Ross from Annaghs, (near the present Kennedy Memorial Park) where they moved in 1684, and " improved, built upon and planted." Here he lived 12 years and " ended his days in great peace and the faithful profession of the Christian faith among the Quakers."[13] Just before his death, Isaac Watts, one of the greatest and most prolific of hymn-writers, penned words whose language and poetry seem exactly to express John Grubb's personal religion and testimony in Ireland:

[12] A "Rapparee" was an Irish irregular soldier or freebooter. From the Irish word "rapaire" describing the weapons carried by bands of Irish peasants, who supported James II in his ill-fated campaign in Ireland.
[13] Information collected by the late Louis H. Grubb, Esq., of Ardmayle, in possession of his son S. L. Grubb, Esq.

Be Thou my Counsellor, my pattern and my Guide,
And through this desert land, still keep me by Thy side.
Lord, let my feet ne'er run astray
Nor rove, nor seek the crooked way.

Should all the hosts of death, and powers of hell unknown
Put their most dreadful forms of rage and malice on.
I shall be safe: for Christ displays
Superior powers, and guardian grace.

Isaac Watts. 1674–1748.

COLLATERAL TABLE "B"

JOHN GRUBBE (SENR.), 1620–1696

He had two sons, five daughters and 40 grandchildren. He was married twice.

By his first wife, MARY TOWERS of Northampton (m. 1643; d. 1681):

1.	SAMUEL	b. 1645; m. Rebecca THRASHER	11 children
1.	Margaret	b. 1644; m. William HUGHES	7 children
2.	Alice	b. 1647; died aged 11 in Ireland	
3.	Elizabeth	b. 1649; m. John CHANCERY	3 daughters
4.	Mary	b. and d. 1650	
5.	Frances	b. 1652; m. (i) James CANNON	4 children
		(ii) Joseph HAWKINS	3 children
		(iii) William HINDE	2 children

By his second wife, ELIZABETH —— (m. 1681):

2.	JOHN	b. 1682; m. 1707, Anne WILLAN	10 children

His elder son, SAMUEL GRUBBE, inherited Annaghs Castle, Co. Kilkenny, and continued in business as a miller and in the linen trade—he had *11 children:* four sons, and seven daughters, of whom:

1. JOHN GRUBBE   Died young
2. WILLIAM GRUBBE emigrated with William Penn to Pennysylvania, settled and died there, leaving three sons—the FOREBEARS OF THE AMERICAN GRUBBS; also of Dr. BARBROOKE GRUBB, F.R.G.S., explorer and missionary in S. America.
3. THOMAS GRUBBE, b. 1683, d. 1738; m. Mary, daughter of Alderman Lamb, of Waterford. They had six children at Waterford, but male descendants died out.
4. JOHN GRUBBE (J)   He left four daughters only; he succeeded his father at Annaghs Castle, which passed out of Grubb hands on his death.

His younger son, JOHN GRUBB (Junr.) inherited Meylers Park, Co. Wexford on his father's death in 1696, when he was only 14 years old. In 1707 at the age of 25 he married Anne Willan, an 18-year-old Quakeress in County Wexford. They had 49 grandchildren; through each of their four surviving sons, branches of the GRUBB family have descended during the following centuries to the present day. *See Chapter Five, and Collateral Table "C".*

John Grubb, Junior. 1682—1731

of Meylers Park, County Wexford; and Magorban, County Tipperary.
(In America 1727–30)

Married Anne Willan, 1707.   10 children
(4 died young)

"By faith he went out, not knowing whither he went."—Hebrews xi.

ELIZABETH GRUBB and her fourteen-year-old son John continued
to reside at Meylers Park after the death of John Grubbe Senior. It
was too much to expect young John to be able to maintain so large an
estate, helped as he doubtless was by his Irish mother, and by his step-
brother and members of that family from nearby Annaghs Castle. Things
were gradually to slip back.

Good labour was as hard to get as it is in Ireland today. The Roman
Catholic peasantry neither took kindly to their new Protestant English
masters, nor had they the will to work, or hope of improvement in their
lot. Their brass sixpences, shillings and half-crowns,[1] which James II had
issued through lack of silver money in his effort to raise and pay an Irish
Roman Catholic army to win back his throne from the Dutch Protestant
King William III (his son-in-law) were now utterly valueless; no new Irish
coinage had been yet issued, and despair had settled on the Irish people.
After James II's defeat at the Battle of the Boyne (1691) all hope of national
freedom from England went underground for a century, and in Dean
Swift's contemptuous words " The Irish people had become simply hewers
of wood and drawers of water." Irish standards of industry and honesty
fell low (their counterparts could be seen in the slums of a large English
industrial town with a large Irish immigrant population until quite
recently), and in contrast there stood out the honesty and plainness of
those English settlers who had become Quakers, like the Grubbs.

In matters of religion the Quakers seldom antagonised the Roman
Catholic population, often fellow sufferers with them under the repressive
regulations of the times.   For their refusal to pay tithes a number of
Quakers suffered imprisonment. For their refusal to take oaths, their
business often suffered. The Quakers had no desire to wield the sword of

---

[1] Known as "Gun-money", because made from the metal of melted down cannon
and coins.

E

the Lord against their Roman Catholic neighbours, nor to attempt proselytism, and in general were inward-looking, quietists, and pacifists, objecting to the use of fire-arms, even for protection, let alone for the killing of animals or bloodsports.

The child of his father's old age, John Grubb was the first of our ancestors to have been born and brought up in Ireland, and he was to be the shortest-lived and the most unfortunate of them all. Whatever little schooling he may have had from his Irish mother, he had to rely on himself, and failure seemed to dog his footsteps. Not in his choice of an Irish wife, however. His marriage at the age of 25 to Anne Willan, daughter of William and Mary Willan, prominent Quakers in County Wexford, was both a sensible and a happy one. It took place after the form of the Quakers in 1707 when Queen Anne was on the throne of England. In all ten little " Grublets " were born of the union, though four died young. They spent the first twelve years of married life at Meylers Park, continuing Sabbath Quaker meetings there, to which several of their religiously-disposed non-Quaker neighbours used to come. This, however, drew upon John and Anne the anger of the clergyman of the parish, incensed at seeing his small Protestant congregation dwindling through the Grubb " House meetings." His opposition spread to some of the neighbouring farmers, and John's trade, not good at the best of times, suffered appreciably. A steady refusal, being Quakers, to take any form of oath to pass goods through customs for import or export, hindered Grubb business the more.

Anne, who went about barefoot as did most of the Irish women, was kept busy about her large kitchen with her youngsters, with butter-making and cooking. She got on well with her mother-in-law, and both of them did a full day's man's work about the farm with the milking and poultry and ducks. But when Elizabeth died, it seemed clear the door was closing at Meylers Park; their funds had fallen very low: but where were they to go?

At last the leading came in 1719 to move to County Tipperary. A certain John Boles, Clerk of the Cashel Meeting (their circumstances and desire for a move would have been notified to all the Quaker Meetings) offered them the opportunity to come and improve a somewhat dilapidated farm on his Woodhouse Estate at Magorban, situated about half way between Fethard and Cashel. To this day the remains of an old Quaker burial ground at Woodhouse evidences the size of the Quaker cause there, held at John Boles' house on alternate First Days to the meeting in Cashel. The Friends had become more firmly and widely established in County Tipperary than anywhere else in Munster. This was the first offer the Grubbs had to move anywhere; like his father before him, John did not wait to view the farm, and review the prospects. Hoping to be " more at liberty " at Woodhouse, with the prospect of closer fellowship with other

Friends, however poor the dilapidated farm buildings might prove to be, John and Anne pulled up their roots at Meylers Park, brought their Sabbath meetings to a close (to the relief of the clergyman at New Ross), and removed their growing family and livestock thither. John was 37, when the Grubbs first came to settle in County Tipperary, the " Devonshire of Ireland."

It had required real courage to maintain their House meetings at Meylers Park in spite of so much opposition. They had not at this time the experience to ask themselves whether their difficulties might lie in themselves; if they were running away from difficulties and opposition on their own volition, or on Divine Guidance. Almost directly after they had moved, a further heavy testing was to face them. Their first winter in County Tipperary was one of the severest of the century. Their only barn was blown down. The dilapidated buildings were quite inadequate to house their stock. Many of the cattle died from exposure. During the next three years Anne lost her next two children through malnutrition. John was never much of a carpenter, let alone a builder. His efforts to improve the farm buildings failed, as did any profit they hoped to make. He fell behind in meeting his debts, and so reduced did they become that their Quaker landlord felt guided to seize the remainder of their stock for past rents, believing that justice so required of a defaulter, be he a Quaker or not. The *second* crisis in John's life was reached one day when their house was burned above their heads. They had to move again, and were forced to accept financial assistance from " Friends " in days when there was no National Assistance or other means to feed the hungry.

The lessons of faith were being learnt in a hard school, although years later Anne Grubb expressed her belief that their removal from Meylers had been an " improper step," which might have produced the " blast which fell upon their outward affairs." Courageous faith, or an improper step? More than a century later their descendants had to ask themselves the same question, after they had moved into the large and palatial Cahir Abbey in 1835 (*Chapters Ten to Twelve*). Had what they believed was the Inward Light truly been Divine Guidance? Whether it was or not, they were being taught that suffering is an inevitable part of life for the Christian.

Now another step of faith was required of John Grubb. Hearing of their difficulties a Quaker in Waterford offered him employment in America if he would migrate there to superintend the building of a trading ship for him. John had no experience of building ships. He had never lived by the sea. Past experience did not suggest he was much of a builder. He could not take his wife. The offer seemed vague, and no arrangements were made for his wages. Was pure philanthropy the only motive behind the offer? Had he known more of human nature, he might have stopped to review the offer. But the door had closed upon them at Woodhouse.

43

Courage and faith were again shown by John Grubb in agreeing to accept this offered employment in a far country, and from a man he hardly knew, except that he was a Quaker, and his name Francis Annersley.

Before leaving Ireland for America, " A Leaving Certificate of Good Conduct and Recommendation " was necessary to take with him from the Friends Meeting of County Tipperary. British or Irish passports were not yet thought of. Its language is revealing, and it is gratifying to observe the improvement that had taken place in John's affairs, and his care to discharge his first debts;

> "Whereas the bearer JOHN GRUBB acquainted Friends of this Meeting that he has intentions of going to America upon business that calls him there, and desiring a Certificate of us accordingly, WE DO HEREBY TESTIFY that for a considerable time past he hath been a member of our Men's Meeting, and we know not *but* that in general he hath behaved himself pretty orderly, *but* that in his wordly affairs he hath run a little behindhand *but* we hope that he will retrieve it, having lately cleared off a good part of it, so that we desire his welfare, and that his behaviour and management be such as will recommend him to the care and notice of Friends."
>
> Signed at our Meeting at Kilcommon this 26th day of the First Month 1727. John Boles, Jos Fennell Jnr, and about 20 other signatures.

John Boles was Grubb's former landlord at Woodhouse, who had taken his cattle to discharge his debts. Some years later one of his daughters was to marry John Grubb's third son, William, and several Grubbs later married into the Fennell family. It is interesting to note there was no form-filling among the Quakers to obtain such a "passport", and the one long punctuated sentence is typical of the language of this century.

The journey by sailing boat across the Atlantic to America took the best part of eight weeks. John's destination was *Ancorns Creek* in West Jersey near Pennsylvania, where so many Irish Quakers had emigrated some 20 years before, including his own nephew William. He had no means of announcing his arrival, and whether he fell in with William is unknown; the pocket book or diary he kept at this time had many blanks. But John recorded in it that he was so well pleased with the New World, that he had already fixed on a situation to which he intended to bring over his wife and family, and permanently settle. A facsimile of one of his "Letters from America" addressed to his eldest two sons in Ireland is reproduced on plate X, and shows he was expecting his wife to join him.[2] Man proposes, but God disposes. This is the only historical occasion of a Grubb dreaming "to build castles in Spain!"

Alas for his hopes! Although John threw himself wholeheartedly into the building of the ship for Francis Annersley, no pay was forthcoming in New Jersey, and a discouraging message from Waterford arrived that no

[2] Original in Friends Y.M. Library, 6 Eustace Street, Dublin.

pay would be forthcoming until the job was done. Next year a dispute arose that the nearly-finished ship was larger than Annersley required, and proving much too expensive. Responsibility for the errors, if such there were, may be judged from the following entry in John Grubb's pocket book:

"YE 10th of 5th month, being 6th day of the week (a Friday) by order of *John Fellows* (who had arrived from Waterford as the newly appointed captain of the ship), Arthur White and Owen Neall took my chest out of my cabin, and carried it away. There was in itt sundry accts, letters, copys of letters, and severall other things."

Whether it was a case of bad workmanship, or bad relationships between John and the men working under him on the ship, the lack of supplies and

parts, or the lack of pay, John Grubb was summarily dismissed, and without wages. Therefore unable to fulfil other business engagements he had made with residents in New Burlington in connection with the purchase of land, he was thrown into prison in New Jersey (1730), and involved in great pecuniary loss until his release and subsequent return to Ireland after his four years in America.

Thus for the *third* time in his life John Grubb went out, not knowing what the future might hold for him in earning a livelihood to support his wife and six children. He was prematurely aged; his constitution undermined; but he was going home to a wife and family he was assured would be waiting for him in the " ould countrie," and were praying for him.

On his second long voyage across the Atlantic, which took two months, John spent long hours, indeed filled his time, proving the excellence and the comfort and the strength of his Bible. True he had little else to do, but in a full life how seldom it is that a man can give to the Bible the time it deserves for unhurried study and contemplation. His faith had been sorely tested. He felt like Job of old. Yet he remembered God had delivered Job; he must not think it strange concerning the trials he had been called upon to endure, as though some strange thing had happened to him *alone*. However low his faith had fallen he had not lost it. He must rejoice that the Omnipotent God of his father and grandfather was still his own God. Though the voyage was rough and the waves high, though tossed about with many a conflict, many a doubt, fightings within and fears without, lacking the security of any firm abiding place (let alone a castle), he could yet learn to rejoice in the promises of his father's God. God has said it. It was written in His Holy Word. Romans v and I Peter iv he came to know by heart, and could repeat to himself when the tossing and spray was too great for him to see to read. He knew within himself that through his tribulations God was working in him patience; through his patience, experience; and through his hard experiences, hope. John Grubb was called to learn the hard way that suffering is an inevitable part of life for the believer: that the Christian whose life is making any impact upon the lives of others must expect to suffer, as a refining of life. He was in the line of God's will; following a path his Saviour had trod. The three periods of his life, he reflected, had each brought to him suffering in different ways. If the result of his faith had been that he was reproached for the name of Christ in his younger days at Millers Park; if poverty, misunderstanding, and then imprisonment had followed his steps of faith to Woodhouse, and then to America, he must return home now rejoicing, and thankful that he had become a partaker of Christ's sufferings, and had loved ones waiting, and dependent upon him. Words later generations were often to sing aptly describe their ancestor's faith, as he crossed the Atlantic.

> "We have an anchor that keeps the soul
> Steadfast and sure while the billows roll;
> Fastened to the ROCK which cannot move,
> GROUNDED FIRM AND DEEP in the Saviour's Love."
>
> (*P. Owens 1829–99*)

PLATE X

FACSIMILE of an early GRUBB FAMILY LETTER from AMERICA

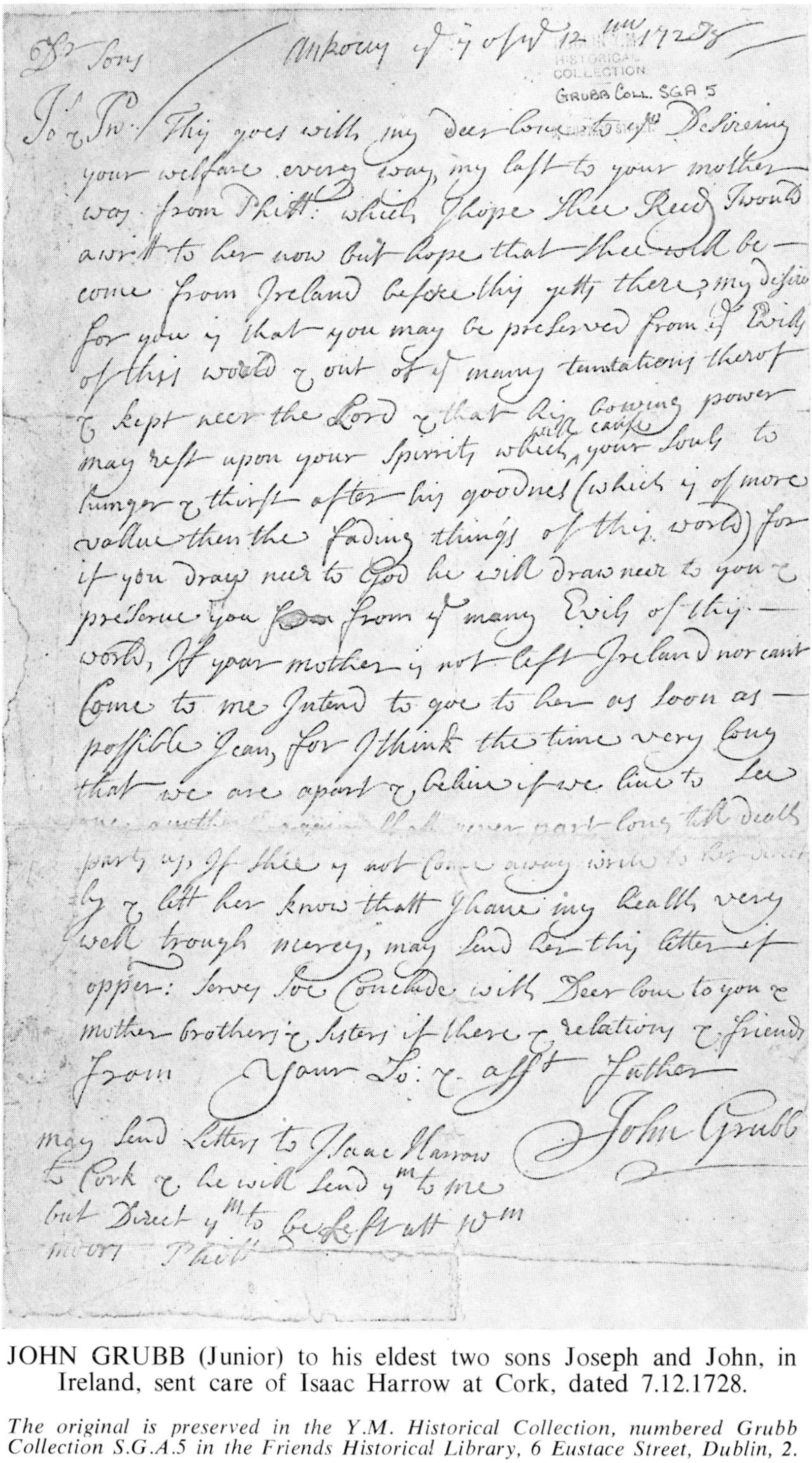

JOHN GRUBB (Junior) to his eldest two sons Joseph and John, in Ireland, sent care of Isaac Harrow at Cork, dated 7.12.1728.

The original is preserved in the Y.M. Historical Collection, numbered Grubb Collection S.G.A.5 in the Friends Historical Library, 6 Eustace Street, Dublin, 2.

PLATE XI

SQUARE-RIGGED BARQUE

CROSSING THE ATLANTIC TO BUILD A SHIP

In faith John Grubb re-crossed the Atlantic, and with hope to bring comfort and cheer to his beloved wife and family, knowing that *all things* must work together for good to them that love the Lord. As he fingered in his pocket the Certificate (or passport) of Good Conduct that the Men's Monthly Meeting of the Quakers of Burlington in New Jersey had given him, John Grubb thanked God that he had not suffered as a thief, or an evil doer, or a busybody in other men's matters.[3] He had no cause to be ashamed, whatever incompetence he had shown as a foreman in shipbuilding. His anchor held. His discovery on that journey across the Atlantic of the deeper meaning of faith was to influence immeasurably the Grubbs in succeeding generations, who sprang from such an ancestor. It was a necessary and fundamental religious discovery about which one of his descendants has recently written a widely blessed book under a somewhat strange title.[4]

Across the seas in County Tipperary, Anne Grubb had equally been learning deep lessons of faith during her three years separation from her husband. She had had to accept the charity of the Quakers, so poor had she become, and to live in a tiny cabin at Rathronan, five miles from Clonmel. It was a time of material distress generally throughout Ireland. John Wesley 20 years later on his first visit to Munster, particularly commented in his diary upon these miserable and common Irish cabins, "built of earth and straw into which no light can enter, save at one hole which is both window, chimney, and door." How great the contrast from the castles where once the Grubbs had lived!

Elizabeth Pease (later to become Mrs. Joshua Fennell, wife of one of the Cashel signatories of the Good Conduct Certificate given to John Grubb) had a desire to pay Anne Grubb a visit. She recorded that she found her and her family " being pretty large, in a miserable cabin with marks of great poverty, and burdened with the nursing of twins."[5] These twins, Anne and Benjamin Grubb, were born in 1727 after their father had left Ireland for America. It is the *only* record of the birth of twins in the Grubb family. Despite the circumstances of their homeless birth, they grew up and married, and were to bless Anne Grubb (their mother), with 17 grandchildren during her widowhood. From Benjamin's later descendants sprang the outstanding Grubb Quakers of the 20th century, Edward

---

[3] See Facsimile on Plate XII of this hand-written Certificate—one of the duties of the clerk of the Burlington Meeting on behalf of the Men's Society, attendance at which, whenever at liberty, was deemed obligatory among the Quakers. Quaker women at this time would not have been likely to make the long sea voyage (cabinless) by themselves. The certificate is in usual form, and testifies to the care and diligence John Grubb had expended on his employer's affairs. Among its 19 signatures are those of *Thomas Scattergood, John Wills,* and *David H. Grubb* who was one of the three sons of John's nephew William (p. 40), a forbear of the American Grubbs

[4] Norman Grubb, M.C., *The Law of Faith.* Lutterworth Press (1947).

[5] MSS. in Friends Library, Eustace Street, Dublin.

Grubb (1854–1939) of East Anglia, J. Ernest Grubb of Suir Island Mills, Clonmel, and Isabel Grubb, for many years Librarian of the Friends' Y.M. Library in Dublin.

Through it all Anne Grubb's faith never faltered. Her zeal for attendance at the meetings of the Friends in Clonmel was such, taking her children with her, that " at one time having omitted to attend a weekly meeting, she came under sharp judgment for the same, during the continuance of which she entered into a covenant with the Lord that if He would forgive her, she would be more faithful in future. [6] The continuing great strength of the Friends lay in their insistence upon every member attending the Sabbath Meetings each Lord's Day . . . just as the strength of Roman Catholicism is the insistence upon every Irish Roman Catholic attending Mass.

A result of the visits of Elizabeth Pease to Anne Grubb in 1728–29 was that she was enabled to move into a nearby farm at Rathronan with the help of the Friends " more commodious for her large family, where her honest industry enabled her to exercise hospitality to her friends, and charity to the poor." Here one happy day next year John Grubb returned to her—as so many Irishmen throughout the centuries come back to their wives after leaving them, perhaps for several years, to find the work abroad that they could not find in Ireland, their pockets full or fairly full. John's pockets were empty, and Anne found him in a poor state of health, run down by his misfortunes, but yet praising God for his goodness. Despite two visits down river to Waterford to meet Francis Annersley face to face; despite the certificate of good conduct he had brought back with him from America, he was still refused his wages for the past three years by Quaker Annersley. The Quakers in the Province of Munster therefore granted John and Anne Grubb the sum of £15 to meet their needs, (the equivalent of £150 today). After the purchase of necessary clothing, the remains of this small patrimony was the only material bequest John could leave his wife and children, when three months after his return to Ireland he succumbed to an attack of inflammation of the lungs on 22nd February, 1731-32, aged only 49.

Anne's circumstances became easier, and she survived her husband by 34 years. Until well over 70 she continued to ride single on horseback into Clonmel to attend her meetings, and see to her affairs. She died in 1756. She had a hard life, but never lost her faith. In the prosperity of her sons and daughters, she lived to see—as her husband in faith had believed—that all things worked together for good under the provision of the Almighty. Her four sons became respectively a leading miller, a leading clothier, a leading grocer in Clonmel, and the third (William) a prosperous farmer just outside. Both her daughters married Quakers in Clonmel, where all

[6] *Ibid.*

of them—with their father and mother and their grandfather's experiences of wandering ever in their minds, remained settled all their lives. One of John Grubb's contemporaries wrote a hymn which exactly expresses the sure foundation of faith that had sustained him during his life and which was to be revealed again and again in his descendants:

" How firm a foundation, ye saints of the Lord,
Is laid for your faith in His excellent Word.
Your God will be with you, your trials to bless,
And sanctify to you your deepest distress.

The soul that on Jesus has leaned for repose,
He will not, He could not desert to its foes.
That soul, though all hell should endeavour to shake,
He never will leave; He will never forsake.   (G. KEITH).

49

JOHN GRUBB (JUNR.) 1682–1731 and ANNE (*née* WILLAN) 1689–1765

They had ten children; six sons (of whom two died young); four daughters (of whom two died young), and 49 grandchildren (40 of them Grubbs)

1.	JOSEPH	b. 1709–10; d. 1782	12 children
2.	JOHN	b. 1712; d. 1779	4 children
3.	WILLIAM	b. 1719; d. 1774	14 children
4.	SAMUEL	b. 1721; *died young at Woodhouse*	
5.	THOMAS	b. 1723; *died young at Woodhouse*	
6.	BENJAMIN	b. 1727 (twin); d. 1802	10 children
1.	Mary	b. 1708; *died young at Meylers Park*	
2.	Elizabeth	b. 1713; m. Gideon TAYLOR	2 children
3.	Lydia	b. 1715; *died young at Meylers Park*	
4.	Anne	b. 1727 (twin); m. Simmons SPARROW	7 children

All of them settled in Clonmel

1. JOSEPH GRUBB, miller and corn-merchant in Clonmel. He married Sarah Greer, 1736. Died aged 72. (*See Chapter Six and Collateral Table "D".*)

2. JOHN GRUBB, their second son, became a clothier and draper in Clonmel. He married Mary Jones of London and died aged 67. They had three sons and one daughter:
   (1) GEORGE GRUBB (1755–1802) Clothier in Hank St., Clonmel. He married, 1779, Anne Morton. They had six sons and one daughter, (Anne), and 35 grandchildren born in Ireland.
      (i) FRANCIS, b. 1780; m. Mary Milner, 1804; three sons and four daughters; d. 1857.
      (ii) JOHN, b. 1781; m. Elizabeth Milner, 1805; 10 sons and five daughters; d. 1852.
      (iii) THOMAS, b. 1783. He went to America and later settled in the West Indies.
      (iv) BENJAMIN, b. 1785. Unmarried.
      (v) ROBERT, b. 1787; m. Susannah Chaytor; three sons, five daughters; d. 1849.
      (vi) GEORGE, b. 1789; m. Hannah Moore; one son, four daughters; (Robert and George were partners as linen-drapers in Clonmel).
   (2) JOSEPH GRUBB, b. 1757. Silk mercer and clothier in Clonmel.
   (3) BENJAMIN GRUBB, b. 1763.
   Their only daughter Sarah, b. 1761, m. Godfrey POWER of Clonmel.

3. WILLIAM GRUBB, their third son, became a farmer. He married Margaret Boles, daughter of John Boles, of Woodhouse, Fethard. He died aged 55 They had six sons and eight daughters (from whom seven died young) viz.:
(1)	Mary	m. George HOWE	4 children
(2)	Elizabeth	m. Thomas CHAYTOR	10 children
(3)	Abigail	m. Thomas McWINN	5 children
(4)	Sarah	m. Joshua MASON (Clonmel Bookseller)	No issue
(5)	Susannah		

   Their surviving two sons were:
   (1) BENJAMIN;
   (2) WILLIAM (Junr.), farmer, who married twice:
      (i) Elizabeth Taylor (d. 1787);
         He had six children; three by each of his wives.
         (a) Margaret, b. 1778; m. Thomas WALSH
         (b) Hannah, b. 1781; d. 1815. Unmarried
         (c) WILLIAM, b. 1784. Unmarried, d. 1860
      (ii) Eleanor Fayle of Dublin in 1791:
         (d) JOSHUA, b. 1795. Unmarried. Killed in an accident.
         (e) Charlotte, b. 1798; d. 1862. Unmarried.
         (f) THOMAS, b. 1800; d. 1878. Fellow of the Royal Society of Dublin, and father of Sir Howard Grubb. His descendants
(*Continued page 86*)

6. BENJAMIN GRUBB, their youngest son became a grocer and provision merchant in Clonmel. He died aged 75. (*See Collateral Table "F".*)

PLATE XII

FACSIMILE QUAKER "PASSPORT"

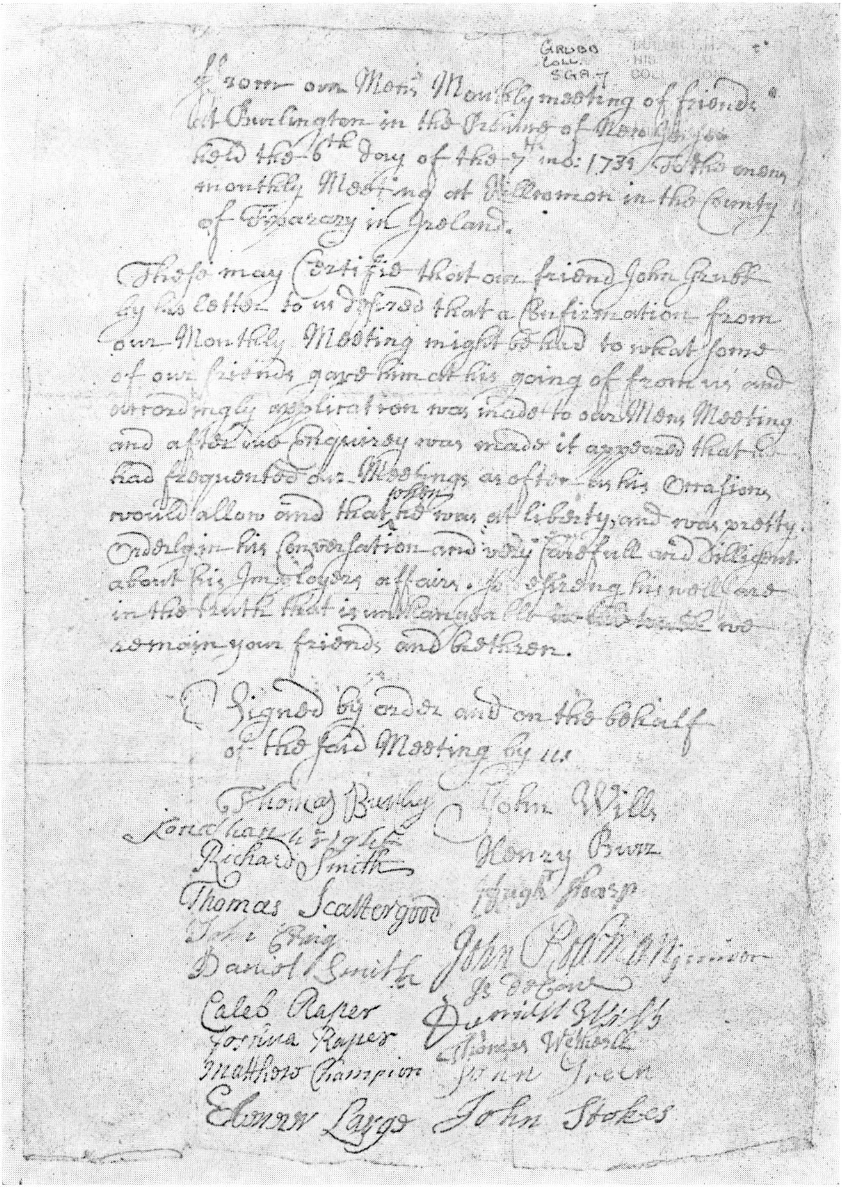

THE CERTIFICATE (The earliest form of Passport) sent by the Quakers of Burlington, New Jersey to the Quakers in Kilcommon in County Tipperary in Ireland, and carried by John Grubb on his return voyage across the Atlantic. Dated 6.7.1730.

Grubb Collection S.G. A.7, Friends Historical Library, Dublin 2.

CHAPTER SIX

Joseph Grubb, of Clonmel. 1709—1782

Miller. Builder of the family fortunes

Married Sarah Greer, 1736.   12 children (4 died young).
46 grandchildren

"A faithful and wise steward, whom his Lord has made ruler over his household."
Matt. xxiv, 45.
and

The eight visits of John Wesley to Clonmel, with an estimate of his influence upon the Grubb family

A GREATER contrast to the life of his parents, John and Anne Grubb, could scarcely be imagined. Joseph Grubb, their eldest son, proved to be the " Dick Whittington " of the family. While they in their distress were in receipt of Quaker relief, Joseph was later to dispense relief to others, and ended his days as owner of all the cornmills along the Clonmel bank of the River Suir, as well as at Anners, two miles along the Waterford road.

Country born and bred, brought up at the farm at Woodhouse with his younger brothers, Joseph Grubb was only 18 when his father left for America to build a trading ship, and had only just reached his majority when his father died prematurely on his return to Ireland. His upbringing had taught him the difficulties and distress of poverty with all the insecurity that frequent moves from place to place can bring. A settled life was his goal, but not as a farmer in Ireland, expecting the best results with worn-out and inefficient equipment and buildings. Through the help of Friends, he was given an opening in the developing corn trade in nearby Clonmel, and he spent all his life in Clonmel as a miller, soon owning his own mill and building or buying others for his sons, as they came to manhood. He was determined to make good, however hard the labour, and he set about it with all the energy of his German blood, his strong broad physique, and his Quaker faith. He was born at the right time, one of increasing prosperity in Ireland (as compared with England across the water) when Irish grain reached increasingly high prices, when business probity proved the exception rather than the rule, and the word of a Quaker could be trusted, when that of others very often could not, so that virtue became in a very

51

practical sense its own reward. It was an age when the upper and middle class Irish Protestants were flourishing at the expense of the always down-trodden Irish Catholic peasantry, living in grinding poverty and hemmed in by the Penal Laws against Catholics. How much he and his brothers who had equally been bound apprentices in Clonmel in the drapery and grocery trades, and equally made good owed to the Quakers, closed and inward-looking as that Society was, who always stuck together and helped one another in times of difficulty, cannot be over-estimated.

At first, Joseph every Saturday forenoon used to trudge five miles home to his mother's farm at Rathronan, riding in again with her to Quaker worship the next day, and lodging the rest of the week in Clonmel. On the road in and out, he would pass the demesne of prosperous Quaker James Greer (1690–) and his wife Ann (née Henderson), and he soon developed a friendship with their only child, Sarah. The Greer family had been established near Lurgan in the north of Ireland from the preceding century, emigrating into Ulster from Leiggs in Scotland, and claimed descent from Margaret, Queen of Scotland. James Greer was a great-grandson of Sir Henry Greer (created Lord Greer in 1592), whose son Henry had come to Ireland with the outstanding Quaker preacher, William Edmundson, and united with him in the first Quaker Meeting at Lurgan.[1] Sarah Greer combined the faith and knowledge of a country woman with the grace of a lady, and had become as much a leader among the young Quakeresses of Clonmel as the burly Joseph had become among the young men. Their marriage seemed made in heaven, and great was the rejoicing when it took place among the Friends in Clonmel in 1736. Joseph was then 27. There were 12 children of this marriage, of whom four died young; and 47 grandchildren.

The ancient Irish name for Clonmel—*Cluain meala*—means " A Field of Honey." The name originated in the foundation of an ancient settlement on the site by one of Ireland's many saints, who was led there by a swarm of bees. So fertile and pleasant was the area, that like bees, the settlement multiplied in numbers. Not far away in the parish of Inislounaght, two miles on the road to Cahir, is an ancient well, known as " St. Patrick's Well," which was to become a popular place for pilgrimage. The Irish say that St. Patrick crossed the River Tar at Clogheen, some 15 miles away, and the Suir at Ardfinan, and so came to Clonmel. He cursed the stream of that place, because " his books had been drowned in them." He said " there would be no mills on those streams for 1,000 years, but the mills of the foreigner would flourish, and the Suir and its banks should

---

[1] Information collected by the late J. Ernest Grubb of Carrick-on-Suir, in a paper entitled "The Three Sarah Grubbs of Clonmel," lent to the author by Mrs. Grubb of Ross-on-Wye. Lord Greer was eighteenth in descent from Sir Henry Greer (b. 1096) who married Julianna, daughter of Sir Robert Maxwell, and lived in Aberdeenshire.

be blessed to the foreigners."[2]   Joseph and Sarah never forgot this particular local legend—one of thousands somewhat similar that have circulated
among the credulous—when within years of their marriage, Greer money
enabled the young couple to buy their own mill on the banks of the Suir,
just outside the old city walls of Clonmel and between them and the river,
and in due course to build and buy others alongside. Were they the foreigners, with their German-English and Scots blood, the foreigners of
whom the Saint was prophesying?

Clonmel town was large enough to have been granted a charter by
King Edward I; its castle was one of the centres of the Earls of Ormonde,
and with its surrounding ramparts withstood many a siege.   In 1616 it
passed into the hands of the Earls of Kildare.   Oliver Cromwell himself
besieged the town in 1650 and suffered there one of the worst reverses of
his Irish Campaign.   It soon became a centre for Quakers before the end
of the century, who recognised its business opportunities beside the swift-
flowing Suir, which runs down into the sea at Waterford, and was to
prove an admirable means for the import and export of goods.   Across the
river stretch miles of rich grazing land—the Golden Vale of County Tipperary—and on the produce of that fertile area, particularly corn and butter,
the town depends still today.   It was the centre for the surrounding farming
community.   Under the shadow of its walls and castle the Grubbs were to
find, if unconsciously, the same sense of security in God, and in the open
profession of their faith, as the family had once known in Northampton,
and later at Annaghs Castle.   Like bees, the descendants of Joseph and
Sarah multiplied in Clonmel, later to be spoken of as "the city of the
Grubbs".   There were over 50 of them settled in business in the town and
neighbourhood before Joseph died, and twice that number whose graves
remain in the enclosed tree-lined Quaker cemetery, established outside the
city walls.[3] Pointing to a row of beehives in her father's large garden, a few
days before they were married, Sarah Greer had said to Joseph, "Shall I
see if there's some honey ready?"   "Don't", said Joseph rather apprehen-
sively viewing the bees swarming round the hives. "Come back, thou wilt
be stung else".   "It's nonsense, that is", replied Sarah.   "Bees don't
sting me!   Hummer bees never will sting a virgin!"   A trill of laughter
passed her lips.   " That's what they say in the country—if a maiden can
walk through a swarm without being stung, that proves she is a virgin,
and when she gets married, she'll have a swarm of children."   Armed with
the simple faith of her beliefs, she strode serenely through the swarm, and
extracted unscathed a comb filled with honey for use at the wedding recep-

[2] St. Patrick's Well has always been Clonmel's most revered place of pilgrimage.
   A notice states "St. Patrick's Day Society, Clonmel, wishes to thank Mr. Sam Vorty
   and Mr. Armand Hammer of Los Angeles, and the Irish Israeli Society of South
   California, whose generous financial aid has made it possible to carry out the
   extensive restorations on this site. 1969.
[3] The Quaker Cemetery, in O'Neil Street, Clonmel is still well maintained.

tion the next week. Joseph never forgot—nor did any of his family to whom he would often recount the incident—this illustration of the simple faith and courage of their mother.

General and increasing prosperity in both England and Ireland under the peaceful reigns of the Anglo-Hanoverian Kings George II and George III formed the background to the 50 years Joseph and Sarah Grubb were building up the family fortunes in the milling world. With his own German origins, it all seemed part of the Divine Plan, thought Joseph, that he should thrive under such kingship, not that he had any connection whatever with royalty in England. Blessed with five able sons, whom he set up in their own mills in or around Clonmel, and strong in his simple Quaker faith, his rigid honesty in business, his care that weights should be exact with no fiddling, his sacks full size without holes, his promises kept (even though it meant long hours of extra work), his premises clean, his deliveries punctual, and no goods overpriced, was all evidence, that the world about them could see, that the Grubbs could be trusted. This good reputation increased business for the Grubbs from all over Ireland, and necessitated expansion of the mills, not merely to provide for each individual son and that son's family. The same held good for Joseph's brothers also settled in Clonmel. The youngest of them, Uncle Benjamin, a tall well-made man, became a leading grocer in the town, where a man could always be sure of getting "good grub". Uncle John became the largest clothier, draper, and silk-mercer in Clonmel, and had a virtual monopoly of sartorial fashions, when he had set up three of his sons with their own shops in the trade. Uncle William had a large farm and a large family of 14 children, though half of them died before they reached their teens. Two of Joseph's married sisters lived close by. Grandmother Greer had come into town to a tall Georgian house in the main street, with a bow window on the first floor above the street, her withdrawing room, from which she could see all that was going on outside —and so could other Grubbs too when they came to visit her! Old mother Anne Grubb continued to ride into town twice a week, covered with her black shawl, to attend her meetings and see to her affairs and her family. And frequently one or other of her more than 40 grandchildren would walk back beside her to stay and help her with her animals. It was a kindly and happy life in which the Grubbs grew up and worked in Clonmel, and God and Quaker meetings were at the centre of it. Again, thought Joseph, the pendulum of life has swung in full measure from the conditions of our boyhood days.

Only gradually did the Grubbs become truly Irish. The bonds of their English or Scottish blood were exceedingly strong among Quakers who lived in Ireland. The strict disciplines under which they lived necessarily kept them apart from their neighbours, whether fellow Protestants, or

Roman Catholics. In England it is said to take 50 years before a newcomer in a small country town ceases to be treated as a " foreigner "; in Ireland it took even longer. Outside the Society of Friends, and perhaps surprisingly, they found closest affinity with the Germans (known as Palatines) and French refugees settled in the neighbourhood, and active and expert in the linen and silk industries. There were congregations of them with their own pastors in Waterford, Limerick, Cork, Kilkenny and Carlow.

Just before his third visit to Clonmel, John Wesley lucidly describes the visits he paid to three such German settlements in the neighbourhood, on Wednesday, July 9th, 1760:

"I rode over to Killiheen, a German settlement near twenty miles south of Limerick. It rained all the way: but the earnestness of the poor people made us quite forget it. In the evening I preached to another colony of Germans, at Ballygrane. The third is at Court-mattrass, a mile from Killiheen. I suppose three such towns are scarce to be found again in England or Ireland. There is no cursing or swearing, no Sabbath-breaking, no drunkenness, no ale-house in any of them. How will these poor foreigners rise up in the judgment against those that are round about them!"[4]

So it became necessary for Joseph and his sons to learn to speak French and German, if they were properly to utilise these neighbours' skills in industry. Towards the end of the century they had their own French tutor for their children, and languages (with their background of German blood) always seemed to come naturally to them. This of course only made the Grubbs seem the more like foreigners in Clonmel, speaking "foreign languages for shure"! Today an ever increasing number of landowners in Ireland come from a German background.

By the middle of the 18th century there were some 50 recognised and regular Quaker meetings in all Ireland, and between 3,000 and 5,000 practising Friends. Their smallness in number was out of all proportion to the influence they exerted in an age when it needed a Wesley constantly to visit Ireland to stir the Protestants from inertia and somnambulance, and some 30,000 Roman Catholic priests, mostly from Spain, to look after the vast majority Roman Catholic population. County Tipperary and its capital town Clonmel were visited frequently by both priests and by Protestant preachers, including Quakers, and by Wesley himself at least eight times. Casual visitors were always coming and going, and putting up at the several inns the town boasted. The town was no backwater before tourists started coming over to fish and hunt. It was on one of the main coach roads from Dublin to Waterford. One such passing visitor, around 1765, thus described Clonmel:

"I left Caher (later to be spelt Cahir) at an early hour for Clonmel,

[4] *Journals of John Wesley*, Vol. iii, 9.

the largest town in County Tipperary, & one of the most important in the interior of Ireland. After a charming drive through very agreeable country, I passed under the main gateway of Clonmel (this is the West Gate which is still standing) & alighted at the Great Globe Inn. For the last 15 years the prosperity of Clonmel has been steadily increasing, and it is at present a decidedly improving town. This is truly refreshing after Kilkenny, Cashel, and the many other wretched places I had passed through and sojourned in.

The chief branches of the trade of Clonmel are the corn trade, the bacon trade, and the butter trade. The corn trade is very large, not fewer than between two and three hundred thousand barrels of wheat being annually brought into Clonmel. It is the great point of export for the County of Tipperary, which is one great granary, as well for parts of other counties, for it is the first point at which water carriage starts.

"The corn mills in and around Clonmel are upon a very extensive scale, and are very numerous. A cornmill in England is generally a picturesque building, crossing a rushing stream which provides the power to turn the mill, and employing the miller and his men, some half-dozen perhaps. Cornmills in Clonmel are very different. They are like the great factories or mills which we find in the English manufacturing districts, and they employ as many persons. The bacon trade is also very extensive here, not fewer than an average of 30,000 pigs being killed a year.

"There are not many able-bodied men out of work in Clonmel, and one sees few ragged and barefooted people in the streets. Three-quarters of the inhabitants are Roman Catholics; there are about 1500 Episcopalians, and a considerable number of the Society of Friends, the members of which in Clonmel are generally prosperous and somewhat aristocratic. I noticed among the Quakeresses more smartness of dress, and a greater disregard for the strict costume than in any other place I have visited.

"Everybody keeps a jaunting car: but then a jaunting car costs but £20 or £25 building, with all its etceteras, and there is no tax on either carriage or horse, and no toll-bars.

"The whole population wears a respectable look: there is an appearance of something doing: a bustle and a throng, evidently arising from people having an objective in view. The shops are well-filled and well-frequented."[5]

We can almost see the aristocratic bearing and pretty silk dresses of Joseph and Sarah Grubb's daughters and nieces, as Grandmother Greer watched them from her window strolling down the main street. They look just like their mother, she mused to herself, when Joseph was courting her: and well they might, as befits the descendants of Scotland's loveliest Queen. "Only I never would let Sarah dress as she now allows her girls to do." We can almost see the activity of Joseph and his sons, always giving the impression to a stranger they had something to do—in comparison to the slouching—any time will do—attitude of passers by in every age.

[5] *My Clonmel Scrapbook.* pp. 58–63. Edited by James White. (1907).

Three of Joseph's nephews set up shop; Benjamin, with his four pretty daughters near the Globe Inn, and another Joseph, who kept a silk mercers business, in which he was to be assisted by his beautiful niece Anne. Here the latest fashions and dresses were supplied. There was much coming and going in his shop, and many were the suitors for the hand of this pretty young Quakeress, Anne Grubb. Far from Clonmel and the County of Tipperary did the fame of her exquisite beauty spread. W. H. Maxwell, the novelist, thus described her under a fictitious name.[6]

> "A lovelier face I never looked at: scarcely nineteen years old, tall, and with gentle hazel eyes. Her golden brown hair was parted Madonna-like, which her silken cap could not fully hide. Notwithstanding her costume the roundness of her arms, and the symmetry of her beautiful waist and bosom could not be concealed. The outline of her face was strictly Grecian—her complexion pale and delicate, whilst her ripe red lips seemed as if some Clonmel bee had stung them newly. Were anything wanting to make her quite irresistible, her voice was so musical and so modulated, that the listener held his breath to hear."

This was the beautiful Miss Grubb who promised her heart and hand to a certain Frederick Close, Lieutenant in His Majesty's 86th Regiment, then stationed in Clonmel. Frederick was over six feet tall, of athletic build, very handsome, the son of a wealthy Manchester merchant. He hardly needed the glamour of his gold-braided uniform to complete his conquest. But alas! The pacifist principles of the Clonmel Grubbs forbade the union of the lovely Anne to a soldier, and a non-Quaker. Many were the meetings between the lovers. Many their surreptitious moonlight strolls along the banks of the Suir, which Frederick, not being an Irishman, would persist in pronouncing as if it were " Sewer," and not correctly " Shure." He always found his " sh's " difficult. Many were the unfriendly attempts of the Friends to break the friendship. But inconsistency has always been common in Ireland, and among the Grubbs' too, it must be admitted. One Sunday evening, when most of her family were at their Lord's Day meeting, Anne slipped away under the excuse of a headache to meet her lover. The couple were observed walking by the river out of town in the Waterford direction, a favourite lover's promenade. Then mystery! Neither was ever seen again.[7] Was it an elopement to America from Waterford! Was it a suicide pact? Was it a drowning accident, in which Frederick lost his life trying to save Anne? Was it murder by a person or persons unknown? Was it murder by a certain Quaker called Strangman, who later brought a libel action successfully against the paper which had more than hinted that his jealous hand had killed them both? A letter from Lieutenant Frederick Close to Miss Anne Grubb is preserved in the Friends Y.M. Library in Eustace Street, Dublin. Had the Quakers been able to

[6] *The Bivouac*, by W. H. Maxwell. pp. 110ff.
[7] "A Munster Mystery," pp. 213–225 of *My Cronmel Scrapbook*.

F

open their doors to the officers and men of the different regiments that from time to time were stationed in their midst, the tragedy, if such it was, might never have occurred.

The plain Quaker dress of sombre black and white, unadorned by costly silks filled a contemporary of Joseph Grubb, and a former Fellow of Lincoln College, Oxford, with admiration. He was John Wesley (1703–1791), the founder of Methodism, whose life-span surrounded that of Joseph by fifteen years, and who visited Clonmel on at least eight different occasions (*see below*). He devoted one of his 45,000 sermons to the specific issue of the right dress for a Christian.[8]

> "Let me see before I die a Methodist congregation full as plain dressed as a Quaker congregation. Only be more consistent. Let your dress be cheap as well as plain. I pray you let there be no costly silks among you, how grave soever they may be. Otherwise you do but trifle with your own souls and with God."

Again this note of inconsistency is struck among the Quaker Grubbs. Had Wesley in mind the smart dresses and costly silks he had noticed worn in Clonmel, and sold by a Quaker Grubb? Was he thinking of the inconsistency of a Quaker keeping a silk-mercers shop? Did some of these perfectly turned out young lady Grubbs attend his meetings, so that he was particularly thinking of them? In matters of clothes and dancing and singing and music, the Grubb descendants of Joseph and Sarah, and from Scotland's lovely Queen, were often to " give concern " to the stricter-minded of the Friends (*see Chapter Eleven*). The Clonmel Quakers by 1771 had become a " wigged " company, and differed from the " plainer " Friends in England by some of them, led by the Grubbs, wearing dark blue coats and waistcoats, black breeches, gay speckled stockings, and large silver buckles on their shoes, with a plain triangular hat above the wig. Inconsistencies are part of that charm so often attributed to the Grubbs and also part of their weakness, at times making them appear to be frivolous and " trifling with their own souls " to the stricter minded.

The Four Volumes of John Wesley's Journals provide a second contemporary source from which much may be learned of life in Clonmel at this period.[9] During his 88 years of life he frequently visited Ireland to proclaim the Gospel, generally for about eight weeks each alternate year in the spring and summer. There was scarcely an Irish town or village that he did not visit on horseback. He visited and preached in Clonmel on at least *eight* different occasions, often outside the barracks, for his chief concern was always the soldiers. On one occasion, and possibly on two, he was allowed by Joseph the use of one of the huge lofts stretching across

[8] "Sermon on Dress," by John Wesley, A.M. in his *Collected Sermons*, p. 10.
[9] *The Journal of John Wesley, A.M. Sometime Fellow of Lincoln College, Oxford.* Vol. ii, 185; 347; iii, 10–11, 92–94; iii, 407; iv, 356.

his six-storied mills, which accommodated 500 people. The first visit recorded in his Journal was on Thursday, June 16th, 1750, when he was 47 years of age, and Joseph would have been 41. " So civil a people as the Irish in general, I never saw, either in Europe or America," he wrote. His usual plan was to cross from Holyhead to Dublin, and after visiting his Society there, to travel either directly south by way of Kilkenny and Clonmel to Waterford, then on to Cork and back by Limerick and the middle Irish towns to Dublin; or north from Dublin visiting Sligo and making his way gradually south, and to as many towns and villages as his time permitted. Inevitably the Grubbs became interested in the Evangelist's intrepid itinerations, in the whole Scriptural gospel that he proclaimed, by his methods and ability to reach the spiritually neglected, and soldiers, and by the hymns based on scripture that he and his brother Charles Wesley (the poet of the Evangelical faith in the 18th century) were almost weekly composing and issuing. Methodism was born in song. Quakers knew no singing in worship. The voice of praise was silent among them. Joseph never forgot hearing Wesley preach that the singing of hymns and psalms does as much as preaching to impress the Word of God upon people's minds; that much more is written in the Bible about praise and thanksgiving than about exhortation and preaching.

Wesley's *second visit* to Clonmel was in May 1756. It is thus described in his Journal:

> "*Thurs 6.* I rode to Kilkenny. One of the dragoons quartered here soon sought us out. A few, both of the Army and the town constantly meet together. I preached in the barracks. Still, in Ireland, the first call is to the soldiery.

> "*Fri 7th.* We rode to Waterford; I earnestly exhorted the Society to love as brethren. I spent a great part of the day in striving to remove misunderstandings and offences. It was not lost labour. We had high and low, rich and poor, 57 on the Sunday evening; the room being too small we were obliged to go into the yard, & the adjoining garden. There seems now to be a general call to this city. So I thought it best next morning, *Monday 10th*, to leave Mr. Walsh there, while I went forward to Clonmell, the pleasantest town beyond all comparison which I have yet seen in all Ireland. It has four broad, straight streets of well-built houses, which cross each other in the centre of the town. Close to the walls on the south side runs a broad clear river. Beyond this rises a green and fruitful mountain (The Comeragh mountains) which hangs over the town. The vale runs many miles both east and west, & is well cultivated throughout. I preached at five in a large loft, capable of containing five or six hundred people: but it was not full: many being afraid of its falling, as another did some years before: by which some of the hearers were much hurt, and one so bruised that she died in a few days.

(This must be a reference to his former visit to Clonmel in 1750).

"Tues 11. I was at a loss where to preach, the person who owned the loft refusing to let me preach there (because of the danger) or even in the yard below. The Commanding Officer being asked for the use of the barrack-yard answered it was not a suitable place. 'Not', said he, 'that I have any objection to Mr. Wesley, I will hear him, if he preaches under the gallows'. It remained to preach in the street, and by this means the congregation was more than doubled. Both the officers and soldiers gave great attention, till a poor man, special drunk, came marching down the street, attended by a Popish mob, with a club in one hand, and a large cleaver in the other, grievously cursing & blaspheming and swearing he woud cut off the Preacher's head. It was with difficulty that I restrained the troopers: especially them that were not of the Society. When he came nearer, the Mayor stepped out of the congregation, & strove by good words to make him quiet: but he could not prevail: on which he went into his house, & returned with his white wand. At the same time he sent for two Constables, who presently came with their staves. He charged them not to strike the man, unless he struck first: but this he did immediately, as soon as they came within his reach, and wounded one of them in the wrist. On this, the other knocked him down, which he did three times before he would submit. The Mayor then walked before, the Constables on either hand, and conducted him to the gaol."

To this day the " four broad straight streets " remain, with the " Main Guard " designed by Sir Christopher Wren as the Town House of the Count Palatine of Tipperary at their intersection. It became the Court House and jail, and was so called because the Main Guard was stationed there. These four streets are known today as—

(1) *O'Connell Street,* which runs west to the West Gate of the old walled city of Clonmel, which still stands.

(2) *Parnell Street,* its eastern counterpart, which ran to the East Gate (now no more), and the later military barracks.

(3) *Gladstone Street,* running north, past the site of the old North Gate to the many new schools and hospitals since erected.

(4) *Field Street,* running south to the River Suir and the large Grubb mills along the quay, but 100 yards away, in which Wesley preached.

These now defunct six-storied buildings lining the river bank and just outside the old city walls, were all once Grubb properties. In the large loft of one of them, still capable of holding five or six hundred people, Wesley preached. It may have been Joseph's predecessor as owner, or Joseph himself (then aged 47) who refused to allow Wesley to preach in the loft again, owing to the danger. Probably Joseph and many of his mill-hands would have been among the concourse in the nearby street to listen to Wesley. His Quaker caution for the safety of those using his buildings, or standing in the yards below, points to another Grubb characteristic, sometimes since assailed—forethought before faith, safety for the

PLATE XIII

THE OLD BRIDGE AND QUAY, CLONMEL, CAPITAL OF
CO. TIPPERARY

Showing the Grubb Mills, and (*on left*) part of those of Robert Grubb
on Suir Island

PLATE XIV

JOHN WESLEY
(A.M. Oxon)

Preaching in Ireland

From a fine proof engraving in Mr. Geo. Stampe's collection of the painting by John Russell (1745–1806), the first Methodist R.A.

Reproduced by permission of the Methodist Archives and Research Centre.

person taking precedence over preaching for the possible salvation of the soul, assured that God will have other time and means for the latter, "who willeth not that any should perish."

The *third visit* of John Wesley to Clonmel in July 1760 followed his preaching in the Old Camp at Limerick. He wrote:

"I was well pleased to see a little army of soldiers there, & not a few of their officers; nor did they behave as unconcerned hearers, but like men who really desired to save their souls."

"*Monday, July 21st.* I left Limerick, & about noon preached near a great house at Shronill, which a gentleman started to build, but cannot afford to finish, having only £30,000 a year, and a hundred thousand in ready money.

'The beggars but a common lot deplore,
The rich–poor man is most emphatically poor!' "

(The age for the building of huge palatial houses in parks all over Ireland had begun, many like that at Shronill being left uncompleted).

At six I preached at the camp at Caire (Cahir) to a large and serious congregation of soldiers. Thence we rode on to Clonmell, where I preached near the Barracks *at eight in the morning to a wild staring people, but quiet perforce, for the soldiers kept them in awe.* We rode in the afternoon to Waterford, where I preached three evenings with great hope of doing good. Why should we despair of any soul whom God hath made?"

The *fourth visit* in the same week, on route from Waterford to Cork, is thus described:

"*Thurs. 24th.* I looked over that well-wrote book, Mr. Smith's *State of the County and City of Waterford.* He plainly shows that 1200 years ago Ireland was a flourishing Kingdom. It seems to have been declining ever since; especially after it was torn into several independent kingdoms. Then it grew more wild and barbarous for several hundred years. In Queen Elizabeth's time it began to revive; it increased greatly in inhabitants and trade until the deadly blow which began on October 23rd 1641. 300,000 Protestants by a moderate computation were then destroyed in less than a year: more than twice as many Papists within a few years following: most of these were adults, & this was a loss which the nation has not recovered yet. It will probably require another century to restore the number of inhabitants it had before."

(See Chapter four on the "Irish Rebellion")

"*Fri. 25th.* I preached once more near the Barracks in Clonmell, and next morning took horse at four. About 11 the sun was scorching hot, till we were near Rathcormuck. Here we rested two hours, and then rode on (mostly shaded by flying clouds) to Cork." Not bad going to cover the 60 miles from Clonmell to Cork in one day in scorching weather. Wesley remained in Cork, Bandon, and Kinsale for three weeks, preaching to "dull careless townsfolk" and to "soldiers in a field, standing so close to the fort that they could hear as well within as without". He urged his preachers always to preach "in the Exchange, as they may do without molestation, instead of in their little ugly dirty garret". A Company of Players were in town, but many of them came to hear Wesley one Friday night, "for a watchnight was newer to them than a comedy"! He was recalled to Dublin for a ship to take him to Holyhead. (One wonders why he did not sail from Cork?).

His *fifth visit* is thus recorded:

"*Mon. Aug 15.* I again passed through Clonmell, and took my usual stand near the Barrack Gate. I had abundantly more than my usual congregation, as it was Assize Week, so that the town was extremely full of gentry, as well as common people." (*See Appendix A (ii).*)

The *sixth visit* came two years later on his next tour of Ireland

"*5th July, 1762.* I rode to Clonmell and preached in the evening near the Barrack-gate *to a wild staring multitude*, many of whom would have been rude enough, but they stood in awe of the soldiers." He went on to Cork, where a well-wisher told him "He shot over the heads of the soldiers in his preaching, who did not understand anything but hell-fire and damnation." "So I strongly applied the story of Dives and Lazarus; they seemed to understand this, & all but 2 or 3 boy-officers behaved as men fearing God." This parable was one of Wesley's favourite themes, which he frequently records he took as his subject in Ireland.

Only two further visits to Clonmel are recorded, suggesting he found the soil barren, and the town indifferent, perhaps due to Quaker influence.[10]

The *seventh visit* (recorded) in 1771 came nine years later on route to Cork.

"*Mon. 29 May.* In the evening *I preached in the Market-Place at Clonmell to a listening multitude.* Some seemed inclined to disturb: but the serious well-behaved troopers held them all in awe."

His last visit (*the eighth*) was in 1787, when he was aged 84, but as active as ever. He was accompanied by three ladies, Mrs. Cookman with her sister (Henry) Moore, and Miss Acton, who probably concerned about his health, had come on purpose to accompany him. He wrote:

"*Mon. 30 May 1787. I preached in the Assembly-Room at Clonmell to a congregation very little awakened.* But how soon can our Lord say to any of these 'Lazarus, COME FORTH'?"

Wesley had the literary knack of expressing what he wanted to say simply and lucidly. " I just set down the words that come first " he declared, and his Journal begun in 1735 and continued for 56 years, is among the longest, if not the greatest, of autobiographies. It was published in instalments, the last appearing soon after his death. It covers his itinerations of over 250,000 miles, in which he is said to have preached 40,000 sermons, and generally at least four or five a day. He always rose at

4 a.m., and attributed his good health to his early rising, times without number recording: " I preached at five in the morning—an unheard of thing in Ireland ".

The Irish day begins late and ends late. Rural shops stay open often until 10 p.m. or 11 p.m., except on Sundays, when the jingle of hoofs and cartwheels on the tarmac road across the field, or the clatter of high-heeled shoes on the pavement underneath the hotel window, are among the earliest impressions the author has retained of good devout people in the land of his fathers making their way to early Mass.

Joseph and Sarah Grubb lived in an age of journal writing. Contemporary Grubb " journals " which have survived, and many letters, particularly the journal of Joseph's nephew, John, written at the impressionable age of 20, (his brother Benjamin, the provision merchant's son), afford a further picture of life in Clonmel among the Friends, their lavish hospitality, the great deal of time occupied in days of leisure by the women folk and young people paying visits, and being visited, and entertained to meals, the woollen market for serges (with but few buyers), and Jos Mason's auction of books, which continued each night of assize week.[10] Their houses were big—the drawing room of John's parents is described as nearly full with 70 persons gathered for a Quaker " opportunity "; their tables lavish—a Grubb characteristic in every generation following. John Grubb seems to have enjoyed the annual Clonmel fair, on one occasion seeing 14 pickpockets and robbers apprehended, and shooting snipe over the Suir. He carefully lists the different companies of troops and Light Dragoons brought into the town to deal with the continuing riots in 1786 of the *White Boys* over the enclosure of common land, their burning of gentlemen's houses, levelling of fences, and digging up newly-made entrances and gates into fields.[11] He writes of attending several hangings on Gallows Hill, chiefly of White Boys, of that of their Captain John O'Flaherty who had " his hair nicely powdered, was well dressed, and not at all affected when going out to his death," and of the frequent whipping of White Boys through the streets. Certainly life in Clonmel was never dull amid the rough and often turbulent life of eighteenth century Ireland surging around the capital of County Tipperary.

Quaker influence in Clonmel, fast rivalling Waterford as the leading Quaker stronghold in the south of Ireland, together with his identification with the forces of government by preaching to the troops, prevented Wesley from founding any permanent Society in the town among its

---

[10] *Sarah Grubb: Some Account of her Life and Religious Labours, and Extracts from her Letters.* Robert Jackson. Dublin. 1792. (This was Mrs. R. Grubb, née (Tuke.) *The Letters of Sarah Grubb (née Pim) of Anner Mills*, in the Friends Library Dublin. *The Journals of John Grubb* (1766–1841) in possession of Mrs. Grubb of Ross-on-Wye. Joshua Mason, the bookseller, had married his cousin Sarah (p. 50).
[11] See Appendix "B".

"wild-staring but quiet people", an apt description, perhaps, of the Quakers among his audiences.[12] Wesley's *Journal* shows he had a very high opinion of the Quakers. Riding one day quite early in his ministry through the Devonshire village of Sticklepath, he records he was stopped in the street, and asked abruptly, "Is not thy name John Wesley?" "Immediately two or three more came up and told me I must stop there. I did so, and before we had spoken many words, our souls took acquaintance with each other. I found they were Quakers, but that hurt me not at all, seeing the love of God was in their hearts".

On another occasion, preaching at Edinderry, he found many of the Quakers were present, it being the time of their General Meeting. " I was shown by one of them the Journal of William Edmunson, one of their preachers in the last century. If the original equals the picture (which I see no reason to doubt) what an amiable man was this. His opinions I leave. But what a spirit was here. What faith, love, gentleness, longsuffering. Could mistake send such a man as this to hell? Not so. I am far from believing this that I scruple not to say " Let my soul be with the soul of William Edmunson '."[13]

In Dublin he records breakfasting in 1756 with " one of the most lovely old men I ever saw; John Garret, a Dutchman by birth, and a Speaker among the Quakers."[14] Years later Garret's great grand-daughter was to marry a great grandson of Joseph Grubb (*see Chapter Eleven*).

At the same time as a churchman, Wesley believed the great weaknesses of the Quakers were their lack of the two Sacraments of Baptism and the Lord's Supper, and of singing and praise in their public assemblies, so that they tended to become much too introspective. From time to time he records, " I baptised (seven) persons who had been brought up and educated among the Quakers." If ecumenicism was not yet, the spirit born in the Grubb family by the influence of John Wesley was to flower in the interdenominational activities of his descendants (*see Chapter Twelve*).

More immediate and positive was the influence of Wesley upon Sarah Grubb, Joseph's wife, and upon her daughters-in-law. Sarah's tender sympathy was aroused at the widespread need in Ireland for the gospel message—the need this visiting clergyman was attempting intrepidly to meet—and by the poverty of the great mass of its population. Except for the Quakers in good business positions, there was as yet no solid Irish middle class. People either had too much or too little. Ireland would have been ready soil for communism, but Soviet Russia was not yet. If

---

[12] *Journal of Rev. John Wesley*: iii, 91 and 266—"Almost throughout the Province of Ulster I found the work of God increasing: and not a little in Connaught, particularly at Sligo, Castlebar, and Galway. But in Munster 'a land flowing with milk and honey' how widely is the case altered. . . ."
[13] *Journal of John Wesley, A.M.* iii. 219, 406.
[14] *Ibid.* Vol. ii, 343.

an Englishman could face so many hardships in riding all over Ireland to proclaim the Word of God, said Sarah one day to her husband, should not Irish Christians do likewise, and become evangelists to their own people? They at any rate would not have all the delays and hazards of that sea crossing from Holyhead to Dublin to face. Roman Catholic priests trudged the highways and byways to give mass and consolation to their own people. " Our own forefathers, Grubbs and Greers, became Quakers 100 years ago " she said, " because men like Edmunson and John Exham (*see Chapter Four*) brought the Truth into their own homes. In those days the Society of Friends flourished and converts were made. Yet earlier Anabaptist Grubbs had itinerated vast distances on the same mission. It is high time we bestirred ourselves, and continued this good work. Only so will our Cause grow. Let Irish Quaker women give the lead that the established church in the kingdom and the presbyterians seem to be forgetting!" Inspired by Wesley, to whom she owed much on his visits to Clonmel, and in assured obedience to the guiding Voice Within, Sarah Grubb was to enthuse other Quaker women in Clonmel and her own daughters-in-law that they must leave home and the comforts of Clonmel to proclaim the everlasting gospel to all Ireland. When her duties as a mother in childbearing were completed, Sarah Grubb travelled over Ireland, [and later with her daughters-in-law, to be known as the Lady Grubb Itinerant Preachers] visiting homes and preaching in assembly rooms and in the open air, distributing also from well-filled pockets, books, bibles and money to the hungry. (*See Chapter Eight*). While Joseph and his sons continued hard at work in Clonmel, building, expanding, and working their mills, and keeping their hands to the plough to supply the spiritual sinews of warfare, the Lady Grubbs on the proceeds had now a God-given objective in view. No pampered idle existence theirs, but to travel far and wide to share the Gospel that meant so much to them with the hopeless and destitute, and to give that consecrated feminine leadership that was to bring revival into the Society of Friends. Quakers and Methodists are alike in opening up to women definite avenues of ministry and service. Sarah Grubb began her ministry 200 years before the established church has yet seen fit to put into practice the equality of women with men in the ministry of God.

By the last quarter of the eighteenth century Clonmel had become jocularly known as the "City of the Grubbs". Not only because of the number of Grubbs who lived, worked, and prospered there . . . nearly all the mills and the corn trade was now in Grubb hands, so was the grocery and provision trade, and they had taken an increasing share in the drapery and brewing trades, and before long developing an interest in boatbuilding and the better navigation of the River Suir, in engineering and piping and the making of instruments (*see* Collateral Tables "C", "D" and "E") . . .

but because of the outward-looking and evangelistic type of Quakerism they represented, and of which the town became the headquarters in the south of Ireland. From Clonmel the Lady Grubb Itinerants were dismissed after prayer on their missionary journeys; to Clonmel they returned, their mission accomplished, to make report to their Society of the great things the Lord had done.

Meanwhile Joseph Grubb decided that the long and frequent absences of his wife from home was the Lord's guidance that he should send his youngest son Samuel away from a motherless home to boarding school— a new departure in the education of young Grubbs. Sharing in the mystic insights and broad-minded outlook of Abraham Shackleton, a learned Quaker who had opened a boys' boarding school at Ballitore in County Kildare, 25 miles south of Dublin, to which many prosperous Quakers were sending their sons to be educated, Joseph placed young Samuel, now turned 12, under his care and that of Mrs. Shackleton. He was to live long enough to see the good results of boarding school education, such as most of his descendants were later to receive. His elder sons had been day-boys in Clonmel, and he had placed them, and Samuel also, when they left school, immediately to work in his mills, and to gain therein their experience of life and their own means of livelihood. As they married, he set each of them up in his own mill. They all married wisely and well, three of them brought another 'Mrs. Sarah Grubb' into the family. Male issue died from the elder four, and it was to be only through Samuel, the youngest, that the Grubb descent from Joseph has continued to this day.

Successful in business, honoured and respected in the Society of Friends, Joseph Grubb died at the age of 73 in 1782. He left all his family in comfortable circumstances, and except for his youngest daughter, Rebecca, happily married within the fold of Quakerism. Rebecca married in 1786 into the Quaker Strangman family, a young man named Joseph, who had been working at Anner Mills. Sarah Grubb survived her husband by six years. Beyond the material legacy of mills and money, what were the outstanding points of character and experience that Joseph was able to transmit to his children? His personal religion and character may be summarised as:

(i) *Authoritative and Assured.* From his Puritan ancestors he had inherited a firm belief in fundamental evangelical doctrines, and the supreme authority of the Scriptures, from which he never wavered. Doubt never crossed his mind. He was a man of swift and confident decisions. If he sometimes wondered what was the right action to take, he never doubted that what he had done was the right thing. He put his whole trust in his Saviour, and in his wife. If Sarah was assured the Light Within was guiding her to leave him to itinerate with the Gospel, Joseph was assured also; to be without her for a while was but a little sacrifice for the sake of his Redeemer who had sacrificed all to save him. As a member of the Society of Friends he had found security in that fellowship, a security that castles and walls and ramparts could never give, strict and confined as at times Quaker " separatism " seemed to him to be. He maintained, in theory at least, if with some Irish inconsistencies, their traditional attitudes to all that savoured of the vanity of life, to the use of firearms and to bloodsports, and their plainness of speech and dress.

(ii) *Experimental and Exacting.* He believed and had proved the continual guiding of the " Light Within," the Spirit of God given in measure to every man—God's " Grace "—which makes for enlightenment and for progress, and is receptive to new leadings, from whatever source they may come. He acknowledged how much he owed to John Wesley, and never admired him more than for his early rising, a secret for his successful life in his mills, and dealing with his many workmen. So he could be exacting upon his fellows and upon his family, as upon himself. Time mattered; there must be fixed times for prayer and Bible reading, for work and for family " togetherness," for Quaker meetings and outside affairs. The very negation of a *laissez-faire* " any time will do " attitude characterised the Grubb outlook inherited from Joseph. They became methodical: lovers of method.

(iii) *Individual and Intelligent.* Believing there is "Something of God in every created being," Joseph saw each individual as a child of God, irrespective of whether they called themselves Catholics or Protestants or Friends or Wesleyans; each is infinitely precious to the Father who created him; to each God will speak directly without the need for rites and ceremonies or Sacraments. He read much: he thought much: he enjoyed the company of intelligent people. Personal religion, sincerity and moral earnestness mattered more to God, and therefore to Joseph Grubb, than institutional or corporate religion, and the routine exercises of an organised cult.

(iv) *Otherworldly and Mystical.* Historically Quakerism has been considered as the "Mystical Wing" of the Puritan movement.[15] When quite a young man, Joseph had been introduced to a book written by one of his contemporaries, and first published in 1729 one of the masterpieces of eighteenth century literature, called *A serious call to a devout and holy life.*[16] Its author, like John Wesley, who also had been profoundly moved by this book, was another Oxford scholar and clergyman, named William Law, A.M. He had been himself inspired by the

[15] Evelyn Underhill [*sic*], the great writer on Mysticism describes Quakerism as a "noble experiment in contemplative corporate prayer, a passionate reassertion of the double truth of the transcendence of God and His loving penetration of life".

[16] In his biography *Once Caught, No Escape* (1969), Norman Grubb, M.C., one of his descendants writes at length of this book as one of the formative influences upon his own life. See pp. 163–168.

German mystics. The book gripped Joseph, despite its long and not always graceful sentences which were familiar to him in Quaker speech and writings, and sent him back to his own German origins in the Hartz Mountains, where mysticism had always been current. The serenity and " quietism " and method of the book appealed to his own Quaker upbringing (as it did to a number of Quakers, including the saintly Abraham Shackleton, to whose school Joseph sent his youngest son). Perhaps it was chapter 17 of this book on " The importance of the right education " that led him to send Samuel to Ballitore. It was chapter 15 of " The Serious Call " on the " Chanting and Singing of Psalms in Private Devotions," which he read again and again and memorised by heart, that explains his own and future Grubb love for hymn singing and music. " As singing is the natural effect of joy in the heart, so it has also a natural power of rendering the heart joyful; it is the true expression of praise and the cheerful heart " wrote William Law. " Let the people sing " mused Joseph Grubb. No wonder he was drawn to John and Charles Wesley, and to the hymns of his father's contemporary, Isaac Watts. He often hummed his words—Sarah loved them too, and would join him:

> "Happy the man whose hopes rely
> On Israel's God. He made the sky,
>   The earth, and seas, the cloud and rain.
> His TRUTH for ever stands secure;
> He saves the oppressed, He feeds the poor,
>   And none shall find His promise vain.

(v) *Understanding and Useful.* The Calvinism of his Puritan antecedents meant to Joseph that God is always choosing *families* because he wants to use those *chosen families* for a special task they only can perform, as well as calling and choosing individuals. God had called in olden days the chosen race of Israel. God in his day had chosen and called his family, the Grubbs, for a task in Ireland they only could perform. Sarah's call to itinerate with the Gospel was a part of that task. So Joseph became more outward-looking and broadminded than many of his contemporary Quakers, serenely confident of the good hand of God behind his meteoric rise to success, practical in good works and charity, and understanding the problems and frailties of his fellow men.

Almost prophetic of Joseph Grubb, builder of the Grubb family fortunes are the oldtime words of the Patriarch Jacob in blessing his son Joseph—

"Joseph is a fruitful bough, whose branches run *over (or outside) the wall* . . . his arms and hands are made strong by the hands of the Mighty God of Jacob, by the God of his father who will bless him in full measure with the blessings of heaven on high, blessings of the deep stretches under the earth (reminiscent of the former Grubb silver mines in the Hartz

Mountains), the blessings of the breast and the fertile body; blessings of sons and daughters unto the utmost bounds of the everlasting hills."[17]

A similar blessing on the descendants of Joseph was given by Moses, but with the added significant words—"His horns are like the horn of a unicorn"[18]—strongly suggestive of the later choice of this fabulous animal by his grandchildren for the Grubb Family crest. (*See Chapter Nine*).

But the greatest blessing God gave Joseph Grubb was his shrewd country-loving aristocratic-looking Christian wife, outward-looking in her itinerant evangelism and care and sympathy for others, and the co-builder of his fortunes; the first of many succeeding Mrs. Sarah Grubbs, she gave him the security and love a castle could never give.

[17] Genesis xlix, 22–27.
[18] Deuteronomy xxxiii, 17.

COLLATERAL TABLE "D"

JOSEPH GRUBB, 1709–1782, and SARAH (*née* GREER), d. 1788

They had 12 children; seven sons (of whom two died young); five daughters (of whom two died young); and 46 grandchildren (27 of them Grubbs)

1.	THOMAS	b. 1736; d. 1809	4 sons
2.	JOHN	b. 1737; d. 1784	5 daughters
3.	JOSEPH	b. 1739; d. 1790	7 children
4.	HENRY	b. 1740; *died young*	
5.	JAMES	b. 1741; *died young*	
6.	ROBERT	b. 1743; d. 1797	No children
7.	SAMUEL	b. 1750; d. 1815	11 children
1.	Anne	b. 1744; m. Jacob HANCOCK	5 children
2.	Sarah	b. 1747; m. Dominick GREGG	10 children
3.	Anna Maria	b. 1748; *died young*	
4.	Margaret	b. 1752; *died young*	
5.	Rebecca	b. 1759; m. (1786) Joseph STRANGMAN	4 children

---

1. **THOMAS GRUBB,** their eldest son, miller and corn merchant; m. 1764 Hannah Allan of Waterford, where they lived until his father's death, when he took over his Clonmel mills (1782). They had four sons, of whom two died young. Two married (Joseph and Thomas, Junior), each leaving sons, from whom male issue died out.

2. **JOHN GRUBB,** their second son, miller and corn merchant of Anner Mills, married Sarah Pim (1746–1832), in 1778. He died early through over-work, aged 47. The most able business man of the family, he built and prospered at Anner Mills; his wife succeeded him (Sarah Grubb and Co., Millers of Anners), assisted by able clerks and managers. They had four surviving daughters (one died), and Anners for over 100 years was a centre of Quaker hospitality.

   (1) Elizabeth, b. 1779; m. John Barclay CLIBBORN (Quaker), who succeeded his mother-in-law at Anners. They had 15 children (most of them buried in the Quaker burial ground in Clonmel). Her eldest son Joseph Clibborn (d. 1880) succeeded, from whom descended the Booth-Clibborn family (descendants of General Booth, Founder of the Salvation Army). Anner Mills, a large house adjoining, land and valuable fishing rights (Anner trout are a delicacy on hotel menues), until 1935 remained in the family; since owned by a German family who have founded there the Irish Falconry, and Restaurant.

   (2) Anna, b. 1780; m. 1808, James Nicholson RICHARDSON (d. 1847) of Glenmore House, near Lisburn, Co. Down, descendant of the Duke of Northumberland through his Nicholson mother, a Quaker, His Richardson ancestors from Gloucestershire purchased large estates in the north of Ireland, and founded the great Richardson linen business in Belfast and Lisburn. He kept bloodhounds, in order to trace thieves who made a practice of stealing linens from the bleach greens; the part played by the bloodhounds of his descendant Lt.-Col. E. H. Richardson in World War I is well known. James and Anna had a large family of seven sons, of whom John Grubb Richardson (1813–1890) married Helena Grubb of Cahir Abbey (*Chapter Ten*), and founded the Bessbrook Temperance Village for 3,000 of his workmen. His family continues to this day, in Belfast and at Moyallon House, Co. Down.

   (3) Rebecca and (4) Jane (twins).

3. **JOSEPH GRUBB**, their third son, miller of Suir Island, Clonmel (partner with his next brother, Robert). He married (1775) Sarah Ridgway (d. 1811). He died aged 51. They had seven children, but male issue died. Joseph and Samuel, his eldest sons, carried on the mills on Suir Island. A daughter, Sarah, married Robert Fayle and had a large family.

6. **ROBERT GRUBB**, their sixth son, Quaker minister, elder, and traveller, of Suir Island (in partnership with his brother); m. Sarah Tuke of York, 1782, clerk of the York Quaker Meeting, also a Quaker minister, traveller, and writer, whose life has been published. She was the daughter of William and Elizabeth Tuke, wealthy and generous York Quakers, who had done much work in securing better treatment for the insane and lunatics.

     English Quakers at this time held a position in the social world which was much higher than that of other Non-conformists, perhaps due to the possession of well-earned wealth. The humanitarian and philanthropic work of the Tukes in York had brought them socially into contact with, and sometimes into conflict with the Prince—Archbishops of York. Being childless, Robert and Sarah were able to devote their wealth to the Lord's work. Robert founded the House of Industry (Workhouse) outside the West Gate of Clonmel, toured France and Germany in the Quaker cause before and after the French Revolution, and turned his large house on Suir Island into a Girls' Boarding School which he also liberally endowed. (*Chapter Eight, footnotes 11 and 12.*) He died 1797. Aged 54.

7. **SAMUEL GRUBB**, their youngest son, corn and butter merchant in Main St. Clonmel. He married (1776) Margaret Shackleton, daughter of Richard Shackleton, Headmaster of Ballitore School. They had 11 children, through whom this family line descends.

71

CHAPTER SEVEN

Samuel Grubb. 1750—1815

Part I. *Corn-merchant and Miller in Clonmel.*

He married 1770, Margaret Shackleton,
daughter of Richard Shackleton, M.A., Headmaster of
Ballitore Quaker School, Co. Kildare

11 Children (three died young) and 60 grandchildren.

"Happy is the man that findeth wisdom, and the man that getteth understanding."
—Proverbs iii, 13.

RARELY does an outstanding man in any sphere of life have as outstanding a son. Fortunate is the man who has a son who will maintain and improve the interests he has worked and stood for. Joseph and Sarah Grubb had been blessed with five. If in every generation of the Grubbs there has appeared wisdom and common sense in business and religious affairs, in their choice of wives, and in organising ability, such gifts were found in all five sons of Joseph whose lives were to show forth the "Wisdom which is from above", and to prove:

" Her ways are ways of pleasantness,
And all her paths are peace."—*Proverbs III. 16*

SAMUEL GRUBB'S acquired wisdom was the result of his parents' decision to send him away from Clonmel and home, to boarding school some sixty miles away in County Kildare under a leading Quaker scholar and mystic, Richard Shackleton, M.A. The expenses of his education were available from his parents' now greatly enlarged income from their expanding mills. True there was a Grammar School of sorts in Clonmel, which his elder brothers had attended. It was very much " of sorts " at any rate at a later date, when Samuel had himself to decide where to send his own sons to school, and when George Borrow attended it during the time his soldier father was posted to the barracks in Clonmel. Never was money better spent than in paying the school fees at Ballitore, the famous Quaker Public School in County Kildare for the 14 Grubbs, shown in the school lists as having been educated there.

Ballitore School, 25 miles south of Dublin, had been founded by an outstandingly wise and saintly Quaker, Abraham Shackleton, in 1726,

72

and had quickly grown into prominence as a progressive Protestant fee-paying school for boys.[1] It was known in Ireland as a " Private School " because fee-paying, as opposed to a " National School "; whereas in England such a school would have been called a " Public School " although, as the Irish saw it, not open to the public who could not afford to pay its fees! If Irish expressions do sometimes appear peculiar to English people, the reverse is equally the case; it must be remembered that during three dark centuries it was Ireland that saved learning to Europe. Protestants from all over Ireland were sending their sons to be educated at Ballitore and not only Quakers: boys were prepared for the University at Dublin, from entrance to which Quakers who could not take the oath were barred. Edmund Burke, the great Irish Parliamentarian and orator, life-long friend of the Shackletons, was perhaps its greatest old boy; the foundations of his life illustrate the broad outlook of the school. A well qualified staff, not necessarily all Quakers, but chosen by the Shackletons for their qualifications, taught the boys the classics and history, mathematics and geography, English literature and the art of writing and composition, boxing and games, and to a standard that would have satisfied the most exacting of educational authorities. For the teaching of French (a language that very strict Quakers feared might corrupt the minds of youth, let alone a visit to France and gay " Paris ") a special French master was employed—William Leadbeater. He was later to marry the younger daughter of the Shackletons, named Mary, who became a gifted and prolific Quaker writer and historian of the school[2], and Samuel Grubb's sister-in-law. Samuel gained from Ballitore his love for reading and the languages, for the mystic and broadminded outlook of his headmaster and future father-in-law, and for the feminine influences in the school (1762–1767).

Joseph and Sarah Grubb were always intensely pleased with the education Samuel gained at Ballitore, the manners and breeding assimilated, the friends he made, and with his choice of his Headmaster's elder daughter to be his wife. His five years at boarding school had taught him to think for himself, to weigh up problems, to see things from differing points of view, and to take time before jumping to a conclusion. If his grandfather John (Junior) had been precipitate and impetuous in the decisions he took on what he believed to be Divine Guidance and an " open door ", Samuel became just the opposite, rather slow to act, but when he did act, to do so with full assurance the step was right. The Quaker background of the school taught him not to be afraid of pauses and silences, to avoid hasty answers and the impatience that can result in

---

[1] *Ballitore.* From the Irish "bally" meaning a village; and "togher" meaning "a bog". The School continued 100 years in the Shackleton family. Sir Ernest Shackleton of Polar fame, was a descendant.

[2] *The Leadbeater Papers and Annals of Ballitore*, Vols. i and ii. Mary Leadbeater.

anger and irritability. Where some boys impulsively ask questions before stopping to think if they can't already find the answer for themselves, Samuel was the quiet if slow thinker. He learnt at Ballitore the sustained habit of attention, of listening, the ability to ignore interruptions, to allow nothing to divert him from his train of thought. So he was to become the wise counsellor of others, to whom during his long life many people would take their anxieties and troubles for disinterested advice and help; had he been a Roman Catholic he would have been outstandingly helpful in the Confessional. Mixing with boys who were not Quakers had the inestimable advantage of broadening his outlook and sympathies, in helping him to take his own decisions upon conduct and morality. His French master, William Leadbeater increased in him an interest in France and the French language. He was later to send his own sons to be educated at Ballitore under their uncle, Richard Shackleton's son, Abraham (Junior).

The school lists at Ballitore record among the contemporaries of Samuel Grubb and his sons, the names of sons of the following well-known Irish families, into a number of which Grubbs were to marry:—

Barcroft	Davis	Gough	Irving	Richardson
Burke	Fayle	Gurney	Phaire	Ridgway
Byrne	Grattan	Green	Pim	Tuke
Clibborn	Guinness	Haughton	Sissons	Yeats

Indeed Ballitore became for the Quakers a natural outlet against the inbreeding which is all too common in small communities.

Sarah and Joseph often used to say of their five sons " The green wood is good, but it needs hardening." Whether in the Grammar School at Clonmel or at Ballitore with all the roughing of a boarding school, their sons received this hardening process. But the difference between their educations was that in Clonmel the Grubb brothers were always wishing for the bell to end school, and to get off to something different for the evening; at Ballitore, Samuel was never ready to pack up his books when the bell rang. He would continue his studies and reading in an empty classroom long after the other boys had left. Difficulties between the brothers there were bound to be with such a temperament, when Samuel left school in 1767, and came home to take his place with his father and brothers in the mill. Where they were punctual and regular, almost like clockwork, in fulfilling their allotted tasks, quick at getting the job done, hardly a day would pass at first but someone would call: " Where's Samuel "? and the cry S-A-M-U-E-L would be taken up around the mill. It was not fair to suggest Samuel had been day-dreaming, or was late. He was only finishing one job to his own satisfaction, checking and rechecking, before he was ready to turn his mind to the next. He could lay no claim to brilliance or speed. The brothers learnt to put up with him, and quicken his labours, but Samuel was never the outstanding miller that his father and his elder brother John became in Clonmel and at Anner Mills. Scholars rarely are. But it was not slackness nor was it idleness that was the cause.

For nine years after leaving school Samuel worked with his father and brothers (the eldest Thomas was already married) in the Grubb mills. It was a valuable experience when from time to time his father would send him out on business journeys to get orders, or to Waterford, Cork, or Dublin to see about import or export matters, much as the representative of a business firm calls on customers today. The chequered history of Irish economic relations with England, varying import and export restrictions and alterations, and the need to obtain Continental and American markets kept the families " on their toes." When there was business to be done County Kildare way or in Dublin or in the North of Ireland, Samuel was always eager to undertake it, and it was not only as an old boy that his visits to Ballitore grew more frequent. Margaret Shackleton came to stay at Clonmel; Sarah Grubb, Samuel's mother went to stay at Ballitore on one of her evangelistic itinerations, and quite enthused Margaret with accounts of her Gospel tours. Never was bride more warmly welcomed in Clonmel, than when the marriage at length took place in 1776 among the Quakers at Ballitore. Joseph set them up on their own in Main Street.

MARGARET SHACKLETON'S own literary interests (like her sister, the writer of the *Leadbeater Papers*), her good birth and engaging society and her liberal Quaker background, made her a most desirable daughter-in-law in an age when it was generally the parents who determined their children's partners in life. That their elder sons married equally suitably filled Sarah and Joseph's cup to overflowing. While the eldest Thomas had married Hannah Allan some years previously (1764) and settled in Waterford, the other three all married Quakeresses named Sarah, from the well-known Pim, Ridgway and Tuke Quaker families; so four daughters-in-law were to complete the Lady Grubb Evangelists' team. Had they not been Quakers, nicknames would have been used to distinguish them. All of them were to continue Grubb Gynococracy in their own homes.

MARY SHACKLETON (soon to become Mary Leadbeater) wrote this account of her elder sister's marriage:—

> "In 1776 my sister Margaret was united in marriage to SAMUEL GRUBB of Clonmel. A wedding was a novel scene to us, and the preparations occasioned no small bustle in the school. Our lovely sister was removed from us a great distance (60 miles in the days of jaunting cars seemed a long distance to the stay-at-home young Quakeress), and we sadly missed her engaging society. But the happiness of her new situation, and the acquisition of many valuable connections compensated in measure for her departure."

75

THE SHACKLETON FAMILY were as pleased as the Grubbs over the marriage. Wrote Grandfather Abraham Shackleton to the new Mrs. Grubb: " Let Christ be thy chiefest joy, my dear, then wilt thou step wisely in thy pilgrimage, little minding what people think of thee, if thou hast but the smile of His Countenance upon thee."

Often in the coming years did Samuel and Margaret Grubb unfold Abraham's letter; the benediction of this saintly old Quaker became engraved on their hearts. His words were reminiscent of his contemporary mystic William Law, whose book " The Serious Call to a Devout and Holy Life " had become a text-book at Ballitore—heavy reading as some of its devotional exercises were—and had become a formative influence upon both their lives. It has been compared to St Thomas-a-Kempis *Imitation of Christ* in spiritual value. (*See p. 195*).

It must not be supposed that Margaret's electric and smiling personality and more liberal upbringing at Ballitore, much as she was welcomed and appreciated by the Friends in Clonmel, turned that " City of the Grubbs " into the new Jerusalem. The devil, " like a roaring lion ever seeking whom he may devour " was as rampant among Christians then as now. It was inevitable that the Grubb brothers and sisters-in-law did not always see eye to eye, or found the Inner Light always led them in the same way. Disagreements there were bound to be, aggravated by the intensity of emotion which the " comings and goings " of the Lady Grubb itinerants produced in a small closely-knit community. Plainness in speech, behaviour, and apparel was a watchword among the Clonmel Friends, that " the plain language of truth might be kept to, with many other things."[3] Excess in everything was to be avoided, and there are a number of minutes of the Monthly Meetings against those who attended race meetings and clubs, music meetings or " Patricks Worship House " (St Patrick's Cathedral, in Dublin), drank healths, doffed their hats by way of salutation, joined political associations, paid tithes, or engaged in other greater or less " conformities to the world." There were regulations about the number of buttons which might be worn on a coat, and the colour of a silk handkerchief, if worn. Mothers were warned against the use of " much beribboned and laced linen " for their babies, fine clothes for their daughters, veneer and garnished furniture and cabinets; a chaise should not be bought, unless infirmity made walking impossible.[4] At the same time poorer Friends were given a weekly dole; Friends stood by one another in time of difficulty, and were regarded by their contemporaries as strictly honest, even if peculiar. They had no extravagances on which to spend their money, hence it was put back into their mills, until a limit of expansion was reached about the end of the century. Samuel and Margaret were to ponder deeply on such " shibboleths "; they must

[3] *Journal of Joseph Pike* (a Quaker public preacher), p. 64.
[4] Rutty's *History of Quakers in Ireland*, p. 89.

face the question for their children how far to conform to the Clonmel ways; how far the broader outlook that was theirs from Ballitore should lead them. The problem became acute after the death of Joseph in 1782. He had been regarded almost with veneration for the past 10 years, as Christian communities the world over are apt to regard a revered and distinguished elder among them, as " *episkopos* " in the New Testament sense of the word, and his death left no recognised leader among the Friends. It speaks highly of the humility (not always the mark of a wise man) of both Samuel and Margaret Grubb, of their sweetness of spirit (sometimes called Quaker " meekness ") that in 1791 Margaret was chosen to be the Clerk of the Clonmel meeting. Despite the antagonisms that might have happened, something of the beauty of holiness revealed in the sweet smiles and brightness of heaven upon her face, seemed to descend upon Margaret; for " Christ was her chiefest joy and she stepped wisely in her pilgrimage " in the words of her saintly grandfather's wedding benediction, " little minding what other people might think of her." Samuel, shared in the blessings radiated by his wife. " Heavenly Armour " it might be called. How could anyone continue to harbour jealousies or entertain suspicions against such a couple, who were obviously living out what they believed, even if they were not quite so strict in trifling details as some of their brethren? In the words of a famous Irish hymnwriter—

> "With smiles of peace, and looks of love
> Light in our dwellings we may make:
> Bid kind good-humour brighten there,
> And so do all for Jesus' sake."   (*Mrs. Alexander*)

Another glimpse into the characters of Samuel and Margaret is afforded by the Christian names they gave to their eleven children, born during the first fifteen years after their marriage. They were years in which Margaret herself was often absent from home about the " Lord's business " with her mother-in-law or sisters-in-law on itinerant evangelism. Three of these eleven died young. Eight of the eleven were given scriptural names, and the others called after Uncle Robert, after Margaret herself, and after her father Richard.[5] (*See Collateral Table "E".*)

When Margaret felt the call to join her " in-laws " in itinerant evangelism she wrote to seek her father's counsel at Ballitore. Wise Richard Shackleton replied to her letter:—

> "I have received thy precious letter, my precious Margaret. I am not for dragging thee, my precious child, from thy domestic concerns, which are many and various and important. But if *Truth* draws thee, follow its leading. He that hath made thee is sufficient to preserve thee. So my dear Margaret, if thou has heard His call, GO FORTH according to Heavenly direction, and there is no doubt that peace will be thy crown."

[5] Possibly also after the first Richard Grubbe of Ravensthorpe.

With serenity Samuel accepted Margaret's call to leave him and her young children for the Gospel's sake for many months at a time, as throughout his life he accepted everything his beloved wife was divinely guided, as he firmly believed, to undertake. She had the God-given knack of making Samuel—and others—feel the decision was theirs, not hers. Samuel's faith was tested—as his father Joseph's faith had been similarly tested—in sparing his dearest for the Lord's work. He knew the cost of missionary endeavour, as in later days many of his descendants were similarly to know the cost of giving their dearest and their best to God.

Often as he returned from the mills at nightfall to a home empty of a mother's care, to be both father and mother to his little children while she was away (though Margaret would have left some woman to supervise as well as a nanny and other reliable servants to look after the chores in their large house), he looked with admiration at the Roman Catholic priests—celibates they were—30,000 of them in Ireland—trudging the roads to give mass to the masses. It did make him wonder whether a woman's place is in the Home, or to be on an equality with men as a minister of the Gospel. But when his darling Elizabeth died with her lovely curly hair in 1788, not five years old, and again two years later his sturdy four-year old little John in 1790—losses he accepted with Quaker resignation—his beloved Margaret (herself suffering equally) was the one who made the decision that her place in God's will was at home, and she must leave it to her sisters-in-law to continue the outreach visitations. Receptive to God's Guidance both of them were throughout their lives, and within a year God had a new task for Margaret, which she could combine with her home duties, that of her election as Clerk of the Clonmel Monthly Meeting. In their high-backed chairs by the open window overlooking the Suir and the encircling hills above the river they would recall in after years the lessons of trust in God their separations had taught them, and Samuel's lips would murmur:

> "Before the hills in order stood,
> Or earth received her frame,
> FROM EVERLASTING THOU ART GOD
> To endless years the same."   (*Isaac Watts*)

Whatever lasting effect her Gospel itinerations had on those she reached, in the goodwill of God her journeys had an immeasurable effect in deepening Grubb Faith, and preparing the family for those later sacrifices when sons and daughters would leave home and Ireland to proclaim the everlasting Gospel throughout the world.

(For some account of the Grubb Ladies' Evangelistic Itinerations and Tours, *see Chapter Eight*).

Margaret Grubb, like her sister Mary Leadbeater, was a prolific writer of letters and diaries, and after her appointment as Clerk of the Clonmel

Meeting, of minutes. Some 4,000 of her letters have been preserved in the Friends Y.M. Library in Dublin. A later facility for writing books, shown by her descendants in the 20th century[6], owes not a little to this further gift God gave their great grandmother.

Throughout their married life Margaret Grubb was the dominant partner and Samuel in his wisdom was content that it should be so, and to lean on her. Among the Irish Grubbs "Mother" proved to be the dominant character in every generation. All the Grubbs had the gift of choosing and marrying highly capable wives. This in no small measure has been their source of strength—a secure home, when castles were no more, built upon Christian foundations of prayer and Bible study. It was of Margaret that Samuel was thinking, when some years later he was to choose a family motto for the Grubb family, and hit on the French words (lover of France as he was): "Bonne et Assez Belle"—in reference to his wife and Grubb ladies: "As Beautiful as she is good," or "She is good and beautiful enough."

When at a later date their marriages took place in Church or Cathedral, Grubb bridegrooms never attempted to enforce the vow of obedience, and more recently the word "obey" has been altogether omitted at their marriages. At Quaker weddings exactly the same vow was taken by both the bride and her groom. This springs from their emphasis on the equality of men and women in the sight of God. Quaker weddings took place during a meeting for worship, when the silence would be broken by bridegroom and bride standing up ("being led" it would be called) to announce their marriage, and to take their vows to each other before the assembly publicly, some of whom would then witness their signatures to a certificate of marriage stating that they had done so. Savouring almost of the Registrar's office, there was no suggestion of the couple having been joined together by God, no necessary reading of a scriptural exhortation or an address to the couple on the meaning of marriage (although there were occasions when a Grubb bride or bridegroom took the opportunity to deliver an address to the congregation of their friends and wellwishers, *see Chapter Eight*), no suggestion that marriage might be a divinely ordained sacrament. The Quakers recognised no need for sacraments, two or seven. Their vows were life-long, for they had publicly said their "yea". A Quaker's word was his bond. Divorces in the family in their Quaker days were unknown.

The Grubb matriarchs position in the family became so commanding that they conceived it their duty to choose the partners whom their children should marry. Not that there was a large selection of families from which the choice could be made. Generally their children dutifully

[6] The Rev. George Grubb, M.A., Norman Grubb, M.C., Sir Kenneth Grubb, LL.B., Henry Grubb, M.A.

acquiesced: "Mother knows best!". When they did not, it was curtly entered in the Family Bible that a clandestine marriage had been made, as in the case of one of Margaret's sons. By and large parental match-making, which dates back to the Old Testament and the time of Abraham, worked well. It is as common in non-Christian religions as in Ireland among both Roman Catholics and Quakers. It covered questions of dowry. It avoided the difficulties of mixed marriages in a country abounding in dissensions between the Protestants and Roman Catholics. It was part of the security and "fence of discipline" among the Quakers. Said a wise old Irishman:—

"You had to face realities from the start,
and keep your dreams for the next world."

It was under such a fence of discipline that the Grubbs lived for some 200 years in their Quaker days. With their "Castle" origins they were well used to the disciplines, even the shibboleths of such a life. Indeed so firm was the Quaker form of discipline—concerning speech and dress and behaviour and music and the amusements of life and marriage—that to put yourself outside the fence, and to refuse to return and obey, meant "Disownment". Quakeresses were more frequently "disowned" than men for "marrying out" or marrying a first cousin, perhaps due to their education and virtue which made them a special attraction to many outside the Society.[7] Quaker "disownments" had a big material effect in reducing the number of members of the Society.

There is also a complete absence among the Grubbs of Tipperary in their Quaker days of any choice of popular Irish christian names for their children, such as Patrick or Patricia, Brian or Bridget, Daniel, Desmond, Gerald, Kathleen, Shane or Terrence. They shared probably John Wesley's view about St. Patrick.[8] They had this in common with their Roman Catholic neighbours, however—so great is the attractive beauty of the Celtic Irish—that large families were the norm, and often twelve. Not that they were consciously thinking of the twelve princes of Ishmael, nor the twelve sons of Jacob, but that feminine physical characteristics among the Irish, as among the descendants of Ishmael or Jacob, prevented larger numbers, although one of the Clonmel Grubbs did have 19 children. " Family Planning " would have been as much taboo among the

---

[7] *The Diaries of Edward Pease.* (1907). Edited by Sir Alfred Pease, p. 26.

[8] *Journals of John Wesley*, Vol. ii, p. 92. "I read today what is accounted the most correct history of St. Patrick . . . I am inclined to believe that St. Patrick and St. George were of one family, but the whole story smells strongly of romance. His success staggers me! I never heard before of an apostle sleeping 35 years, and beginning to preach only when he was 60. Nothing is to be heard of but kings, nobles, warriors bowing down before him. No blood of the martyrs is here. No reproach; no scandal of the Cross; no persecutions of them that will live godly. Thousands are converted without any opposition at all."

Quakers as among the Roman Catholics. The Tipperary Grubbs had this in common with the Pope. Ireland has always seemed to need large families, whether to replace the thousands killed in internecine struggles, or to carry the Irish "gay green beam of sunshine" all over the world. By 1800 its population had reached 5 million. By 1850 it was up to $8\frac{1}{2}$ million. The Grubbs of Tipperary made a praiseworthy contribution to these figures, if a decreasing one, when they left the Friends. The Irish peasants naturally made the greatest contribution, as happens when people are poor and careless for the future. Today about 95 per cent of the Irish population are Catholics.

All important to Samuel and Margaret Grubb was the proper education of their children. Naturally they would send their sons to Ballitore where Samuel's brother-in-law Abraham Shackleton (Junior) had succeeded his father-in-law Richard Shackleton as Headmaster. Abraham Grubb (b. 1777) was admitted by Abraham Shackleton in 1787, when he was only ten; Richard Grubb (b. 1780) in 1791, and Samuel Grubb (Junior) (b. 1787) in 1795, when only eight.[9] But alas for their plans. The outbreak of the Irish Rebellion in 1798, so soon after the French Revolution, and the severe fighting all over Ireland and in Ballitore itself, compelled Abraham Shackleton to close the school, and send all the boys home. There was no choice therefore for Samuel and Margaret, but to put their two youngest surviving sons, Robert (b. 1790) who was later to make a clandestine marriage and migrate to Canada, and Thomas (b. 1792), at the Clonmel Grammar School near the west gate of the town, where their uncles had been educated. The school had seen better days. The boys seemed to spend more time in its school yard, recessed behind tall railings close to the road, than in the school building. No wonder, for the schoolroom was a long, high, stonefloored hall, "dirty and dilapidated" when George Borrow attended the school in 1815, "in which the boys used to crowd on stools and benches round a roaring fire, and the only master at that time, an old clergyman who taught the most elegant Latin, sat at a desk of black Irish-oak absorbed in an enormous Elzevir Flaccus. Occasionally he would raise his head, mumble out a few instructions about Latin or Greek tastes, and then bend again to his own reading. Nobody paid any attention to him. The boys held their books on their knees, and talked in low voices among themselves. They were not construing Latin or Greek. They were telling each other wild stories of adventure, or playing cards."[10] True this quotation was 17 years later, and Borrow's flowery style and exaggerations must be allowed for. Within

[9] Ballitore School lists.
[10] *In the Steps of George Borrow*. Eileen Bigland. 1951. pp. 57ff. George Borrow was a pupil of Clonmel Grammar School in 1815, when his father, Capt. Borrow, was posted to the barracks. He attempted to learn Irish from a boy called Murtagh in exchange for a pack of playing cards.

two years Samuel and Margaret were to pull up their roots in Clonmel, and move away to the life of country gentry. (*See Chapter Nine.*)

Writing from Clonmel on New Years Day 1796, an American visitor and a public preacher among the Friends formed this impression of the Clonmel Quakers he had met, and the prospects facing their children:—

> "They seemed to live like princes of the earth, much more than in any other country I have seen. Their gardens, carriages, horses and various conveniences, with the abundance of their tables, appear to me to call for more gratitude and humility than in some cases it is to be feared is the case. The easy situation of some is an injury to themselves and to their families. Many of their brethren have been much shaken & seriously tried."

Two days later he visited a Quaker's home in Clonmel, which in his Journal he described as "a very sumptuous establishment indeed, which I did not omit to tell him was quite too much so." He contrasted this with the poor Roman Catholics, many of whom, he said "did not get meat six times a year, and had barely anything to eat save potatoes and salt.[11]

"PRINCES OF THE EARTH". The words of the American challenged Samuel and Margaret, as they sat in their comfortable Clonmel home with its lavender lined lawns, the carriage at the door, and a well-stocked larder and kitchen. The words rang a bell in Samuel's mind as he recollected as a boy at school at Ballitore being present with Margaret when the sepulchre of a young Danish prince had been unearthed close by on Max's Hill. (*See Chapter Two.*) Could it be that there was truth in the visitor's words? Was his family indeed descended from those forgotten Danish princes, who had invaded Ireland so many centuries ago? There are certainly a number of Grubbs who held this view. In this case, he ruminated, he would have both Danish and Scottish royal blood in his vein.

"PRINCES OF THE EARTH". William Savery's words were but an enlargement of the earlier impressions of the traveller Inglis to Clonmel some 30 years previously. The early Puritan strain was fast disappearing in the general and increased prosperity of the Grubbs in Clonmel. The Lady Grubb preachers (Margaret and her sisters-in-law) would hardly have failed to offer entertainment and hospitality to a visiting American Public Friend. Was he perhaps thinking of the obvious wealth at Anner Mills, which had been built by John Grubb in 1770 and the following years on land purchased by his father Joseph in 1763 some two miles out of Clonmel on the Waterford road? It had taken ten years to complete, with its comfortable Anner House close by. Since John's death through overwork in 1784, the mills had been run by his widow under the business

[11] *Journal of William Savery*, pp. 267–268.
[12] *History of Clonmel*. Rev. W. P. Burke. (1907). p. 199ff.

name "Sarah Grubb and Co. Millers of Clonmel". (On the marriage of her eldest daughter, Elizabeth, during the Napoleonic Wars, to John Barclay Clibborn, her manager, they then took it over)[12]. Was it Joseph Grubb's comfortable establishment on Suir Island, in which Ridgway money from County Waterford had assisted in the furnishing? Or Robert Grubb's home on Suir Island (he and Joseph were partners in maintaining the huge mill buildings on the island that they had built in 1775) later turned into an expensive girls' school? Was it Benjamin Grubbs lovely home, whose drawing room was large enough to accommodate 70 for a Quaker meeting?[13] Or was the sumptuous establishment, "quite too much so", that of Samuel and Margaret themselves?

"PRINCES OF THE EARTH".—"In some cases lacking in gratitude and humility—their easy situation a cause of 'trial' to their poorer brethren.'

The impressions of an outsider are valuable, be they only based on a visit of two or three days! Here was a challenge to the Quaker Grubbs of Clonmel indeed. They knew their bibles: knew how easily money can corrupt: knew too that it is not money, but the "love of money" that is the root of all evil. On succeeding Lord's Days (called by the Quakers "First Days") it was noticeable how many of the Grubbs were led to stand up in the silences, led by the Spirit within them to read such passages as:—

> "Do not save riches here on earth, where moths and rust destroy, and robbers break in and steal. Instead save riches in heaven, where moths and rust cannot destroy, and robbers cannot break in & steal. For your heart will always be where your riches are."
> "No one can be a slave to two masters. You cannot serve both God and money. This is why I tell you; do not be worried about the food and drink you need to stay alive, or about clothes for your body. Look at the birds flying around: they do not plant seeds, gather a harvest, and put it in barns: yet your Father in Heaven takes care of them. Are you not worth more than birds? Who of you can live a few more years by worrying about it?"

As one and another expounded such passages and others similar to them, wise Samuel and Margaret pondered over their lives, their family, and the future they believed God had in store for them. It seemed to them much easier to exercise a living faith in God when you are poor, and have no material possessions of your own, on which to rely. They thought again of the trials and testings of grandfather John Grubb in America, and grandmother Anne Grubb bringing up her children in a veritable hovel. They looked at their own healthy growing family, so similar in position to the rich young ruler, it might appear, who was challenged by their Master to sell all he had, and give it to the poor, and to follow Him. They

---

[13] *Journal of John Gubb* (1786–87).
[14] "History of Clonmel" Rev. W. P. Burke. (1907) p. 199.

thought of brother Robert Grubb—true he was childless—who had been responsible for building a "House of Industry" (the Irish name for a workhouse)[14] outside the West Gate of the town, to be a place for the confinement and lodging of vagrants and an asylum for the poor and helpless.

The succeeding chapters of this book illustrate how far the Grubb family had learned to make wise use of the gifts and money with which God had endowed them; how well or how badly their spiritual life grew under prosperity in the next century: how they held to their resolve expressed in a new hymn by Charles Wesley, which was published just before they left Clonmel:—

"Forth in Thy Name, O Lord, we go
    Our daily labour to pursue:
Thee, only Thee, resolved to know
    In all we think, or speak or do.

The task Thy wisdom hath assigned,
    O let us cheerfully fulfill:
In all our works Thy presence find
    And PROVE Thy good and perfect will.

For Thee delightfully employ
    What e'er Thy bounteous grace hath given,
And run our course with even joy
And closely walk with Thee to Heaven."

COLLATERAL TABLE "E"

SAMUEL GRUBB 1750–1815 and MARGARET (*née* SHACKLETON) d. 1829.

They had 11 children; six sons (of whom one died young); five daughter (of whom two died young), and 60 grandchildren (41 of them Grubbs)

1.	ABRAHAM	b. 1777; d. 1849	4 daughters
2.	RICHARD	b. 1780; d. 1859	12 children
3.	SAMUEL	b. 1787; d. 1859	9 children
4.	JOHN	b. 1788; d. 1890, *died young*	
5.	ROBERT	b. 1790; d. 1882	3 children
6.	THOMAS	b. 1792; d. 1885	13 children
1.	Anne	b. 1778; m. Robert FAYLE	
2.	Sarah	b. 1782; m. her 2nd cousin Francis DAVIS (One of her children married his 1st cousin.)	
3.	Elizabeth	b. 1783; d. 1788, *died young*	
4.	Margaret	b. 1786; m. Thomas FAYLE	
5.	Deborah	b. 1794; d. 1795, *died young*	

Their five sons, and three sons-in-law were all educated at Ballitore Quaker School, and a number of their grandchildren. The Fayle family were prominent Dublin Quakers.

———

1. ABRAHAM GRUBB, their eldest son, corn and butter merchant, and later life and insurance agents in Clonmel; m. 1800, Susannah Banfield. Died aged 72. Four daughters; their only son, Samuel died young.

   (1) Anne, b. 1802; m. 1824, Thomas Murray.
   (2) Margaret, b. 1810; m. William Bell; d. 1881.
   (3) Elizabeth, b. 1814; m. William Davis (her 1st cousin, see above).
   (4) Rebecca, b. 1818; died 1880; m. (1) Sydney Brown; m. (ii) Rev. John Sargent.

2. RICHARD GRUBB, their second son. Miller of Cooleville, Clogheen, and of Cahir Abbey. He married Susanna Haughton 1807, daughter of John Barcroft Haughton, Esq., of Cleave Court, Co. Cork; they were spared to celebrate their golden wedding. He died aged 79. (*See Chapter Ten and Collateral Table "H".*)

3. SAMUEL GRUBB, their third son, miller of Clashleigh, Clogheen, and of Castle Grace, Clogheen. He married Deborah Davis, 1819, his 2nd cousin, daughter of Samuel and Mary (*née* Grubb) Davis of Clonmel; she had become his sister-in-law, when her brother Francis married Sarah Grubb (see above). He died aged 72. (*See Collateral Table "G".*)

5. ROBERT GRUBB, their fourth son. He went to Limerick, and later to British Columbia, where his descendants multiplied, and remain today. He made a clandestine marriage in 1812 to Anna Fayle, his young sister-in-law. They had three children:

   (1) SAMUEL GRUBB, b. 1813.
   (2) THOMAS HENRY GRUBB, b. 1817.
   Sarah Fayle, b. 1814.

6. THOMAS GRUBBE, their youngest son. Boat-builder, iron, oils, and colour merchant, of the Quay, Clonmel and Richmond Mills, Clonmel (which he built in 1830). He added an "E" to his surname, and a second christian name, Samuel. The cleverest of the family, he married, 1819, Elizabeth Haughton, his sister-in-law, second daughter of John Barcroft Haughton, Esq., of Cleave Court, Co. Cork. They lived at Parson's Green, Clogheen for some years before moving back to Clonmel. She died 1849, aged 45. He died aged 91. His large home, Quay House, Clonmel, is turned into solicitors' and doctors' offices. Thirteen children, seven sons and six daughters.

(*continued next page*)

H

COLLATERAL TABLE "E"—*continued*

Not to be confused are the two outstanding THOMAS GRUBBS of the nineteenth century, conspicuous over Ireland for their initiative and inventiveness in an expanding age, viz.:
- (i) THOMAS GRUBBE of Clonmel. 1792–1885. Boat-builder and merchant.
- (ii) THOMAS GRUBB of Dublin. 1800–1878. Optician, and Fellow of the Royal Society.

They were second cousins, and great-grandsons of John Grubb Jr., boat-builder in America.

(i) THOMAS GRUBBE of Clonmel (*continued from previous page*), youngest son of Samuel and Margaret Gubb devoted his life to make the River Suir navigable for barges and boats from the sea at Waterford up to Clogheen and Cahir. Brought up to work in his father's mills at Clogheen he had quickly realised the difficulties of transport and export from the Golden Vale of Tipperary. His marriage in 1819 (the same year as that of his brother Samuel) to Elizabeth Haughton, the younger sister of the wife of his brother Richard, gave him an equally liberal endowment. While his brothers Richard and Samuel occupied their lives in the purchase and building up of large estates at Cahir Abbey and Castle Grace, he invested his money in the purchase of a large frontage of the Quay at Clonmel, where he built up a flourishing river transport export and import trade. He placed the eldest of his seven sons, SAMUEL THOMAS on his majority in charge of the Waterford end of his rapidly expanding river-transport business, and his third son THOMAS CAMBRIDGE in charge at the Cahir end. For his second son JOHN BARCROFT, knowledgeable on roses, and with his " green fingers " quite expert on plants and gardens, he built a great expanse of glass houses on land he bought near the old gaol, and gave him charge of the horticultural side of his business. The four younger sons were fully occupied in boat-building, river conservation, drainage, and the mechanical side of the Grubb business. With their 12 cousins at Cahir, and nine at Castle Grace and Chassleigh, it became well known that on occasions as many as 60 Grubbs could find the time to turn out for a day's hunting in the surrounding districts. The family of Thomas Grubbe was:

(1) SAMUEL THOMAS GRUBBE, b. 1821; m. 1845, Eliza, only child of Rev. Alexander Alcock, T.C.D., d. 1863. He became J.P. for Counties Kilkenny and Waterford; High Sheriff of Waterford, 1863. With other issue, his eldest son was Thomas Alcock Grubb, of Waterford, whose descendants are still living in Waterford today.

(2) JOHN BARCROFT GRUBBE, b. 1823. Owned horticultural gardens near the gaol.

(3) THOMAS CAMBRIDGE GRUBBE, b. 1824, of Goose Island, Clonmel. His young wife Mary was buried in Cahir Church in 1851, aged 27.

(4) ABRAHAM GRUBBE, b. 1828. (6) ALBERT GRUBBE, b. 1830.
(5) RICHARD GRUBBE, b. 1828. (7) EDWIN GRUBBE, b. 1835.
(1) Sara Haughton, b. 1820.
(2) Margaret Butler, b. 1827; m. 1851, her first cousin, Richard Davis Grubb, of Castle Grace, Clogheen. Two children. She died 1855 in childbirth.
(3) Susan, b. 1832. (5) Eliza Emma, b. 1837; d. 1838.
(4) Elizabeth, b. 1833. (6) Eliza Haughton, b. 1839.

(ii) THOMAS GRUBB of Dublin (*Continued from Collateral Table "C", p. 50*). Youngest grandson of William and Margaret Grubb, he interested himself in the moon and stars, and in astronomy. He was a creator with his fine delicate fingers, a Fellow of the Royal Society of Dublin, and became a noted optician and constructor of reflecting telescopes and fine instruments. He married 1826, Sarah Palmer (d. 1883), and had nine children; five sons and four daughters (of whom three died young). Annabel b. 1827; Mary Anne b. 1831, m. 1860 Romney REMBRANT; Emily (1838–59). Surviving sons were HENRY GRUBB, b. 1833, m. 1860, Anna Hunt; and

Sir HOWARD GRUBB, F.R.S., Dublin (1844–1931).
Graduate in Science, Trinity College, Dublin; a leading astronomical instrument maker. Knighted 1887. He married Mary, daughter of Dr. G. H. Walker of U.S.A. They had four sons and three daughters (three died young). Ethel b. 1872, m. Frank CARLISLE; and Mary (1889–1969). GEORGE GRUBB, b. 1878 and ROMNEY R. GRUBB, b. 1879, m. 1915, Ada Pearson.

86

PLATE XV

PIGOT'S MAP OF IRELAND

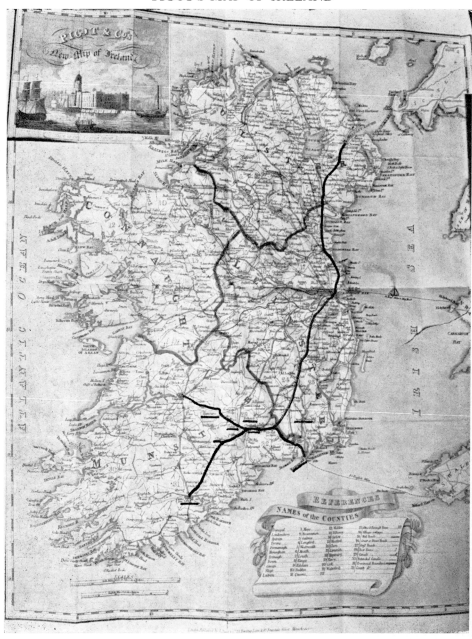

Showing the principal coach-roads and the Customs House, Dublin.

CHAPTER EIGHT

The Lady Grubbs
and their Irish and Continental Tours

"Ambassadors for Christ."—II Corinthians, v. 20.

REMINISCENT of Naomi and Ruth in Old Testament days is the affection that bound Sarah Grubb (Senior), Joseph's wife, to her daughters-in-law as they toured Ireland at first together, and later on their own, or in the case of Sarah (Tuke) Grubb with her husband Robert in journeying on the Continent and in Scotland. They all had the same motive—to bring succour to the poor and needy, and to tell abroad the "Truth" of the Everlasting Gospel. Inspired by John Wesley, Sarah Grubb Senior had begun her Gospel itinerations soon after her eldest son Thomas was married, and had moved to Waterford. It became almost a ritual in her family that as her sons became engaged to be married and settled down, their wives should (wish to) accompany Mother-in-Law, one or other of them (if only to keep an eye on Mother's health) when she obeyed her leadings to set out on another journey. Three of them were "Sarah's"—true Princesses of God, distinguished by the use of a maiden-name before their married surname—Sarah (Ridgway) Grubb; Sarah (Pim) Grubb, and Sarah (Tuke) Grubb. At a later date; when their own touring days were over, Sarah Lynes of Wapping (*see pp. 94ff.*) who had been a companion and nurserymaid to Sarah (Pim) Grubb in the days of her widowhood, felt the same call to itinerant evangelism, and on her subsequent marriage into the Grubb family, became a "fifth" Sarah Grubb, and perhaps the best known of them all, in her missions for the Saviour.

In retrospect, never did the centuries-old influence of their "Castle" origins in the Grubb blood reveal itself more clearly than in quickly knitting their Quaker wives into the family, and then inspiring them out to the attack on the citadels of Satan, from within their security in the Quaker "fence of discipline". They became knit together into a team; all their energies enlisted for the Lord's work, even at times it might seem at the expense of domestic duties and responsibilities. True, nannies and servants were plentiful and cheap, and Mother-in-Law Sarah had already brought all her children up, while Sarah (Tuke) Grubb and Robert her husband were childless, and so well able to be away on tour for consider-able stretches of time. It was natural that the itinerations of Margaret

87

and of Sarah (Pim) Grubb were shorter, and less regular, occupied as they were with young and growing families. Sarah (Lynes) Grubb after her marriage is recorded as sometimes taking a child with her.

Beautiful and cultured women were the Lady Grubbs, sensitive, sympathetic and active. The Grubb male has always seemed to have a knack of finding or choosing a wife "as good as she is beautiful" in the words of the Family Motto. Some who met them on their tours spoke of them, as once men spoke of Stephen, as having the faces of angels. Two of them, by all accounts, were outstandingly lovely—Mother-in-Law Sarah herself, and Margaret, Samuel's wife, through whom the Watkins Grubbs are descended. With her smiling Irish eyes, noticing everything, and breathing sympathy and interest to everyone she met, she had inherited from her grandfather Abraham Shackleton the Mystic and Scholar, something of the beauty of sanctity and of clear thinking and expression. No one could overlook her, or mistake her for anything but a perfect lady. She possessed also a physical grace of form and movement and a rich auburn colouring inherited through her Mother from her Grandmother Rachel Carleton, both of them outstanding beauties in their time. Grandmother Rachel Carleton was a daughter of *George Rooke*, a native of Cumberland. He was one of the earliest Quakers, and on settling in Ireland built up in Dublin a large timber business. After his marriage to *Joan Cook* of Limerick, they were spoken of for years after as "The handsomest couple ever to have been married in Limerick." Rachel Carleton's wealth was great; after her husband's death she moved to a large house in Ballitore in 1759 near the school to be close to her daughter and grandchildren. Her elder daughter Deborah Carleton (another beauty of lively and cheerful temper, some 14 years older than Margaret's mother) lived with her. Mary Leadbeater thus described her grandmother in her Journal:—

> "Grandmother Carleton knew what was what; her stately reserve was sometimes censured as height (the softened term for 'pride'): she was the remains of a fine old gentlewoman." [1]

Samuel and Margaret were both very fond of her, and benefited considerably on her death. It gave Margaret a degree of financial independence, and they were both in agreement it should be primarily used in the Lord's work and the propagation of "The Truth" among Ireland's needy and poor. In the use of money, there was no "communism in Quakerism"; each member was responsible for the wise and charitable use of that which he (she) had earned or inherited.

---

[1] *The Leadbeater Papers*. "Annals of Ballitore". Vol. i, pp. 53–58. The surname Carleton later appears as a christian name among several of Margaret Grubb's descendants. The best known is the Rev. George Carleton Grubb, son of Richard Grubb, Jnr. (*Chapter Twelve*), who was so well known as a Keswick Speaker, and for his Australian missions.

The Lady Grubb's evangelistic tours of Ireland, and later on the Continent of Europe, form an often overlooked feature of Irish social life in the last decades of the eighteenth century. They were known as "Public Friends" or public preachers. In areas they were visiting for the first time they would be accompanied by a Provincial Friend, as it were to vet them, and to introduce them to isolated Quakers who would appreciate a visitation, or offer hospitality. Welcome and hospitality in hospitable Ireland they were constantly to receive. They had never a doubt but that God had chosen them, with the gifts He had given to them, for such pastoral and evangelistic service. They believed their married status fitted them the better to go to the homes of Ireland, than if they were celibate. In their trim Quaker travelling cloaks, bonnets, white blouses and collars, they formed an attractive and compelling picture of uniformed gospel workers, comparable only to Salvation Army lasses today. Non-conformists as they were, they recognised the need of a distinctive religious dress or uniform on such missions across Ireland, as easily recognisable as the clerical dress and collar of a Catholic priest. But their success depended not on their clothing, but on their outward looking and charming capacity for quickly making their hearers feel they were indeed FRIENDS, really interested in them, and caring so much as to be ready to face the difficulties of travel to be of service to them. So were opened hitherto closed hearts to listen to what they had to say. If they were somewhat overpowering, and almost masculine in the courage they showed in overcoming all obstacles standing in the way of the achievement of their missions, they were successful in pioneering new avenues of ministry, and in the deployment of women's special gifts in the Master's service.

The Lady Grubbs' mission tours, following as it were in the steps of St. Paul or John Wesley, spring from four main causes in the leading of God:

(i) Unceasing travel from place to place had been the method of the Saviour of Mankind: He sent out his disciples two by two, to go where the people lived, rather than to expect them to come to a building or church or temple to hear the Message. It was the method of St. Paul, and of the Celtic Saints. It was the method of George Fox, William Edmundson, John Exham and others to spread the Quaker teachings. It was the method of John Wesley. The Grubb family have never placed overmuch importance on church and chapel buildings in themselves, and have found the reality of worship and of witness also in open-air or tent gatherings, or in private houses. The Lady Grubbs had a calling to go where the people were, to their homes or to the market-place, to proclaim the good news of One who loves and cares and delivers from sin. They were by no means the first "Public Friends", or wandering evangelists, but they were among the first women evangelists in Ireland. Travel seemed to come naturally to them; it was no hardship, but rather an adventure and crusade for their Saviour. They cared little if the tongue of gossip ran before them, if numbers attended their open-air ministry out of curiosity. It is easy to draw a crowd in Ireland.

(ii) The poverty and need of the Irish people cried out to heaven for some one to help. Ireland, always mindful of past wrongs and grievances and at loggerheads with England, now expected little help from English people; both the established church and the presbyterian church seemed concerned only for their own well being in these Anglo-Hanoverian days, and completely out of touch with the people. Wrote the poet Spenser:—

> "It is a great wonder to see the difference between the zeal of the papist prelates and the ministers of the Gospel. For they do not spare themselves to come out of Spain and from Rome by dangerous travelling, where they know the peril of death may await them, and where no rewards or riches are to be found, only to draw the people to the church of Rome. (There were always close affinities in Irish history between Spain and the six south-west counties of Munster). Whereas some of our ministers, having the resources of the Kingdom offered to them without pains and without peril, will neither for the same nor for any love of God, nor zeal for religion, be drawn from their warm nests to search out into God's harvest."

Exaggerated as Spenser's strictures often were, the Lady Grubbs had seen with their own eyes the misery and sinning all around them. Being themselves non-conformists, they were never antagonistic to Rome, but they believed that what Roman priests could do, surely they could do better with the pure Gospel and an open Bible. They must answer the cry for help from Ireland's starving thousands, whatever the cost of leaving home and families would mean. But for their intervention, as Irish women to Irish women, their sympathy and practical generosity, and the divine message they preached, Ireland could well have turned Communist before Russia. They went out to storm the citadels of Satan and to bring lost sheep into the stronghold and fold of the Lord.

(iii) Their own study of the Scriptures had challenged them to leave all for their Master's sake. They just could not enjoy the tea parties and visiting in prosperous Clonmel, and all that wealth could give them; a still small voice within insistently reminded them of the desperate need of the poor of Ireland for the healing and deliverance of the true Gospel of Christ which would not be proclaimed to them unless they themselves were to take it. They knew within themselves for a certainty that they were chosen and called of God to be His messengers for just such a time as this. Their godly husbands, when consulted, put no hindrance in their way. They rather provided the "sinews of war", the funds needed, to bring material benevolence to the starving—at a time when national assistance was still unknown. Their tours were rather those of the

PLATE XVI

ON TOUR THROUGH IRELAND

IRISH JAUNTING CARR.

By Irish Jaunting Car

"Grande-Dame" than of the bare-footed friar, and the repeated references in their Journals to the hard-hearts and indifference they encountered, suggests that their combination of charitable belief with gospel preaching —generally typical of the out-going religious efforts of Anglo-Hanoverian days—cannot be compared to the evangelistic missions of a succeeding century.

(iv) In the call of Sarah Lynes, a charismatic (or prophetic) gift known as "Speaking with Tongues" is also noticeable. The Voice within said "Cry out, and spare not". She could do no other than obey the Inner Light and use these gifts she was conscious to have received from the Lord, even if it meant preaching uninvited one Christmas Day in St. Paul's Cathedral. All the Lady Grubbs went out in faith that God was calling them to their missions for Him. To leave loved ones and children did not seem to them to be a sacrifice. If God should call any of their little ones to Himself during their absences from home, it would not be their neglect, but the Master's Higher Wisdom in teaching them priorities. He had some better thing in store for their dear ones in His own good time. They must not count life dear unto themselves, but face cheerfully and with a smile the hardships of separation, if by any means they might be used to save some, and extend the Kingdom of God.

Moved by the Holy Ghost as they believed, in apostolic fervour and plainness of costume and life, the Lady Grubbs went forth from Clonmel between 1770 and 1810, sometimes singly, sometimes in twos or threes, allowing no domestic or feminine duty to deter them from their high calling. In John Owen's words of the previous century that had inspired the first Grubb to come to Ireland, they sought to be faithful in this one thing—to do their utmost for the preaching of the Gospel in Ireland. Good organisation—ever a Grubb characteristic—determined the mileage for each day. Their stopping and preaching centres were largely determined by the hospitality they were likely to be offered by other Friends, or by the needs for visitation of the sick or isolated. It must not be supposed they ever had to sleep under the hedgerow. Their purses were filled for expenses and benevolence when they started out; when funds were exhausted, it was time to return to Clonmel. They would cover anything up to 20 miles a day. For "Public Friends" called to such itinerations and not so comfortably off as the Lady Grubbs, the Local Meeting sending them forth would provide a horse and clothing for the journey, and a sufficiency of cash for such nights as hospitality was not available. There was little of the faith of the methodist preachers[2] and many a

[2] John Wesley records on route to Ireland on one of his visits he overtook on the road to Holyhead a certain John Jane, one of his Methodist preachers, who had set out on foot from Bristol with only thirty-six pence in his pocket. "Six nights out of seven, since he set out, he was entertained by utter strangers, and he reached Holyhead with still one penny in his pocket". *Journals of John Wesley.* Vol. ii, p. 170.

missionary, who go forth not knowing where they will sleep, or how the Lord in whom they trust, will provide for their daily needs.

It was such itinerations and preachments that kept the Society of Friends alive in Ireland in the latter part of the eighteenth century, and that in the previous century established it, when the preachers were few and had to prove the meaning of faith in every detail of their journeys. It was by such visits and preachings that converts were made, and weak Society meetings strengthened. Only by the influx of new blood and converts can any church or religious society fulfil its mission and truly thrive and live. When any particular or local church ceases to be outward-looking and evangelistic, it surely withers and becomes as dead, lacking all inspiration, useless to God and the people around it. The Quakers have always been ahead of most other Christian denominations in encouraging and employing the ministry of women. It uses their gifts as pastors and counsellors, as well as evangelists. "Mother Confessors" the Grubb Ladies frequently were to become, as unhappy and sin-beset souls poured out their griefs and troubles to them. It is little wonder they wrote so many letters, and kept so many diaries!

Was it the example and earnestness of these Lady Grubbs that inspired another lady evangelist of the next century to pen those well-known words, that so exactly summarised their purpose and their missions?—

"RESCUE the perishing—duty demands it,
Strength for thy labour the Lord will provide:
Back to the narrow way patiently win them;
Tell the poor wanderer a Saviour has died.

Down in the human heart, crushed by the tempter,
Feelings lie buried that grace can restore:
Touched by a loving hand, wakened by kindness
Chords that were broken will vibrate once more.

Rescue the perishing, care for the dying,
Snatch them in pity from sin and the grave:
Plead with them earnestly, plead with them gently
Tell them of Jesus, the mighty to save.
Frances Van Alstyne.

What then, did the Lady Grubb Evangelists find on their missions throughout the countryside of Ireland? It was usual to visit about twenty places a month, and to travel at least 1,000 miles before thinking of a return home to Clonmel to give a report to the local meeting of all they had seen and done. The usual route adopted would be by the main coach road to Dublin, where they might stay some weeks, attend monthly or yearly Friends Meetings, visit other Quakers, and attend to necessary shopping before riding north into Ulster. They would make detours from the coach roads to visit isolated families, and to search out those they had heard to be in need, preaching in the open air or in assembly rooms, as the Spirit led them, and attending on Lord's Days the local meeting of the Society. Invitations would have reached them previously to attend week evening meetings in various places of the Quakers. They would proceed west to Sligo, as Wesley used to do, always an important town to visit. Southwards along the borders of Connaught, an almost entirely Roman Catholic Province, and along the "Celtic Fringe" to Galway, County Clare (called by Wesley "Clara") and to the Limerick region. There was no hard and fast itinerary, and they would either return home to Clonmel, to visit County Cork and the South West on another mission, or continue their itinerations southwards. Time mattered not. They might continue in one place until the Spirit led them on, when their mission seemed completed. They were not dependent upon time-tables. Should their horses need reshodding, it was the Spirit's guidance to remain in ministry at that place another day or two. If sickness beset them, they lived in faith that the Lord would provide the necessary cure, and continued quietly waiting on Him until better. They knew the Lord was continually guiding them in such ways. It was the apostolic method of travel. They were content, and therefore never lost their serenity. To use an "Irishism" it was not always necessary for the preachers to preach, if not so led, or if prevented by sickness or loss of voice. Sometimes Quaker meetings of worship were held in complete silence week by week, no one being led to offer praise or prayer or exhortation.

Quiet Quakers. This was the original concept of members of the Society of Friends. "The silence of all flesh before God", the suppression of strain and effort in listening to words and the flow of words by whomsoever spoken, the hushing of all faculties of thought and wandering thoughts, the "Quiet Time" for listening to the Spirit of God within, a mystical stillness before God in company with others equally minded—this had been the original distinctive ethos of the Society, as George Fox had founded it. John Griffiths, a much travelled "Public Friend" wrote in his Journal of his visit to the Quaker meeting at Birr: "I found it my place to example the Friends with silence . . . I had all the people called Methodists and their preacher at one meeting than whom, I think, no people are more at a loss what to do with silence in worship. Oh, that they might be as happy to be emptied . . . then would they come to experience true poverty of spirit, to abhor the active self, whose time is always ready."[3] His words reflect the growing division in method and practice among the Quakers in the latter half of the eighteenth century, largely

---

[3] *The Quakers in Ireland* by Isabel Grubb, M.A. Chapter 6.

I

as a result of the influence of the Methodist movement, and the succeeding Evangelical Revival.

The Lady Grubbs represented this other side of Quakerism. Like the Methodists at Birr they were seldom at a loss to speak, but at times it might seem rather at a loss what to do with silences. The "Kerugma" or proclamation by voice and word of the Divine Message was an essential part of their ministry. Wrote one of them, Mrs. Robert Grubb (née Sarah Tuke, once Clerk of the York Quakers Meeting, and like her husband, an Elder among the Quakers)[4], in 1784:—

"For Zion's sake we cannot rest nor hold our peace, until they (her audiences) are at least informed of their state . . . We have not only travelled far and hard, but found much work at places where we have come, finding it more than usual in the line of our duty to bear a testimony, not only to the Truth, but against the numerous evils *and inconsistencies* which have generally overspread the professors in these parts. As our peace much depends upon our being honest and speaking the Truth without parables, we have been enabled pretty tolerably to discharge our duty, and to show them how far they are from what they pretend to be. But 'tis hard work, and we find that the more abundantly we manifest our love in this way, the less we are loved by many, who have been used to smooth things, and have fought to make truth conform to them, instead of their conduct being brought to, and regulated by the Truth. So that indeed many are blind in error, and those that see will not exert themselves to search their own houses, and *remove the inconsistencies* that are there. Under these impressions we seek not great things for ourselves, but rather are disposed to consider it a favour if we give our lives for a prey, from one place to another. They that have the seed to sow, must expect to dwell in a low spot."

There is this same emphasis on the inconsistencies among Quakers in Sarah Grubb's *Journal* that John Griffiths reported with sorrow he also had found among the Irish Friends—"an indifference, a lukewarmness, and insensibility to the life of religion, a prevailing disposition to compromise, if thereby peace at any price might be obtained, and covetousness sheltering behind a cloak of plainness." But inconsistencies are common in Ireland and among the Grubbs of Tipperary themselves, and among the Sarah Grubb preachers, who (conveniently) overlooked the Scriptural injunctions of St. Paul that women should keep silent in worship. One of them, as a bride was to give an hour's address at her own wedding!

Mrs. John Grubb (née Sarah Lynes of Wapping, who married one of Samuel Grubb's first cousins), a petite English girl, came over to Clonmel at the age of 14 to be companion to Widow Sarah Grubb (née Pim) of Anner Mills, and nursemaid to her orphaned daughters after the death

---

[4] *Some Account of the Life and Religious Labours of Sarah Grubb*, p. 85.

of her husband, John Grubb, an elder brother of Samuel's. She had been recommended by the Friends School and Orphanage at Islington, where she was one of its brightest pupils, and had been drawn to a religious life from an early age. At the age of 17 she made her first appearance in the ministry at Clonmel (1790), discovered her own charismatic gift for discourse, generally rather long and most expressive, and made some preaching itinerations with her mistress (who now had her sister to help with the children, and gave her "nannie" all the help she could). Sarah Lynes was formally acknowledged as a minister in Clonmel in 1794, where she had found support from another Grubb family, that of the grocer Benjamin Grubb, and in particular his eldest son John (1766–1841), not yet 30 and her ardent admirer. He used to visit her frequently at Anner Mills, and later to take leave from his grocery duties to stand by her side in her open-air preachments. But no thought of marriage would deter Sarah Lynes from the peripatetic ministry to which she believed she was called. After several Irish tours, she felt the need in England for her ministry. It is recorded by the biographer of her grandson, the eminent Quaker teacher and preacher, Edward Grubb[5]:—

> "One Christmas day she entered St. Paul's Cathedral in the afternoon. When the bishop of London had delivered 'something called a sermon', she stood up from her chair, & in a loud voice asked if the service was over? Led out of the Cathedral by an official for disturbing the service (the precursor of many who have been similarly outsted from St. Paul's) she turned at the Great West Door 'to address the audience to the relief of my mind'. . . . At Bath she had no fear in entering the Pump Room to declare the truth 'to the gay people who resorted there.' "

John Grubb waited seven years for his Sarah Lynes, like Jacob of old for Rachel, until she felt herself more free from her exacting commitments. Their marriage took place after the manner of the Friends at Isleworth in Middlesex. It was probably the one and only Grubb wedding at which the bride gave the sermon to the assembled congregation and guests! Wrote John Grubb to his sister next day that when Sarah and himself had completed the usual form of contract:—

> "A considerable silence ensued; then the meeting seemed about to break up, when I found my dear Sarah was under considerable exercise. She then stepped up into the (ministerial) gallery, and was, I think I may say, favoured in a remarkable manner to expound the gospel to the people. She said it was unexpected and a cross to her to have to move into that line that day. She spoke a considerable time, so that it seemed like one of her public meetings. She sat down a short time in the gallery, and then returned to a seat beside me."

Usually at Quaker meetings, (except at weddings) the sexes were divided, members of the same family likewise. John added:—

> "My bride was again engaged in the exercise of her gift after dinner."

[5] *Life of Edward Grubb* by James Dudley, pp. 22ff.

CHAPTER EIGHT—THE LADY GRUBBS

It is little wonder that "the exercise of Sarah Grubb's gift" was to occupy her all her married life, sometimes to the exasperation and trial of the congregations who heard it, at least in East Anglia in the latter part of her life. Wrote that eminent Quaker Edward Pease in his Journal in 1840[6]:—

> "I was exasperated at a meeting, one of the most trying I have ever attended, by reason of S. Grubb occupying nearly the whole time in ministry. It is to me no small trial that young Friends should have to remark to me that which I cannot defend upon the clearest and soundest grounds."

and again the same Edward Pease had this to say of Sarah Grubb's constant speaking:—

> "Feeling and hearing how much trial there is in S. Grubb always occupying the time in meeting, I was bold enough to offer a few observations not to exceed the measure of their gifts. [7] I was followed by S. Codner and Samuel Gurney, [8] but whether the Friends were cowardly in touching such a character, or deemed us radical, I know not; but we were not followed up. This I deplore, because I am certain we are suffering under a domination, which if continued, will come out in open revolt."

With the departure of this John and Sarah Grubb from Clonmel in 1818, having disposed of their share in the family grocery business, to a wider field of ministry in East Anglia (where a family of continuing Quaker Grubbs grew up and flourished), there came an end to the Lady Grubbs gospel tours of Ireland. Clonmel by this time had become a most convenient base for the start and terminus of itinerant evangelism, which was carried on by others less expensively by means of the Irish-Car-Service. Early in the new century there had been a day when an unknown Italian picture-seller and door-to-door hawker of rather florid pictures of the Madonna and the "Ascent of Mary" (such as the Irish Roman Catholic peasants loved, and their women-folk purchased to cover their bleak cabin walls) was given a lift on a passing wagon, and set down in Clonmel outside one of the Grubb mills as a likely place where he might be given hospitality. Seeing his distress, and true to their Quaker principles, the Grubbs befriended him.

Charles Biancini was in no hurry to move on. The Clonmel district proved a fruitful soil for the sale of numbers of his paintings on religious subjects. From his own experience he realised the hardship of pedestrian itinerations into the villages and hamlets, still unprovided with any kind of public transport, whether to sell pictures or to preach the gospel. He

---

[6] *The Diaries of Edward Pease.* Edited by Sir Alfred Pease, p. 74.
[7] *Ibid.*, p. 165.
[8] The Gurneys of Norfolk were prominent English Quakers, and Samuel Gurney was one of the founders of the British and Foreign Bible Society. It was his influence that obtained for young George Borrow, as equally loquacious as Mrs. Sarah Grubb, an appointment with the Bible Society.

conceived the idea of an Irish-Car-Service to link up the smaller inland towns and villages, unprovided for by the long-distance coach service from Dublin to Cork, or to Waterford. His initiative was immediately successful, aided by capital from some Clonmel residents. Charles Biancini's cars increased rapidly over County Tipperary, and into the south and west of Ireland, Clonmel being his headquarters and the start and terminus of his transport system. The present HEARN'S HOTEL was his first headquarters, and the clock by which his cars were timed to depart and arrive is still to be seen in the wall of the hotel yard. His "cars" as they were called, were of the Irish jaunting-car type, drawn by good horses with the passengers facing the sides of the road, back to back. They were run at 2d per mile, and made short gospel itinerations possible for the successors of the Lady Grubb itinerants and other travelling evangelists or public friends. Biancini himself became another of Clonmel's rich men, the friend of Daniel O'Connell, to whose struggle for Roman Catholic emancipation he contributed generously from his Clonmel fortune, and as an old man the third Catholic mayor of Clonmel in the nineteenth century.[9] He always spoke of the Quakers with appreciation.

Voltaire, the Frenchman, with a similar Roman Catholic upbringing to Biancini, was another to look kindly upon the Quakers, and to look to Clonmel. After the overthrow of the French monarchy, there were many French intellectuals and reformers who wanted to know more of the practice of Christianity without bishops, priests, elaborate ritual, costly churches and sacraments, as well as of the *Republican ideals* of the Quakers as Penn's settlement in America seemed to them to be. Again it was to be from the Grubbs of Clonmel that this questing after God was to be answered. Robert Grubb and his wife Sarah, of Suir Island, Clonmel, who shared in the Grubb love for all things French, had already paid a first visit to France in 1789, as Public Friends, to preach and encourage the few Quakers established in Congenies

> "We are all striving for the same object," they affirmed; "We are striving for Universal Fraternity and Friendship, for the Brotherhood of Mankind. We by gentleness and the refusal to bear arms; you by resistance to a corrupt monarchy. We share your impatience and your sufferings; for long we have suffered in Ireland in the same way."

On their second visit in 1791 they assisted Madame Roland and Monsieur J. de Marsillac and others at Congenies in drawing up and delivering a petition to the French National Assembly for recognition and freedom of worship for the people called Quakers, and their exemption from military service. Their mission and itinerations made no small stir

---

[9] For a fuller history of Charles Biancini's cars, see *The Stranger in Ireland*, pp. 239–249, by Constantia Maxwell, former Lecky Professor in Modern History at the University of Dublin. (1954.)

in troubled France. On their third visit in 1792 after the Revolution, they went to negotiate for the purchase of one of the former Royal palaces at Chambord with a view to establishing therein a Quaker school on an extensive scale, to which they felt guided to contribute generously from their Clonmel fortune. They had wide contacts in France, and before returning to Ireland went on into Germany to preach and enlist interest in their French project, spending some months at Minden, a garrison town in Westphalia, and at Pyrmont, a German health resort in Waldeck, of which places and their activities Sarah wrote much in her Journal.[10] They also visited the Hartz mountains and Brunswick. In Ireland they secured the active interest and support of the Shackletons at Ballitore, on which school their new venture was to be copied, and of Samuel and Margaret Grubb. But alas the outbreak of war between England and France was to put an end to their design. Instead they decided to devote the funds already collected to opening a girls' finishing school at Clonmel, and turned their own large home on Suir Island to this purpose.[11] Anne Tuke, Sarah Grubb's sister, a qualified teacher, came over from York to assist in the teaching, and they soon recruited a well-qualified staff. Grubbs have always been interested in education and teaching, a profession in which through the nineteenth and twentieth centuries many of them were to find their life's work. Margaret Grubb also assisted in the teaching for a while; Grubb daughters were sent there; and Margaret's already voluminous correspondence grew yet more voluminous. The French and German languages, English literature, astronomy, deportment, exquisite caligraphy, the making of samplers (many of them worth a lot of money today), mathematics, the keeping of accounts, sewing, mending and household duties formed the larger part of the curriculum, at a time when there were no external school inspectors at work. The teaching was

[10] See Appendix "A".
[11] *Life of Sarah Grubb.* Third Edition. 1796. Ch. VI, p. 183. The full quotation reads:

"The subject of opening a Boarding School for Girls in Clonmel had for some time been deeply pondered by Robert and Sarah Grubb, and at length 'so matured in our minds as to afford evidence it would be right to set forward this work'. Their motives were purely disinterested, and with a single view to promote a guarded and religious education for female youth, and to use inherited money for this plan, being themselves in easy circumstances.

" 'My dear R.G.', wrote Sarah, 'has kindly condescended to make ample provision for a Boarding School for girls, and has built a considerable addition to our present dwelling, which stands upon an island in a navigable river called the Suir. It is about 100 yards across, and over a quarter of a mile long; it has on one side of it the Quays and town of Clonmel, and on the other cultivated mountains, which seem almost to hang over it. The prospect from the front of the house, is through the garden and a pasture to the river and valley, and is terminated by a very high and rugged mountain, which is several miles distant. The place is altogether very commodious and pleasant for its intended purpose, but how shall we meet with suitable disinterested persons for undertaking the immediate care of the children is not clear. A hope, however, cheers us, that if our views are right, and deserving of blessing, all things needful will be afforded us in the needful time.' "

broadly based, as might be expected of Grubbs with so many interests, and not confined to books written by Quakers. Suir Island School became one of the leading Quaker Finishing Schools for Girls in Ireland, and in 1846 was transferred to larger premises at Prior Park.[12]

---

[12] Robert Grubb, in his WILL dated December 20th, 1796 "BEQUEATHED his premises on Suir Island, now used as a Girls Boarding School, to 12 Trustees to hold for the purposes of the school". He left them an annual rent of £60, derivable from his flour mills that were held by Thomas Grubb (his brother), such rent to be paid to the Governors of the School for the time being, whom the Trustees shall appoint. The buildings accommodated 32 boarders. His character and strength can best be assessed in the frequent references to him in the *Life and Journals of Sarah Grubb*, his wife.

THE CONTINUING QUAKER BRANCH OF THE GRUBB FAMILY

BENJAMIN GRUBB (1727–1802) and SUSANNA (*née* MALONE)

He was the youngest son of JOHN and ANNE GRUBB (*Collatteral Table "C"*). Benjamin was a tall, well-made man, described as pious and helpful in meetings. He married Susanna Malone, who came from good Quaker stock at Ballyraggin in County Kildare.

1.	JAMES	b. 1763; d. 1766, *died young*	
2.	JOHN	b. 1766; d. 1841	4 children
3.	JOSEPH	b. 1768; d. 1844	7 children
1.	Anne	b. 1759; d. 1818	
2.	Mary	b. 1760; m. Samuel DAVIS. Two of her children (Francis and Deborah) married into the family of SAMUEL GRUBB of Clogheen	
3.	Elizabeth	b. 1762; d. 1829	
4.	Hannah	b. 1764; d. 1812	
5.	Susanna	b. 1771; d. 1805; m. James MOORE	7 daughters
6.	Sarah	b. 1772; *died young*	
7.	Abigail	b. 1774; d. 1816	

---

2. **JOHN GRUBB** (1766–1841) married, 1803, Sarah Lynes (1773–1842), of Wapping, one-time nursery maid to widow Sarah Grubb of Anner Mills. He was in partnership with his brother Joseph in the family grocery business in Main St., Clonmel, which they expanded to a second store in Gordon Street. They had four children born in Clonmel, but "his wife did not allow family cares to restrict her ministerial activities". She was a recognised Quaker minister for 48 years, a tremendous traveller and speaker, and one of the most remarkable women in the Society of Friends. John's life was ordered by her "leadings", which led them to leave Ireland in 1818 for a wider ministry in East Anglia. They settled at Bury St. Edmunds, later moved to Chelmsford and Stoke Newington and ended their days at Sudbury, looked after by their children. They had two sons (the second JOSEPH (1809–1810) died in infancy while they were taking missions), and two daughters—Susanna, b. 1806; m. William KING, bank manager at Sudbury, and Hannah (1811–1875).

JONATHAN GRUBB (1808–1894), their surviving son, had all the energy and evangelistic gifts of his ancestors. He married (a) Elizabeth Gripper, of Layer Breton Hall, Essex (1837), who died of consumption (1838), and (b) Elizabeth BURLINGHAM (1844), a quiet home-making woman, whose surname was given to many of his descendants, who became known as the BURLINGHAM GRUBBS. Selling his water-mill and corn business at Lexden in Essex, they made their home for 50 years in a large country house on the River Stour, called Holgate, outside Sudbury (where his married sister lived). He gave himself to religious work as a Quaker minister and evangelical preacher, and took Gospel Missions all over the Eastern countries, and in Ireland 1858–1862. His activities bear comparison with those of his mother. He often preached to 1,000 people at a time, and travelled widely. He did outstanding work in the Vaudois Valleys, in Piedmont, and in the Shetland Islands, and against such evangelical background his three sons and two daughters were brought up. Sarah, b. 1846; m. 17 July 1877 as his second wife, Stanley PUMPHREY, of The Cross, Thornton, Worcs. (See *Burke's Landed Gentry*, 1952); and Elizabeth Lucy, b. 1852, married Gawen KENWAY. His three sons were educated at the Friends Boarding School at Sidcot, in Somerset, and became distinguished Quaker ministers.

(*Continued next page*)

THE CONTINUING QUAKER BRANCH OF THE GRUBB FAMILY
(*continued from last page*)

(1) THOMAS BURLINGHAM GRUBB, b. 1848; m. Sarah Frame.

They had two sons: THEODORE GRUBB, b. 1873
BENJAMIN GRUBB, b. 1877

(2) JOHN GRUBB, b. 1850; m. Madeline Kenway. They lived at Winscombe in the Mendips, and had one son—DAVID BURLINGHAM GRUBB (1878–1964), who followed his father in Quaker ministry, and as a Governor of Sidcot. Of his three children—Elizabeth (b. 1904), married John PULSFORD; and has three children and two grandchildren.

> (i) JOHN GRUBB (1906), became Senior English Master at Ross-on-Wye Grammar School; he married Mollie Coomber, has one son PAUL GRUBB (b. 1944), and three grandchildren: MICHAEL, Elizabeth and DAVID.

> (ii) GAWEN GRUBB (b. 1907), his second son, married Evelyn Mercier, and has one son, ANTHONY (b. 1936), married Enyl Hughes (1960), they have one daughter; and a daughter Gillian (b. 1946), married to Andrew EVANS.

(3) EDWARD GRUBB, M.A. (LOND.) (1854–1939) became a school teacher, editor of *British Friend* and a great traveller in America and Germany in the Quaker ministry. In complete contrast to his contemporary and cousin the Rev. George Grubb, M.A. (1856–1940), and to his own father, he was a leader of that section among the Friends who revolted from their older evangelical doctrines in favour of all that modern research and evolutionary theories, Biblical criticism and psychical research could offer the Society. See the biography of his life entitled *A Spiritual Pilgrimage* by James Dudley (1946). He was a keen fisherman and naturalist, and a prolific writer of religious books, hymns, and poems. He married Emma Housnail in 1877, and had three daughters and two sons,

> (i) HOWARD BURLINGHAM (b. 1881);

> (ii) NORMAN HENRY (b. 1883) and Edith (b. 1878), Music Mistress at the Quaker "Mount School", York; Mrs. Margery WALSH (b. 1892); and Elizabeth (b. 1893). His sons were sent to their father's old school at Sidcot, and the scholastic profession and scholarship has continued to characterise the family.

3. JOSEPH GRUBB (1768–1844), the younger son of Benjamin and Susannah, married Lydia Jâcob in 1804, and remained in Clonmel all his life, carrying on the family grocery trade, when his brother John left in 1818 for England. They had three daughters—Anne, b. 1812; Lydia, b. 1818; Susannah, b.1820. And four sons—

BENJAMIN GRUBB	b. 1805	⎫
JOSHUA GRUBB	b. 1807	⎬ all educated at Ballitore Quaker School
JOSEPH GRUBB	b. 1814	⎭
JOHN GRUBB	b. 1816, who married Rebecca Strangman, his second cousin, a granddaughter of Joseph GRUBB (*See Collateral Table "D".*) Their only son J. ERNEST GRUBB (1843–1927) of Carrick-on-Suir, a scholar of no mean repute, and his daughter, Dr. Isabel Grubb (b. 1881), the noted Quaker historian, exerted great influence and became widely known in Quaker and historical circles. Dr. Isabel Grubb is the author of many books (see Bibliography) and now lives at Waterford.	

101

CHAPTER NINE

Samuel Grubb

Part II. *The Squire of Clogheen, Co. Tipperary*
(1800–1815)

"A wise man, endowed with knowledge, showing out of a good conversation his works with meekness."—James iii, 13.

TO be able to discern the right time to retire, and leave your work in other hands, is a mark of a wise man. Life never stands still. It can never be lived again. The record has been written in the Books of Heaven. To leave retirement too late may be to undo much of the good work a man has done. To retire too early can be bad for the soul, and deprive others of a man's accumulated experience, while he is still in his prime. Unhappy is the man who can never afford to retire, or whose failing health, or accident, renders his early retirement inevitable. Not easy the choice for a self-employed man, who is able to retire just when he likes. After some years of cogitation, Samuel Grubb retired from his work in Clonmel at the turn of the century, when he was only just turned 50. True he had developed a limp, which made progress slower than he liked, and necessitated the aid of a stick.

There had been six or seven matters much on Samuel's mind during the last years in Clonmel. Pointers there were, he mused, of God's guidance that the time was fast coming when he should go out, like Abraham and Ishmael of old, and with a similar faith he hoped, to a new home and new if less arduous work. Carefully he weighed their significance as he said his prayers, and read his papers, and took counsel with his wife and sons. It was no sudden decision he made to leave Clonmel; to Samuel as to most wise and prayerful men, God's guidance came gradually but surely and unmistakably.

(*i*) *On the Family Level* his sons were growing up, and it was his duty to settle them in life, as Joseph Grubb, his father, had settled him and his elder brothers. But there was a limit to the number of mills in Clonmel that Grubbs could own and man, in competition with one another. His miller brothers all had growing families of their own (except Robert) to maintain, and carry on their respective businesses. As Quakers there was still little else his sons could do, but to go into trade or farming. It would seem wise to look elsewhere to start them on their own.

102

(*ii*) *Letters from America* had been reaching him for some years from his relatives and friends, telling him of the growing discontent in the New World at the apathy of successive English governments to do anything really constructive to improve the lot of the Colonists. Visiting American "Public Friends" at the Clonmel meeting had been giving similar reports, and warning of the cruel choice confronting Quakers if war should break out in Ireland, where discontent with England was as widespread as in America.[1] Lord North's Government had lost America in the American War of Independence, and it seemed quite possible would lose Ireland as well. "Where do our loyalties lie?" mused Samuel. "The Grubbs have been in Ireland over 100 years now, yet within the confines of Clonmel where we live and work, we are still regarded as English; probably we always shall be, while we live in this 'City of the Grubbs'. Are we still English or are we now Irish in our hearts?" Margaret added, with the experience of her contacts all over Ireland in her itinerations; "Master (she always called him that publicly), I think we ought to throw our lot entirely with the Irish people of this country where we live. That we can best do, if we move out of Clonmel".

(*iii*) *Daily Newspapers*, both English and Irish, had been obtainable in Clonmel since 1780. Responsible and intelligent journalists had superseded the "hacks of grub street"[2], and were inspiring Irish patriotism with a spirit of complete independence from England. Avid readers as were both Samuel and Margaret, as well as writers, how could they do otherwise than eagerly absorb the almost daily reports of the speeches of that brilliant old boy of Ballitore, Edmund Burke in the Irish Parliament in Dublin, in England, and up and down the country, and as eagerly read articles from his pen? Grattan was another. They realised the growing power of the Press. That indefinable spirit of loyalty produced by a good school in its pupils and old boys (there was no "old boys' tie" for Samuel to wear to lighten his dark clothing—had there been it would have stretched Quaker puritanism almost to breaking point), enthused in Samuel and Margaret a wholly Irish support for Burke's efforts. Even Ballitore School had recently produced its own school magazine[3]: Burke supplied his old school with an occasional article. Were they not still Quakers, Margaret certainly and perhaps the more cautious Samuel might well have taken up politics. But their interest in such matters gave increasing concern to some of their fellow Clonmel Quakers.

(*iv*) *Divisive Loyalties among the Friends*, not only over matters to do with politics and the future of Ireland, but more pressingly over Biblical Interpretation and the guidance of the Inner Light, became an increasing

[1] Especially Job Scott and William Savery. See *Later Periods of Quakerism*, Rufus M. Jones, pp. 282ff.
[2] J. R. Green. *A short history of the English People*, p. 776.
[3] *The Leadbeater Papers*, "Annals of Ballitore", pp. 309ff.

trouble to Samuel. Margaret was never troubled what others might say or think of her, with her Shackleton assurance that a devout life was of more importance in the sight of God than definition and rigid orthodoxy. As clerk of the Clonmel Meeting she had become conscious of how inward looking were so many of them, and of the gap left by the early deaths of brother-in-law Robert, and sister-in-law Sarah Grubb (née Tuke), who had been in the forefront in the stirring of a social conscience for the poor and ailing in the House of Industry he had founded, and in education both in Clonmel and in France. Visiting American friends seemed by their testimonies only to widen the gulf. With Job Scott, a mystic and welcome guest at Ballitore (where he later died of small-pox), and a man of singular piety, she felt much more at one, than with William Savery for instance. Like the majority of American Quakers he had been intensely influenced by the preaching of Whitfield, and shared their views on fundamental Biblical interpretation[4]; but with his brilliant and acute mind he seemed so stern in the manner he testified to such interpretation. She had come to know almost exactly how the various members of the Meeting would be led to speak, and yearned for the Fire and Wind of the Spirit to come among them. Nor was it always easy to accept the frequent and often impassioned testimony of young Sarah Lynes from Anners, her sister-in-law's nursery maid, who had been recognised in 1794 as a minister among them.

(v) *Discontented Employees and Servants.* Both Margaret and Samuel felt a certain amount of sympathy with the grievances of the Irish national-ists, much as they had deplored the murders committed by some of the White Boys. (*See Appendix B*). They realised that most Irishmen were discontented because poor, and poorer, so they believed, because of the apathy of the English Government and the restrictions placed upon Ireland. Samuel and Margaret knew the reason why some of the mill-hands in their brother's mills failed to turn up on time—due to the nightly drills they were expected to attend in preparation for an expected French invasion of Ireland[5], to overthrow British domination and to bring about a similar revolution to that which had taken place in France. They were aware of the manufacture and concealment of pikes and other weapons in nearly every blacksmith's shop, and found weapons one day hidden behind bags of corn in their own store. They read in the papers of the murder of local magistrates in the county and of neighbours regarded as informers, and were aware of the increasing number of fires in the houses of their friends. They saw the English garrison in Clonmel growing in numbers, and knew that the hanging of insurgents on Gallows Hill was no answer to the problem. Unease filled their hearts for the future of the "City of the Grubbs".

[4] *Quakers in Ireland.* Isabel Grubb, pp. 117ff.
[5] The French actually landed at Bantry Bay in 1797.

(*vi*) *Declining Irish Finances, and a Drop in the Value of Money.*—Inflation it would be called today. To read of the English Viceroy in Dublin dispensing most lavish hospitality, such as the Irish love, day after day, and even his own neighbours laying out great expenditure on ten-course meals (whatever might be written by William Savery of his own sumptuous table), while their servants were paid next to nothing, shocked Samuel's moral consciousness. Then the banks stopped payment of cash, and the wherewithal to pay his own millhands and staff became doubtful. Would it be wise, he thought, to pack up from Clonmel, and sink his earnings in landed property?

(*vii*) *The debacle of the Irish Rebellion* in 1798 clinched matters, and a state of affairs not dissimilar to that in Belfast and throughout Ulster in 1969 onwards developed-widespread murders, the burning of houses and mills, floggings, suspicions, and a great increase in the British troops stationed in the kingdom. Wrote the historian Lecky:—"When a half-disciplined yeomanry and a militia irritated by many outrages came to live upon a hostile peasantry, who regarded them all as "Orangemen", who had been taught that every Orangeman had sworn to exterminate the Catholics, it was not difficult to anticipate the result!"[6] Torture was systematically employed to discover hidden arms, and blacksmiths were the special objects of suspicion, being scourged to reveal what pikes they had made, and to whom they had consigned them. It was the habit of Republicans in Ireland—as it had also been in France—to have their hair closely cut or cropped, as a distinctive sign. Torture and scourging of "the croppies" (as the Republicans were called) became a popular amusement among the soldiers. Quakers also used to keep their hair close cut; with their age long dislike of fighting, and therefore of professional soldiers taught and paid to fight, it was generally suspected that their sympathies lay with the "croppies". The Grubbs in Clonmel had indeed to move carefully, if they would keep out of the fighting and consistent to their pacifist views. It troubled Samuel and Margaret—as well as many others among the Friends—to find that some Quakers were ready to carry and use arms in self-defence of their homes and children.

(*viii*) If County Tipperary suffered less than most other counties in Ireland, it was due to the successful if unscrupulous energy of the High Sheriff, *Thomas Judkin Fitzgerald*. Collecting a number of well-known insurgents together, in a three-hour speech, partly in Irish, he told them what the French would do if they landed, promised a free pardon to all who delivered up their arms, and he ordered free hospitality to be provided, wherever asked, for His Majesty's troops. As a result day after day the inhabitants of Clonmel watched cartload after cartload of surrendered pikes and other arms being moved into the town, and unloaded

[6] Lecky. *History of Ireland in the XVIIIth Century.* Vol. iv, pp. 268–272.

in the castle. But even skilled leaders make mistakes in times of emergency. Acting on unchecked information he had received, the High Sheriff suspected the Grubb's French tutor, a little man called Wright, who like all the Quakers kept his hair cropped, to be the leader of the "United Irishmen" as the insurgents were called. He had him arrested, condemned without trial, and ordered him to be publicly flogged in the streets of Clonmel, and then shot.

What were the Grubbs to do? What could they do as Quakers, and themselves suspected of siding with the insurgents? They could do absolutely nothing. They felt themselves quite helpless, yet the older Grubbs in that moment realised their kinship to the few followers of Jesus who accompanied him to Calvary. Their very presence and their silence might avail to help their condemned French tutor. It was not out of curiosity, nor like those "wild staring people" in Clonmel who had watched Wesley preach outside the barracks 40 years before, that Samuel and Margaret and some other of the Grubbs congregated outside his rooms, as the pious Wright was dragged into the street outside the house to undergo his sentence. Wright knelt down to pray with his broad-brimmed hat before his face, (his usual custom, and as Quakers did), thus revealing his close-cut hair. They saw the High Sheriff himself snatch Wright's hat from his hands, trample it on the ground, kick him, and strike his forehead with his sword. They saw a ladder carried to a position against the house. They watched as Wright was stripped, tied to the ladder and receive fifty lashes, until the blood covered him and the roadway. As they turned their faces away, and prayed, the crowd itself became uneasy. They saw an officer in the town approach Fitzgerald, and ask the reason for so dreadful a punishment. They saw the High Sheriff hand the British major a note—as the great Irish historian records the scene[7]—which he said he had taken from Wright's pocket, written in the French language, and that although he did not himself understand the language, he believed the major would find in it "what would justify him in flogging the scoundrel to death." The officer read it, and found it to be a perfectly insignificant note to one of the Grubbs, postponing an appointment to give a French lesson. Notwithstanding the Sheriff ordered the punishment to proceed, and a hundred more lashes were administered. Wright uttered never a word, and the major in charge of the troops ignored the Sheriff's order to shoot him. He was put into the Assize prison and "remained in a cell with no other furniture than a straw pallet for six or seven days without any medical assistance."[8]

So dreadful a spectacle and punishment upon a friend of theirs, lived in the memory of Samuel and Margaret Grubb all their days, and troubled their conscience. Their feeling of helplessness—of shame that such a

7 *Ibid.*   8 *Ibid.*

thing could happen in Clonmel within yards of their own home in Main Street, together with a new found respect for the British officer who (like the centurion at the Cross, thought Samuel) had done his best for the condemned Wright, and refused orders to shoot him. It was no satisfaction that Fitzgerald's actions were called in question by the British Parliament at Westminster, and he was arraigned, proceedings against his conduct dragging on for several years. It was brought out in his favour that 8,000 rebels had been ready to attack Clonmel but for his vigilance, and their fears inspired by his treatment of Wright.[9] Sister-in-law Mary Leadbeater wrote (as she also recorded in her Journal) that 15,000 Irishmen were assassinated or exiled during this year, and described the sufferings and atrocities around Ballitore.[10]

Such circumstantial guidance confirmed the ever cautious Samuel in the more direct leadings of Margaret that leave Clonmel they must. They felt they could never hold their heads up and walk its streets again. Where then should they move? What effect would these sombre events have upon their children?

The River Suir runs westwards from Clonmel through Ardfinan to the lovely village of Clogheen, some 15 miles away, today a neat market town of some 2,000 people in the foothills of the Knockmealdown Mountains (pronounced KNOCK-ME-DOWN), and the fertile Golden Vale of Tipperary. It lies at the foot of one of the beauty spots of Ireland, at the commencement of the wonderful "V" (Vee) Road, that winds and turns "up and over" into County Waterford on the other side. The area had always appealed to the Grubbs for holidays and as a centre for walks and rides, and it was still largely undeveloped. They had their eye for some time on the area, and at the opportune moment were able to secure land beside the river, and a commodious house known as *Clashleigh*, and to build mills close by. In many ways the area was not dissimilar from Ballitore, where Margaret had been brought up. She loved country life. It was like coming home. Margaret and her sons saw to all the details of the move, and the arrangements and furnishings of the new home. Samuel was content to have it that way. He was beginning to suffer from lameness, and walked with a stick. He left his eldest son Abraham, married the same year (1800), to take over his corn and butter business in Clonmel, and put his younger sons Richard, Samuel, Robert and Thomas to work in the new mills, as they left school. Seven years later when Richard married in 1807 a lady of some substance from County Cork, Samuel secured for him a newly built Georgian residence at the other end of the village, called *Cooleville*, approached by a long driveway from the village street, and built another huge mill by the river. Twelve

[9] *Ibid.*
[10] *The Leadbeater Papers.* Vol. i, pp. 223ff.

years later (1819) on his marriage to his second cousin, Deborah Davis, and with the help of his mother Margaret, who remained at Clashleigh on her husband's death, and of his Davis in-laws, Samuel Grubb Junior was able to buy the huge estate of Castle Grace, some two miles outside Clogheen, its ground running up to the top of the Knockmealdowns and to the border with County Waterford. During the next ten years he built a new mill on the adjoining River Tar which flows into the Suir, and a considerable and substantial Georgian residence not far from the old castle ruins which covered more than an acre (1829–30). The Grubbs had indeed taken possession of Clogheen, as they had of Clonmel!

Castle Grace has remained in the hands of Samuel Grubb's descendants to the present day, more than 150 years: Cooleville for 125 years, Clashleigh for not quite 100 years. The countryside around Clogheen is vividly described by Lynn Doyle in 1935 in his book *The Spirit of Ireland*.[11]

"On my first day in Clonmel by the courtesy of a man I only met that morning, who in warm-hearted Irish fashion was my friend by the afternoon, I motored to Mellory, the monastery of the Trappist monks in the Knockmealdowns. Our route was by the wonderful "V" (Vee Road), that rises from Clogheen in the Tipperary plain, and winds for endless miles through the heather and peat and barren desolation of the Knockmealdowns. Gradually we passed beyond the arm of the Comeraghs that enfold Clonmel. In the distance on our right lay the Galtee mountains. Between them the Golden Vale of Tipperary—the farmer's paradise. I need not attempt to describe those Elysian fields, that magic chequerboard of grass and tilth, the cattle and flocks and the comely homesteads, but I will use the language of an Ulster man who had done chauffeur work on this road. "Man, sir", he said. "I never knowed there was land in the world like this. If I tell my ould father about it when I goes back, he'll cut my throat."

Turning to the mountain slope I saw what appeared to be a cyclopean tombstone. It marked the grave of a Mr. Grubb, a Quaker, who had lived and owned property in the Golden Vale, and wished to be buried in sight of the Paradise he had quitted for another. There is a local tale he had given orders to be buried at the very top of the hills, but his six strong bearers could struggle no further up with his coffin. What matter? He would have seen no better from the top!"

This Mr. Grubb was a great-grandson of Samuel and Margaret, an outstanding character, and High Sheriff of County Tipperary in 1914, who left instructions he was to be buried standing up in this tall cairn of local stone, as though like Moses he might view the landscape o'er.[12] His

---

[11] *The Spirit of Ireland.* Lynn Doyle. (1935.) pp. 39ff.
[12] Samuel Richard Grubb, Esq., J.P. (1855–1921).

PLATE XVII

" 60 Grubbs out hunting together in the Golden Vale of Tipperary."

(Dr Violet Grubb)

position in his tomb bears perpetual witness to his faith in the Resurrection as expressed by his favourite hymnwriter, Isaac Watts:—

> "Could we but climb where Moses stood,
>   And view the landscape o'er,
>   Nor Jordan's stream, nor death's cold flood
>   Would fright us from that shore."

No wonder the Irish name for Clogheen—"CLOICHIN" means a white stone. The area, with the eternal hills surrounding it, brings out that Petrine rock-like determined character with the firm chin (and rather oversize nose) that has since been found among so many of the Grubbs. The area is not dissimilar from the Hartz Mountains in Brunswick, from which the family first sprang. There was something in his blood— heredity we may call it—that surely led Samuel Grubb to choose Clogheen for his new home, when he removed from the security he had once known under the city walls and castle of Clonmel. It was also hunting country.

A further description of the Clonmel they had left, is also given by Lynn Doyle in the same book.[13] "The Irishman is the best farmer and stock-breeder in the world, and some of the best land in the world is in County Tipperary. Clonmel, its capital, is an excellent example of a southern Irish town. The streets are wide, well-kept and busy. The children seem well-fed and happy. Its most striking feature is the swift-flowing River Suir, which washes one side of the town. Flat-bottomed boats used to come up the Suir to take away the flour manufactured in the many mills of the town, and in the country outside. The quays are still there, and the great stores and mills. . . . There is little outward sign of the political revolution that has taken place in Ireland."

Today bats occupy the once flourishing Grubb mills in Clonmel. A rather different picture, written after the Second World War (1947) is given by Frank O'Connor, who stayed a night there on a cycle tour.

"We took a room in a hotel, and walking up the long main street, passed three pairs of good-looking girls unattended, and a group of women in black shawls, who jeered at us. We passed a boarded-up pub, which always signifies in Ireland the beginning of the end. We came to the old grammar school that George Borrow attended, and found that to be deserted, too. 'Maybe you'd be wishing to look around inside, sir?', said a man's voice behind me. 'Is not anyone living there?' I asked. The voice replied: 'Well, no sir. One time there were people thinking of taking it for a school, but the teachers' rooms had a bad aspect. Then the military were thinking of taking it over; but their officers said there's no place for artillery there.' 'That's bad,' said I. 'It is, sir. Will I show you round?' 'We'll see tomorrow', I said, and

---

[13] *The Spirit of Ireland.* Lynn Doyle. (1935.) p. 36. Another writer speaks highly of Clonmel's interesting buildings—the Court House; the Main Guard, designed by Christopher Wren; the West Gate, and the old walls.

felt I had had enough to depress me. To get away, we crossed the river, and came down the further bank . . . we re-entered the town by a foot-bridge, and found ourselves in a complete suburb of eighteenth century mills and warehouses, all in ruin. Standing by a tall rusty gate to look at a handsome old mill house, with the weeds growing like thatch on its parapet, the bats swooped down upon us."[14]

Wise old Samuel Grubb. Did he have a presentiment of what the future held for the mills in Clonmel? Certainly with the turn of the century a completely new form of life as Country Gentry opened up for the Grubb family at Clogheen. Necessity as well as desire required they should live as good neighbours; there was no regular Quaker meeting at hand; inevitably the old "separatism" was on its way out. The Grubbs at Clogheen became truly Irish (though they never learnt the old Irish language), with the charming intonations of Irish accent and Irish brogue, and they gradually took up all the pursuits of country life, and especially including riding and hunting. The young folk after a day's work in the mills, could not be expected by Samuel and Margaret to decline every invitation they received from the neighbourhood to dance or ride or hunt, or to attend the local church on Sundays. Quaker farmers in the previous century had objected on principle to payment of tithes to the clergyman of the parish, and some had been prepared, on refusal, to endure imprison-ment for not doing so. Not so the Grubbs, who in their wisdom were content to pay their tithes to the Rector of Clogheen, and in due course one of Samuel's grandsons married a daughter of the rector.

Expanding leisure expanded their horizons at this period of great expan-sion of the British Empire. It was during these years at Clogheen that many of the great Evangelical Societies were being founded in England, such as the British and Foreign Bible Society which they supported generously, and the Church Missionary Society, of which a century and a half later one of their descendants, Sir Kenneth Grubb, K.C.M.G., was to serve as President for 25 years. These were the years also of the Napoleonic Wars, of the Battles of Trafalgar and Waterloo, and of the exploits of a great Irishman, Sir Arthur Wellesley, later to become the Duke of Welling-ton. Quietly their horizons were broadening in the fresh air of the glorious countryside, in their walks and climbs up the slopes of the Knock-mealdowns, in their rides in the Golden Vale of Tipperary. After Family Prayers one morning, when Samuel—as he often did—had been enumerat-ing their many blessings, counting them one by one as it were before God with thanksgiving, said Margaret: "We are closer to God in this clean countryside than ever we were in the security (and seclusion) of our lives in Clonmel."

There was the supreme joy of their family growing up in such an

[14] *Irish Miles.* Frank O'Connor. (1947.) pp. 86–87. Macmillan.

PLATE XVIII

Armorial Bearings of Samuel Grubb (1750–1815) and his Descendants.

Arms: *Per chevron ermine and gules en bas a harp or, stringed argent on a chief crenellée of the last three roses proper.*

Crest: On a wreath of colours, a griphon's head erased per chevron crenellée sable and argent charged with two roses in pale proper.

Motto: *Bonne et assez belle.*

atmosphere. Richard was just 20 when they moved from Clonmel; Thomas their youngest surviving son, only eight. Clashleigh provided the space, the comfort, the feeling of elegance that formed the perfect background to family life. The mills provided constant income, and occupation. Significant of their changed situation, and perhaps egged thereto by the family, the Grubbs took to themselves a Coat of Arms, together with the motto:—

"Bonne et Assez Belle."

Was it the influence of their brother-in-law, William Leadbeater the French master at Ballitore, or of Wright, their French tutor in Clonmel, that they chose the French language, rather than English or Latin? Certainly since Ballitore days both Samuel and his sons talked French, even if at times (they spoke fairly fast) it sounded almost like "double dutch." Uncle Robert and Aunt Sarah also spoke German. The motto can be variously interpreted, and was chosen in reference to the beauty of the Grubb ladies, and the unfailingly wise choice of Grubb males for their spouses. They were as good as they were beautiful—a preferable translation to "Good and beautiful enough", reminiscent of the Grubb Puritanical and Quaker background. Not that the Grubb men were not well-made and good looking also.

In the Register of the Office of Arms in Dublin the arms of Samuel Grubb and his descendants are thus described:—[15]

Crest: a griphon (or griffens) head erased per chevron, crenellée sable et argent, charged with two roses in pale proper. Per chevron ermine et gules; en bas a harp or, stringed argent, on a chief crenellée of the last three roses proper.

In keeping with this new crest, which later was to be worn on signet rings by his descendants, Samuel and Margaret ordered two large canteens of cutlery in Dublin for use by the family at Clogheen, and on their marriages, his children were each presented with George III silver mint-marked with the Grubb crest. Such tableware has been passed down from generation to generation; some has found its way into the auction room, and the writer has been able to secure several large spoons at auction, bearing this crest.

Said King James I: "The King can make a noble or a knight; but he cannot make a Gentleman." This is not the place to discuss the definition of a Gentleman, an Esquire, a Knight. Nature's Gentlemen are born, not made. Titles, abhorred by the plain and simplicity-loving Quakers, have alway been and will always be with us. Knighthood largely passed the Grubbs by until after World War II. Certain it is that historically the bearing of arms, not of titles, has been considered a distinctive mark

[15] Vol. J. Folio 141. G. O. Bentehaill, Athlone Pursuivant, Register of the Office of Arms in Ireland. These arms were confirmed 25th August, 1903 and appear on Plate XVIII with the authority of the Office of Arms, Dublin Castle.

of noblesse. Samuel's greatest gift to his posterity was that the world has looked upon them as gentlemen. This can justifiably be said the Grubb's never became snobs; nor did they forget that "to whom much is given, from them will much be required" during the passing years, in which their names have appeared in publications such as *The Landed Gentry of Ireland*, *The County Families of the United Kingdom* and in *Kellys Directories*.

All their past experiences, and their respective heredities, fitted Samuel and Margaret together for their new responsibilities and life among the country gentry. Responsibilities before pleasure—this remained their outlook. Continuing Quakers as they were, they became easy of access, and hardly a day passed but some guest or business acquaintance was entertained to Grubb hospitality at Clashleigh, where it was easy to obtain as much staff and as many servants as they needed among the poor peasantry, eager for work and pay. Although semi-retired, Samuel's advice on business matters was sought by many old friends from Clonmel, and with his widened horizons he was ever quick to see new openings in the business world.

Yet it was the same man at Clogheen as in Clonmel, and the trials and troubles of life can never be escaped where ever a man may live. In the fifteen years of life that remained to him—Samuel died at the comparatively early age of 65—anxiety over the prolonged war with France (he just lived to hear of the British victory under Wellington at the Battle of Waterloo, June 18, 1815), and over the effect that this war and the changed circumstances under which they now lived must be having on his children—hastened continued bouts of ill-health. It is one thing to hold definite and pacifist principles when living among like-minded folk in a closely-knit and confined community, as at Clonmel, with every hour of the day occupied with business or religious affairs. It is another thing, with time on your hands, in a changing and progressive world, mixing through one's family and their friends with men and women of different upbringings and outlooks, to justify to oneself, let alone to one's family, every shibboleth, even every principle, with which one has been brought up and lived. Not that Samuel and Margaret minded what others might say! But they were wise and forward looking enough not to bury their heads in the sand, like ostriches, or unnecessarily to be deemed the nineteenth century equivalent of the modern day " square ", unless convinced there was strong and sufficient reason for such a course. Nor for them to swing the pendulum of life too far in one direction or the other, but as far as possible to steer a middle course, even at the risk of others continuing to condemn them as compromisers, or inconsistent. They grew their own tobacco. French wines they had always enjoyed, and though Margaret never forgot the evils of Irish gin and whisky drinking among the poor, were they right to frown on their sons in the hunting field or of an evening enjoying their cups? Anxious at times Samuel continued to be, but through his wisdom and knowledge of his Maker always trustful and prayerful; even through three years of often painful lingering illness, when he was much in bed, until on August 9th 1815 he breathed his last at Clashleigh, in his sixty-fifth year.

Sister-in-law Mary Leadbeater wrote this description of his death in her *Journal:*—[16]

"1815, August. My brother-in-law Samuel Grubb after three years of lingering illness was now rapidly declining, and died 9th of 8th month. His last words were:—

' My spirit is going where the wicked cease from troubling, and where the weary are at rest.'

"Most of his children were with him at the last, and his sons with affectionate tenderness performed every office in their power for one of the best and beloved of fathers. My dear sister Margaret, his companion for nearly 40 years, was much shaken by this stroke, but her mind resting on the Rock of Ages knew where to seek consolation.

"My dear brother Grubb was remarkable for his disinterested friendship. He counselled his friends in their business—and highly qualified he was to do so—with as much earnestness and anxiety, as if it was himself who was to profit by the means pointed out. He left his family in very comfortable circumstances, most sincerely regretted by them, and by his neighbours and friends. He was buried among the Friends at Clonmel. There was a very large and solemn funeral."

Large funerals characterise most families, and certainly the Grubbs. Friends and relatives wish to attend as a mark of respect, and in token of sympathy with the bereaved.[17] However seldom the Grubb family are able to meet as the years pass, however far separated their homes may be, they never miss a funeral if they can help it. That sense of "Belonging to a family to be proud of", and of real loss when one of its members dies, manifests itself at family funerals.

A plain slab marks Samuel Grubb's grave, among some 60 other Grubbs, in the Friends Burial Ground in Clonmel—a small enclosed garden. His widow Margaret lived another 14 years at Clogheen, to rejoice in more than 50 grandchildren. Enough has been said of her character to suggest how greatly the nineteenth century Grubbs were to benefit in one way or

[16] *The Leadbeater Papers*, Vol. i, p. 352ff.
[17] All unnecessary displays of mourning, and all ceremonial pomp at Quaker funerals was discouraged, no "mourning clothes", and no rites at the graveside, save prayer or an address by some worthy Friend present. At first only a flat stone over the grave was allowed, with names and dates, but no epitaphs. Tombstones were later permitted, of a uniform plain type; the dead were often buried in their own gardens, or orchards.

another from the admixture of Shackleton blood into their heredity. The writer of more than 4,000 letters (still preserved in Dublin) brought into the Grubb lineage a genius and wit, a lightness of touch and intellectual ability to write clearly, to think deeply, and to speak convincingly, fluently and without hesitation, which readers of the two recent *Grubb Biographies* (by Norman and Sir Kenneth Grubb) will not fail to recognise.[18] The thoroughness, energy, honesty and puritanism of the Grubbs from their German days in the Hartz Mountains, needed such enrichment. Margaret Grubb was indeed *Bonne et assez Belle*. She was buried beside Samuel in 1829.

No apter expression of their lives and experiences, and no better message to their descendants could they offer than verses from their own well-thumbed copy of Tate and Brady's version of the Psalms:—

> Through all the changing scenes of life,
>   In trouble and in joy,
> The praises of our God shall still
>   Our heart and tongue employ.
>
> Of His protection we will boast.
>   Let all that are distressed
> From our experience comfort take
>   And charm their griefs to rest.
>
> The hosts of God encamp around
>   The dwellings of the just:
> Protection He affords to all
>   Who make His name their trust.
>
> O make but trial of His love,
>   Experience will decide
> How blest are they, and only they
>   Who in His truth confide.
>
> Fear Him, ye saints, and you will then
>   Have nothing else to fear:
> Make you His service your delight:
>   Your wants shall be His care.
>
>   *Nahum Tate, 1652–1715.*
>   *Nicholas Brady, 1659–1726.*

[18] *Once Caught: No Escape*   See Bibliography.
   or *Crypts of Power.*   See Bibliography.

PLATE XIX

CASTLE GRACE HOUSE

(after 1830)

"THE GRUBBS OF CASTLE GRACE", CLOGHEEN, CO. TIPPERARY

Castle Grace, with between 1,000 and 2,000 acres of land at different times, running up into the Knockmealdown Mountains, has remained Grubb property for 150 years to the present day. It is so called from the ruins of a twelfth century Anglo-Norman castle built by the Norman Raymond Le Gros on the banks of a small river, formerly known as the Ountearr, shortened to the "Tar" which flows into the River Suir, near to which a grist mill used to stand. The estate was bought on the marriage of Samuel Grubb, third son of Samuel and Margaret Grubb (*Chapters Seven and Nine*) to his second cousin, Deborah Davis (d. 1885), in 1820. (*See Collateral Table "F"*.) Samuel Grubb built new mills in 1829, and a large gracious and imposing "E" shaped house. The castle occupies over one acre in extent, is remarkably well preserved with a tower at each angle, and is regarded as one of the finest of Irelands 3,000 ruined castles.

SAMUEL (1787–1859); m. 1819, DEBORAH (*née* DAVIS) d. 1885
They had six sons and three daughters:

1.	RICHARD DAVIS	b. 1820; d. 1865	2 children
2.	SAMUEL	b. 1823; *died young*	
3.	HENRY SAMUEL	b. 1824; d. 1891	1 son
4.	ARTHUR	b. 1827; d. 1882	
5.	ROBERT	b. 1830; d. 1864	
6.	EDWARD	b. 1838; d. 1878	
1.	Sarah Strangman	b. 1822; m. 1865, Thomas ANDREWS	
2.	Elizabeth	b. 1832; m. Edwin TAYLOR	
3.	Louisa	b. 1836; m. Charles BARRINGTON	

1. RICHARD DAVIS GRUBB (1820–1865), their eldest son, m. 1851, his first cousin Margaret Grubbe, daughter of his Uncle THOMAS of Clonmel. She died 1855. He outlived his father six years only. They had two children:

    (1) MARGARET, b. 1853. She married John Russell Mechem.

    (2) SAMUEL RICHARD GRUBB, J.P. (1855–1921); m. 1885, Alice Hannah, daughter of E. W. Binney, F.R.S. of Ravenscliffe, Isle of Man. He was High Sheriff of Co. Tipperary, 1914. A Quaker, he was buried in the Knockmealdown Mountains, a large stone cairn marks his grave. They had two children:

    (i) RICHARD RAYMOND DE CRUCE GRUBB, M.C., J.P. (1886–1970). Wellington College, Berks.; R.M.C. Commanded 3rd Hussars 1932–36. G.S.O. 18th Div. 1939–45. He married, 1914, Ruth, daughter of Alfred Leney, J.P. of Saltwood House, Hythe, Kent. Colonel Raymond de Cruce and Ruth Grubb had two sons:

    (a) RICHARD DE CRUCE GRUBB (1915–1934), R.A.F. Test Pilot. Killed in a flying accident over the Irish Sea.

    (b) PATRICK DE CRUCE GRUBB, b. 1918. Wellington College, Berks.; Lieut. 3rd Hussars. P.O.W. 1941–42; m. 1947, Vivien Anne, daughter of Robert Woodhouse, Esq., of Dungarven, Co. Waterford. He is a director of "Tipperary Products and Packaging Business" of Castle Grace; also Horse-box Building. They have two sons:

    (*i*) RICHARD, b. 1948. Educated at Wellington College, and Belfast University.

    (*ii*) NICHOLAS, b. 1950. Ditto.

    (ii) JOAN MARY (1889–1969); m. Francis de Sales le Terriere, of Dunalstair, Perthshire. She lived at Kiltynam Castle. One daughter.

3. HENRY SAMUEL (1824–1891), their third son, inherited Clashleigh after his grandmother's death. He married 1864, Martha, daughter of Thomas Hughes, Esq., of Ystrad, Denbighshire, sister of Col. Hugh Hughes, M.A., High Sheriff of Co. Tipperary; died 1891, leaving one son:

    LOUIS HENRY (1865–1929), of Ardmoyle, Co. Tipperary. Educated at Rugby and B.N.C. College, Oxford (1888), M.A., D.L., J.P. High Sheriff 1897; m. 1899 his distant cousin Sarah Mary Watkins Grubb, eldest child of Col Alexander Grubb, R.A. of Stone Castle, Kent. They lived at Ardmayle and had four children. (*See Chapter Fourteen.*)

The three younger sons did not marry. They lived at Maryville, Cashel, a large house, since turned into the Deanery of Cashel, and now a hotel.

115

CHAPTER TEN

Richard Grubb (Senior) 1780—1859

Born in Clonmel. Miller and Gentleman,
of Cooleville House, Clogheen, 1807–1835.
and Squire of Cahir Abbey. 1835–1859.

He married 1807.

SUSANNA HAUGHTON, daughter of John Barcroft Haughton, Esq.
of Cleave Court, Co. Cork.

They had 12 children (one died young and four during their lifetime).

"Constantly on guard lest any fall back from the Grace of God."—Hebrews, xii,15.
(Weymouth)

"Some men are born great: some achieve greatness: others have great-ness thrust upon them." Substitute for greatness the word "OPPOR-TUNITIES" and it may be said of RICHARD GRUBB that he was born with many opportunties in an age of opportunity; he had many oppor-tunities thrust upon him in his 79 years of life, when many of his contem-poraries achieved greatness; but he never seized the nettle of opportunity to achieve a greatness he was without ambition to aim at or to covet for himself.

The second son of Samuel and Margaret Grubb, Richard was born in 1780 at Clonmel, and named after his grandfather Richard Shackleton, whose Boarding School at Ballitore he attended. He lived in a fascinating age in British history, with the same opportunities as his contemporaries David Livingstone, Lord Nelson, Lord Shaftesbury, Lord Wilberforce and the Duke of Wellington. If maternal ambitions that he might become a creator in the worlds of poetry or philanthropy, authorship or exploration or medicine were never fulfilled, for any of which he had the talent, he never grasped the nettle of opportunity to strike out as the Spirit within him might lead from the security of his confined Tipperary upbringing among the Quakers. He was brought up to follow the ways of peace; a military or naval life was not for him, had he desired it, which he did not. He was content to carry on as a miller, as his father and grandfather before him, and later to become an Irish landowner and esquire. In the life of any nation there can only be a small and limited

116

PLATE XX

RICHARD GRUBB

of

Cooleville, Clogheen, and Cahir Abbey

PLATE XXI

SUSANNA GRUBB

(*née* Haughton), wife of Richard Grubb

number of outstanding men and women in any generation, with a multitude of commoners, necessary, faithful, and helpful as they are to the achievements of the really great, but whose names history has no reason to remember. The excellent talents he inherited from a wise father and a gifted, witty and beautiful mother, from his scholarly and saintly Shackleton forbears, and his industrious and prosperous Grubb grandparents, Richard has bequeathed to his descendants—talents to achieve the greatness he never strove for or attained himself.

Within a year of his birth, Margaret Grubb his mother wrote strangely prophetic words, though she knew it not, of her second son:—

> "I have kept little Richard mostly on bread and milk, since he was weaned, which he is very fond of: he is stout and very healthy, but the itching frets him at night." [1]

Five strands in the future character of Richard Grubb are to be found in these mundane, but inspired, if not exactly inspiring words of his proud and intelligent mother.

(i) A life-long assurance that he was kept secure in safe hands. They were the hands of God, mediated to him first through his mother, and later through a good and dominant wife. He never had to stand on his own. From babyhood he was conscious of the protection of his devoted if dominant mother. Not that she consciously spoilt or pampered him, but Grubb gynocracy in two generations meant that Margaret's children came to rely upon her, and to obey and later humour her wishes more than in many another family. In his intellectual and moral education in schooldays as a boarder at Ballitore, his uncle (the headmaster) and aunts kept all the boys from "unwise reading", and securely within the "Quaker fence of discipline."[2] Brought up in Clonmel among Nonconformists, he was kept from the general mixing and "rough and tumble" of Irish lads, from cards and dice and playing in the streets or by the river, perhaps "too prim and proper by far." But he never forgot his parents uplifted hands in prayer for himself and his brothers and sisters in the family prayers of each day. Throughout his life he knew he was kept by the Power of God, securely upheld in Divine Hands. His inbred Quaker submissiveness kept him trustful in God's control of his life.

As a grown man Richard chose a wife (or Margaret his mother did for him), Susan Haughton, of Cleave Court, County Cork, who was to prove as dominant as his mother and grandmother, both of him and of their twelve children. His life was to be spent in a close family circle. His four brothers and their families all lived not far away, and frequent were the "get-togethers" between the families, and visits paid one to another. His eldest brother Abraham and four daughters, and his youngest brother

[1] Letters of Margaret Grubb, preserved in the Friends Y.M. Library in Eustace Street, Dublin.
[2] *The Leadbeater Papers.* "Annals of Ballitore". Vol. i, p. 294.

Thomas Samuel and his thirteen children lived in Clonmel. His brother Samuel and his nine children lived almost next door to him in Clogheen. True brother Robert and his three children lived in Limerick, but that was not all that distance away. There were also his three married sisters and their families close at hand. Amid the changes of Regency and Victorian England and the general disturbance to faith through Biblical criticism and Darwin's teaching on the evolution of mankind (Richard would never believe that the Grubbs were descended from monkeys) that he lived to see, he remained completely assured that the love of God would never let him go, but "was infallibly pledged to his support." St. Augustine or John Calvin would have called his faith an assured belief in the fact of predestination.[3] Richard knew that there is more in heredity than some men suppose.

(ii) An appreciation for the essential simplicities of life, both for the body and for the spirit. His Mother's use of the word "mostly" (on bread and milk) was in reference to the daily ration of beer, given in Ireland and indeed in Quaker homes, to young children to encourage growth— a practice encouraged by the Irish doctor. There was no lack of delicacies of life in his home in Main Street, Clonmel, but Samuel and Margaret brought up all their children to find the "bread and sufficiency of life" in the simplicity of Quaker worship, Lord's Day observance, family prayers, and the "pure milk of God's Word." So Richard's faith from earliest days became simple and sincere; the advanced Biblical criticism of his manhood's years (which was seriously to split Quakerism) never troubled him.

(iii) He was stout in build and character, as were most of the Grubbs of his father's generation and his own (a result of the "good grub" mother or wife provided for them); perhaps also of the Irish stout they drank. In middle life he was to prove stout hearted in facing the clouds of bereavements, the storms of Quaker controversies and the disownment or ostracism of one of his sons by the Quakers (see next chapter), and all the problems of purchasing landed estate and properties in Cahir, that could have overwhelmed a weaker man.

(iv) He was very healthy, his body disciplined by regular hours and outdoor exercise, always "on the go"; he lived to be nearly 80, with hardly a day's illness. He was fond of riding. The Grubbs had always much to do with horses, their only means of transport for a great many years; in the country at Clogheen and Cahir they had more time to devote to their stables, to hunting and riding, and became experts in cracking a whip. There was a period when as many as 60 Grubbs were to be seen in the hunting field together.[4] Richard's brother Samuel and his descend-

[3] *The Tractarian Movement.* Bishop E. A. Knox. p. 69.
[4] Dr. Violet Grubb D.Sc. in a letter to the author.

ants at "Castle Grace" especially distinguished themselves in this field, and in the breeding of ponies, as did also their Richardson cousins in Ulster until 1850 circa. Healthy also was Richard in his many cultural interests in the palmiest days of English novel writing, the 1840's and 1850's, when "the great star in the firmament of Queen Victoria's reign" as the late Dean Inge once described the English novel, was making its appearance[5], and Charles Dickens vied with Thackeray, George Eliot with Charlotte Bronte, Charles Kingsley with Anthony Trollope (who incidentally lived at Clonmel for some years) in the number of new books that were appearing. All the Grubbs enjoyed books, and often saw themselves and their homes in the writings of these great novelists. Bookshelves were in constant demand to house their increasing library . . . "Would that I could write like these great authors," said Richard on more than one occasion.

(v) "The itching which frets him at night" in his mother's words was to remain with Richard Grubb throughout his long life, and became perhaps his most outstanding characteristic. It showed itself in an intensity of concern for other people in trouble and need, in tensions imagined or real that fretted him over many things and choices he had to make, and so in a restlessness of spirit, which at times can so easily spoil much that should be harmonious. This intensity of spirit inherited from his mother Margaret and Shackleton grandparents has shown itself from time to time among his descendants. Two illustrations may be given:

(a) He often questioned how as a Quaker he could reconcile pacifist views with the fact that his parents before him, other Quaker property owners, and himself had had resource in troubled Ireland to call in the protection of the soldiery and armed guards on occasions of insurgence or hooliganism. Ought they not to have turned the other cheek? His father-in-law once told him that during the rebellion of 1798 he had felt led as a Quaker "for the cleansing of my own hands to break in pieces my fowling piece in the street publicly outside my door." Richard knew some Quakers refused to keep guns or other weapons. Similarly how could he join with his brothers and sons in hunting and bloodsports, if he really believed that animal and human blood should not be shed by the hand of man. Yet when his eldest son Samuel was killed in the hunting field, Richard would never believe this was a just retribution on the sin of hunting; Samuel was his own flesh and blood, and his grief was unbounded. Inconsistency was the only answer, and this huge moral issue always fretted Richard.

(b) Over the matters of the luxuries of life and alcoholism there was incessant conflict in his mind whether he ought to become a

[5] "Diary of a Dean" by W. R. Inge, K.C.V.O. D.D. p. 222.

teetotaller, as his beloved daughter Helena and his Richardson relations repeatedly urged him to do. Should he by his own example draw a hard and fast line against what he believed in his heart had become one of the curses of Ireland, at the risk of his whole family and himself being regarded as "peculiar" by their neighbourhood?

The social Ireland in which he was born and grew up, is thus described by the great Irish historian Lecky[6]

"Among the gentry of Ireland drunkenness and extravagance went hand in hand, especially among the lesser gentry. The immense consumption of French wine was deplorable as a national calamity. Berkeley noticed that while in England many gentleman with an income of £1000 a year never drank wine, this could hardly be said of any in Ireland who had an income of only £100 a year. 'In Ireland nine gentlemen out of ten,' wrote Chesterfield, 'are impoverished by the great quantity of claret, which from mistaken notions of hospitality and dignity they think it necessary should be offered and drunk in their houses.' They tell stories of decanters, which having no flat bottom, would never stand on the table, and had to be passed from hand to hand and emptied immediately; of wine glasses with their stems broken, that they should be emptied in a gulp as soon as they were filled; of carousals which were prolonged until daylight, & the most hardened drinkers were under the table."

Was it possible to be moderate in all things and to take a little wine only for the stomach's sake, as the Bible said? Richard remembered his parents had imported French wine, in their liking for all things French. Was it really necessary to become a teetotaller, and if so was he to try to prevent his own sons from the cups? His future son-in-law John Grubb Richardson from the North of Ireland used often to come and stay with him while courting his daughter Helena, and told him how much more serious in Ulster than even in County Tipperary was the tremendous drink problem that confronted them in their large Richardson linen and flax-spinning businesses in Belfast and Lisburn. He told him that spirit-drinking among their workpeople was undoing all the good that habits of thrift and industry could achieve. He enthused Richard Grubb with their plans to build a Temperance Village or Colony (such as the Quaker William Penn had built in Pennsylvania) for about 3,000 people out of the fortune that they had inherited from Anna Grubb (of Anner Mills, Clonmel) his mother, and Richard Grubb's first cousin. He told him of the discovery of the ideal site and his later purchase (1845) of 6,000 acres of land at Bessbrook (or "The Brook" as those who lived there used to call it) from the Earl of Charlemont, in a flax-spinning area near Belfast, including the Clamlough lake and mountain, where the motive power for his new mills water supply could be collected and brought down

[6] Lecky's *History of Ireland in the XVIIIth Century*. Vol. i, 287ff, quoting Chesterfield's Miscellaneous Works iv. 39.

to the valley by the River Bess. Here John Grubb Richardson built a model village complete with electricity to house his own employees and their families. (It was the forerunner of the creation by another Quaker, George Cadbury, of the much larger ideal suburb of Bourneville, for his chocolate workers). Richard was thrilled with the development and success of his son-in-law's plans. It was tritely said that "Bessbrook wanted the three P's (wanting in the Irish sense of lacking)—Public Houses, Pawn Shops and Police."[7] Could he have seen ahead 120 years to the Ulster government closure in Belfast (1969–70) of all public houses at night time in face of the riots and killings, he could have had no doubts or further tensions about John Grubb Richardson's conviction that where strong drink was absent, Irishmen would need no police to keep order, no large English garrisons, and even on Party Days there would be as little need for the "gomboon man" as the pawnbroker or moneylender was called.[8] Yet when his own daughter Helena begged Richard to become a teetotaller as she and her husband had done, he hesitated, put it off, and never did. So he remained uneasy in his mind, always wondering if he had lost his opportunities for Christian witness by his hesitations to renounce drink and bloodsports that "purchased pleasure at the expense of pain." Had Richard known the experience of sudden conversion that came to a Lord Wilberforce or Lord Shaftesbury and others of his contemporaries, his wealth, his time, his whole life, might have been devoted to as creative and lasting effect as theirs.

When Richard Grubb went to Ballitore in June 1791, his uncle Abraham Shackleton had succeeded his grandfather as headmaster, and had stopped the practice of taking boys from any Protestant families. Only the sons of Quakers were admitted, and it had become compulsory to attend the Quaker Sunday meetings, and to "conform in dress and language to the simplicity of our profession" as his aunt Mary Leadbeater wrote in her Journal.[9] Abraham Shackleton was intent on tightening things up at Ballitore, and he objected to the study of those authors who "treat in seducing language of the illusions of love and the trade of war." He published an advertisement to this effect in the Irish papers "thus relinquishing the credit and profit of preparing lads for college" wrote Aunt Mary with apparent disapproval.[10] This tightening of Quaker discipline at school, compared to what he found during his holidays at home, increased the tensions on young Richard, and had its effect upon him in

---

[7] *Life of James Nicholson Richardson.* (1925.) pp. 34–49.

[8] John Grubb Richardson was a great athlete as a young man, a fine swimmer, a good fives player. He did not hunt much, and disapproved of his son James N. Richardson so doing, who wrote: "My father used to carry some sherry in a flask out hunting, but this was later exchanged for a concoction of peppermint and ammonia, a tipple we did not like". He was later offered a knighthood by Mr. Gladstone, which he declined.

[9] "Annals of Ballitore", by Mary Leadbeater, pp. 40, 175, 186ff, 294, 309.

[10] *Ibid.*

later life when he hesitated to walk the path of complete renunciation, as urged upon him by his daughter Helena and her husband Grubb Richardson. However he enjoyed the hours he spent at school learning carpentering with his grandfather's servant, David Doyle, an expert in making bookcases, sash windows and the like, and who understandably made a special favourite of "his young master". Each boy had also his own garden, which they were encouraged to maintain, and Richard's lifelong love for his gardens and hot-house plants dates back to this beginning.

On leaving school at Ballitore, Richard started work in his father's mills in Clonmel. It was impossible for him to have gone to College in Dublin, had he wished it, owing to the policy of Shackleton in tightening up the disciplines and the literature taught there. At an impressionable age he never forgot the sight of cartloads of captured pikes and arms rattling through the Clonmel streets during the Rebellion of 1798, the bright and gaudy uniforms of the soldiery (many of them soon to be moved to Spain to serve under the future Duke of Wellington in the Peninsular War), and the merciful action of one of the officers in saving the family French tutor from death. The tensions of life but increased; he had no desire to break away from his Quaker pacifist heritage. He became as anxious as his parents to break away from Clonmel however, now of unhappy memories; none was happier than he when the decision was finally taken in 1800. Life at Clogheen was quite different and much happier. His three years' experience of milling in Clonmel enabled his father to entrust him with increasing responsibilities in the family's new mills, built just opposite the entrance drive into Clashleigh on the River Suir.

Seven happy years were these early years of a new century at Clashleigh in which he learnt much of country life, mixed widely as an eligible young bachelor, and paid a number of visits to old school friends all over Ireland, but especially in Cork. His marriage took place in 1807 to Susannna Haughton, elder daughter of the rich Cork Quaker John Barcroft Haughton Esq. of Cleave Court, Cork, who owned one of the largest demesnes and mansions in the county. The Haughton family, like the Grubbs, had come over to Ireland during Oliver Cromwell's Protectorate; they were the descendants of Wilfrid Haughton, Gentleman, of Haughton Hall, Lancashire, and had remained as Anglo-Irish and as broadminded Quakers as the Grubbs. Their marriage was judged highly suitable by Margaret and Samuel his parents: it lasted 52 years.

After a widely attended and lavish wedding in Cork, their links with Cork remained close, and in later years two of their twelve children were also to find their life's partner from the city of Cork. Their parents, true to Grubb tradition, settled them in a very large house, judged by modern standards, newly erected, at the other end of Clogheen village to Clashleigh;

PLATE XXII

COOLVILLE HOUSE, CLOGHEEN

The first married home of Richard Grubb

COOLVILLE MILL BUILDINGS ON THE R. SUIR *in 1971*

(*Looking up to the House beyond the lawns*)

situated on the banks of the River Suir, and facing the towering Knock-mealdown mountains some five or six miles away, it was approached by a long drive, a courtyard of stabling where a new mill was now built, and then a further curving drive around well-cut lawns. Cooleville was its name, a glorious house that was to remain in Grubb hands for 120 years. It was spacious enough in all conscience for the 12 children to be born here to Richard and Susan.

With such a background as Cooleville provided, Richard and Susan could not help expanding their interests, succeeding in their business, and playing an increasing part in the life of the County of Tipperary. Cooleville rang with laughter as the children grew up. The schoolroom walls were covered with drawings and water-colours; here diaries and later love-letters were written. Beautiful pieces of furniture found their way into the withdrawing room and halls. Oil paintings of the family adorned the dining room walls. Grubb-crested silver and china—gifts from Cork—were in use; a far cry from the plainness of Quaker life in Clonmel. Richard kept his guns; dogs and ponies frollicked in the paddock. The gardens became a blaze of colour; each of the children were given their own part therein to tend. Susan, tall and of ample proportions especially loved hollyhocks and delphiniums, tall like herself. Friends came to stay. It seemed to the outsider a perfect life for an Irish country gentle-man and his family.

So some 25 years passed. As the marriages of her children became imminent, Susan decided their large house had insufficient bedroom accommodation and must be enlarged. An L-shaped wing was added; building was cheap, and builders plentiful at this time. Enough bedrooms were added to accommodate Haughton, Barcroft, Shackleton, Grubb and Richardson relations, as well as Ridgways invited to the marriage of their eldest daughter, Miss Sarah Grubb, to Henry Ridgway, Esq., of Garry-gowan in 1833. It was an *Age of Expansion* all over Ireland, of pulling down barns to build greater; when ruins or half-ruins of castles and houses, of abbeys and churches and cottages, were either repaired and tidied up, or pulled down completely, and larger buildings erected from their stones for human habitation. Rates were levied in Ireland on any and every building, so long as it was habitable, whether inhabited or not. This had the result that the owners of such properties would take the roof off their former home, when they moved into another, if they could not sell it, leaving it derelict to avoid rates. Sometimes they would use rafters, beams, window frames, panelling for a new and larger house they were building, again leaving the old one derelict. Castles were being restored, new houses were being built alongside ruined abbeys. Richard's younger brother Samuel had just completed his spacious new Georgian house at Castle Grace, two miles away, and faithfully restored the castle close by.

Until about 1790 Irish houses had been generally mean in proportion to the income of their owners, with little about them of the domestic economy and the quiet comfort and beauty of their counterparts in England.[11] It was a period in the history of the Quakers in Ireland when large numbers of their families were giving the impression they were too busy and occupied in worldly cares and building up family homes, to be as zealous as their forefathers for the plainness and simplicities of their beliefs. It was a testing time for Richard Grubb, of renewed tension whether such an outlay of money was justifiable; but as with his forbears Grubb gynocracy was irresistible, and Haughton money had become available to Susanna.

The Grubb-Ridgway wedding in 1833 marked the peak of Richard and Susan Grubb's life at Cooleville, Clogheen. So successful was the organisation of the event, and so widely talked about in the county, that whether they liked it or not the Grubbs had reached a pinnacle in public esteem among the gentry of Tipperary. The pendulum had indeed swung from their confined "separatist" Quaker life in Clonmel. The Ridgway family[12] were delighted with Grubb hospitality and charm, and another marriage was arranged between the families for next year between their eldest daughter Eliza and Barcroft Haughton Grubb, the second son of Richard and Susanna. 1834 was also to see the wedding of Samuel Grubb, their eldest son, to Anna Watson, an athletic girl he had met on the hunting field. This meant the setting up of new Grubb homes in the neighbourhood. It was inbred in Richard to do as his parents and grandparents had done, and provide such homes for the oncoming generation. Since the beginning of the reign of William IV, he and Susanna had been considering the matter. The family had begun to call her Susan.

Susan Grubb was a lady of strong character and determination, large in dimensions, and with a very powerful voice. She was credited with the power of second sight, and ruled her large family, her husband, and her many servants with some firmness and originality. In her widowhood in later life she used to keep a megaphone beside her bedroom window,

---

[11] Arthur Young and Mrs. Delaney, two English visitors to Ireland in the last quarter of the XVIIIth century, have given interesting accounts of the meanness of Irish homes and country houses, in which on their different journeys they stayed. See Lecky's *History of Ireland in the XVIIIth Century*, p. 289. Arthur Young, *Tour of Ireland* in 1776, p. 236ff. *Mrs. Delaney's Correspondence*, p. 351ff.

[12] The Ridgways were a Quaker family (some branches spelling their name with an "e" —Ridgeway), who originated in South Devon. There is a fine memorial to Thomas Ridgway in Tor Abbey, Torquay. They came to Ulster at the time of the Cromwellian Settlement of Ireland, and from thence to Queen's County, and then to Waterford. See further *Burke's Landed Gentry of Ireland* (4th ed.). One of Richard Grubb's aunts was a Ridgway (Aunt Sarah was one of the Lady Grubb itinerant preachers), and his eldest grandson, Richard Grubb Ridgway, born the next year, was later "read out" or disowned by the Quakers for marrying outside the Friends. He became a member of the Church of Ireland, and in due course with his descendants "pillars of the church" in Waterford. There are many memorials to the Grubb Ridgways in Waterford Cathedral, and the family continues in Counties Waterford and Cork to the present day.

through which she would shout her orders to her outdoor staff—orders which could be heard half a mile away on the road, or in the yards.   She had been brought up to have her own way; she knew no fear, and would allow no opposition; she became the gracious and charitable "Grande Dame" to the poor.   Her charity, and the payment of the millhands, was always distributed in bright new gold sovereigns.   Susan was driving alone to the Bank at Clonmel one day with her coachman through thickly wooded country to fetch a new crate of sovereigns, and on her return journey a notorious highwayman waylaid her in the wood.   At the point of his pistol he demanded the money she had just withdrawn from the bank.   "What's befallen ye, Ryan?" Susan angrily asked.   Ryan was the most dreaded ruffian in County Tipperary, always in debt, always drinking too much, with a family of 20 little Catholic children (some illegitimate) whom Richard and Susan Grubb had often assisted.   "For shure, Mistress Grubb, is that your blessed self? Why, oi wouldna hurt one white hair of your ould head.   It's you, for shure, who will feed my bairns, when no one else'd lift a finger to help a good Catholic.   Oi can't go home to the missus without taking them some grub; just one of them sovereigns'd be plenty enough!"   Touching his cap, while Susan reasoned with him of the evil of his ways, he led her horses out of the wood, and with a knowing wink pocketed the sovereign Susan gave him.   Susan often used that road—old Ryan well knew it—when she was visiting her sister in Clonmel, the wife of Richard's youngest brother Thomas, boat builder and machinery maker at the Quay, Clonmel.   He had gone one better and added an "E" to the family surname: "Grubbe sounded more distinctive," her sister had argued; "besides we have 13 in our family, and we must distinguish ours from your twelve!"

It had become quite customary in the nineteenth century among the Grubbs to give a bride's surname as a christian name to one or all of their children, and in both Richard and Thomas Grubbe's family, Haughton, Barcroft and Cambridge were so used as christian names.   There were the Watson Grubbs (Samuel and Anna Grubb gave all three of their children the name Watson), the Grubb Richardsons, the Grubb Davis's, the Grubb Ridgways, and later the Watkins Grubbs.   In so large a family, it was a convenient way of distinguishing the different branches.

Although they had already spent so much money in enlarging Cooleville for their eldest daughter's wedding, it had become clear to Richard's business eye that Clogheen was now really too small for any further Grubb expansion.   Indeed with the purchase of Castle Grace by his younger brother Samuel, who had eight children growing up, and had been in charge of the Clashleigh Mill since his father's death, and inherited that estate for his second son after his mother's death in 1829, which he ran in conjunction with Castle Grace, Richard and Susanna felt somewhat dwarfed. They cast their eyes further afield, and circumstantial guidance gradually accumulated that the neighbouring market town of Cahir, with its famous castle[13] dominating the town, and but nine miles away at the apex of a geographical triangle whose other points were Clonmel and Clogheen—all on the River Suir, and all in the fertile Golden Vale of County Tipperary—was the obvious centre, where new Grubb mills should be established. Cahir lay on the main coaching road between Dublin and Cork; numbers of passing travellers frequented its inns; John Wesley had often stayed a night there on his journeys and preached to the troops in its barracks—the principal centre for Irish cavalrymen in that rich Tipperary pastureland. With the coming of railway services all over Ireland, Cahir lay at the junction of the lines east and west to Clonmel, Waterford and Limerick, as well as north and south to Dublin and Cork, very convenient therefore for the dispatch of goods. Furthermore Richard's youngest brother Thomas was seeking to open up the Suir for navigation as far as Cahir. Professional men, such as the doctor and lawyer used by the Grubbs had their offices there; it was a town of some 4,000 people, described in a current brochure at the time as "built in a style very pleasing to the eye with a very uncommon uniformity of design and a degree of taste and finish that reflects much credit on its inhabitants and builders." Unless they decided to pull up their roots in County Tipperary, and move away to Counties Cork or Waterford or Limerick, and begin afresh, "what better centre," said Richard, "could we find to build new mills and settle our sons?"

There was further "guidance" which attracted them to Cahir. Beside its famous Castle on the river in the centre of the town, "The only Irish castle thought to be impregnable and the bulwark of Munster" as it has been described, a beautiful specimen of mediaeval architecture and one of the residences at that time of the Earl of Glengall, there lay at the top end of the town the ruins of a "Canons Regular" abbey, founded in the reign of King Richard I overlooking the Suir. CAHIR ABBEY had been an Augustinian Foundation, dedicated to Our Lady, founded by Geoffrey de Camoell. It was an extensive ruin, with a 70 ft. high central tower, and outbuildings reaching the river's edge. Five lancet windows on the south aisle, and the mullions of the East Window remained perfect, but the conversion of the central tower into a dwelling house had obliterated other interesting features. At the end of the previous century, a fellow Quaker, named Joshua Fennell, whose wife had been a Miss Grubb, had built a spacious rambling Georgian house close to the abbey, beautifully set in rolling parkland of some 750 acres, and a large six-storied mill on

[13] Its original Fort on an island in the Suir (in the centre of the town) is recorded in the *Yellow Book of Lucan*, as having been destroyed in the III Century A.D., and successive castles were built on this magnificient site.

the Suir between the house and the abbey ruins. A small Quaker cause used to meet on Lord's Days upon his premises at his invitation, which the Grubbs from Clogheen sometimes attended. Fennell's business dealings however, had earned him unpopularity in Cahir, and the Quakers had been turning to Richard Grubb in nearby Clogheen as a man of standing to act as their spokesman and scribe on various occasions. Fennell's death in 1830 had raised the question of a future meeting place for the Society of Friends. At last a slice of land on the Cahir Abbey Estate adjoining the road and the new railway line was rented from the Executors and representatives of Joshua Fennell through the generosity and instrumentality of Richard Grubb for the erection of a small barn-like Quaker meeting house. It was Richard Grubb who signed the legal document on May 11th 1832, (now in the Friends Y.M. Library in Dublin) which reads:—

> "On behalf of the Society of Friends we propose to take from the representatives of the late Joshua Fennell of Cahir Abbey, that part of land of Upper Cahir Abbey situated on the west side of the Tipperary road, for a Meeting House, containing about a hundred feet in front, at the rate of Twenty Pounds per annum."
>
> Signed. Richard Grubb. May 11, 1832.

Attached to this document are the account sheets of the expenses that attended the erection of this rather ugly meeting house, amounting to £838 3s. raised by public subscription, a sum which included the erection of surrounding walls and gates. When the Quaker cause died out in Cahir at the end of the century, the building became a Presbyterian chapel. This is the one and only instance in the long history of the Grubbs there is any record they spent money on the building or the adornment of places of worship. Worship in the home, the assembly rooms, the open-air was always as real to them as the outward aids of a consecrated and set apart particular place of worship.

Having seen so much of the Cahir Abbey demesne, inevitably Richard and Susan discussed its purchase after the death of Fennell, and moving in themselves. It was large enough in all conscience. With his younger brother's recent purchase of the Castle Grace Estate at Clogheen, and his erection of a large commodious house there (1830), was there perhaps the thought in his mind he must launch out to do as well for his family? In after years Richard realised that this was the moment of crisis in his life. Should he sink his capital in buildings and more land—with all the possibilities and interests it would give him—or as his Richardson cousins were later to do, devote it to charitable and evangelistic purposes? Blessed with so large a family he put their interests first, as a good family man, and bought Cahir Abbey Estate.

The winding up of an estate in Ireland takes even longer than in England.

It was two years after Fennell's death before Richard was able to get the slice of land for a meeting house leased to him on behalf of the Cahir Quakers. It was to take three years more before the Executors of Fennell completed the sale to him of the Abbey, its mills, and its land. Helped— as was Samuel at Castle Grace—by the compulsive and comprehensive operation of the "Incumbered Estates Court"—a deservedly popular tribunal which wrested an enormous amount of property from the hands of helpless and insolvent owners into those of new and energetic and wealthy proprietors—Richard in the course of the years was to extend his new estate to include between 750 and 1,000 acres of land, valuable fishing rights on the River Suir, a valuable frontage of half a mile on both sides of the Tipperary-Cahir Road, farm buildings and a square courtyard of stabling adjoining the house. Front and back-drive "lodge cottages". and two barrack-like semi-detached houses, double fronted, between the mills and the main road, and but 50 yards from his own front drive, together with another pair of similar houses a little further down the road (turned into St. Joseph's Boys' School in the twentieth century), with gardens behind running down to the mills, and also across the road on which tennis courts were laid out and old fashioned wall-gardens created, completed the Grubb property. All these houses became known in the course of the years as Cahir Abbey; all of them (save for the lodge-cottages) were to be occupied by his family, as they married.

Richard settled his eldest son Samuel at Cooleville, when he vacated it. There were thus two Samuel Grubbs—Millers—in Clogheen (as at Clonmel the previous century there had often been as many as three or four John Grubbs, Joseph Grubbs and Samuel Grubbs in business at the same time) differentiated only by their addresses or mills. His second son Barcroft Haughton was ensconced on his marriage in one of the "Barracks" as the family jokingly called their houses on the main road, and his third son Richard two years later, on his marriage to Maria Garrett, in the adjoining one. Upon them was to lie the main responsibility of running the mills, just behind their homes and adjoining the old Abbey ruins. When his fourth son Frederick married Anna Haughton his second cousin, in 1842, the third of these "barracks" was ready for him, and the fifth son Alfred was settled in the fourth, on his marriage to the Rector of Clogheen's daughter. Full credit must be ascribed to the brain and organising power that could thus plan and provide, both for his own family, and for the housing in other cottages and homes on his estate of the increasing number of mill-hands and assistants he was to employ in his expanding mills. Like Julius Caesar of old (Richard Grubb had extended the Grubb love of languages to the classics, and gave his three youngest children classical names—Augustus, Octavius, and Helena— a new departure from the generally Biblical names chosen by his forbears

PLATE XXIII

CAHIR ABBEY

Co. Tipperary

From a photograph by W. Hubert Poole, Esq. of Abbey Lodge, Cahir in 1930

PLATE XXIV

CAHIR CASTLE

Reflected in the fast-flowing River Suir.

By courtesy of the National Parks and Monuments Branch of the Office of Public Works, Dublin

for their children—perhaps it was also because he had already exhausted the "Sarahs" and "Samuels" and "Susans" and "Margarets", so common in every Grubb family), he could say "VENI; VIDI; VINCI"—"I came; I saw; I conquered." His family had taken possession of that half of Cahir which lay across the river Suir, divided by the Castle of Cahir on its island site from the town, the shops, Cahir House and other substantial buildings, the property of the Earl of Glengall, the successor to the Butlers as lords of Cahir.

Whenever Richard walked or drove down the hill to the town, the shops, or later to the Parish Church of Cahir, a graceful handsome cut-stone building by Nash, with a beautifully proportioned spire often reflected in the fast flowing waters of the river, and very similar in its setting and style to that of Stratford-on-Avon, he would pause and gaze at Cahir Castle. A sense of deep security and thankfulness filled his mind. However inconsistent it might seem to have spent so much money on enlarging Cooleville, only to leave it after a year, however secure and contented his brother Samuel might be with his new house beside Castle Grace, he had the comfort of Cahir's famous castle to inspire that something in the Grubb blood that always yearned for castles.

The very name Cahir is derived from the old Irish CATHAIR, which means a stone fort or fortress. Similar roots are found in many ancient languages, and looking at Cahir Castle Richard's mind would often turn to the Lord's words to Simon Peter: "Thou art Peter; and on this rock (i.e., rock-like faith you have shown in me), I will build my church, and the gates of hell shall not prevail against it." He and Susanna had their full share of the bereavements and sorrow of life, which few escape. Five of their children died during their lifetime, Samuel his heir in a hunting accident, Alfred through fever caught after bathing in the Suir, Helena in childbirth, Margaret not yet 18, and baby Augustus the first. Despite such bitter loss, a rock-like faith "that will not shrink" upheld him "in the hour of grief and pain" to lean upon his God. Two things had to be done at once, and he did them. It was impossible for Samuel's widow to manage the large estate and mills at Cooleville and bring up three small children. It needed a capable man to run their lovely old home. He must send one of his married sons from Cahir, and bring Anna and his three grandchildren over to the vacated "barrack house". Why his choice fell on Frederick, the fourth son, and not on Richard the third, we shall never know, except that Richard had been married six years and already had five children, and had just been "disowned" by the Quakers. (*See Chapter Eleven.*) So Cooleville remained in Frederick Grubb's family for the next 80 years. As quickly on his daughter Helena's death, he immediately offered to bring up her two motherless children, an offer their father John Grubb Richardson was ready to accept for his baby girl, named Helena after her mother.

Life at Cahir Abbey was never dull, and gave Richard and Susanna much the same pleasure and freshness in middle life, as had come to his own parents on their move from Clonmel to Clogheen. He was fully occupied with his rolling acres, and the expansion of his estate, and buildings, leaving the running of the mills to Barcroft and Richard Junior. He had over 20 grandchildren growing up about him, running about the park, getting in the way sometimes, as children do. It was a happy life. Wrote his grand-daughter Helena Richardson years later:—

> "I grew up among my rollicking uncles at Cahir Abbey. It was an atmosphere in which practical jokes were the order of the day. The 'Cahir Abbey Laugh' won for itself a name throughout the County. It was long and hearty. One day my grandfather was waiting in his carriage outside the front door for his youngest grand-daughter, who did not appear. At last she came demurely down the steps and took her place in the carriage with the rest. Not until they reached their destination was it discovered that an uncle had dressed up in the gown, bonnet and cloak of his niece, and left her in bed in the Abbey."[14]

Irish fun and Quakerism made an unusual combination. It was almost inevitable that a break must come. Nowhere in Ireland were there stricter Quakers than in County Tipperary, and the suspicions that the Cahir Quakers had entertained against the former owner of the Abbey, Joshua Fennell, were increased at the hunting, riding, dancing, music and amateur dramatics of the younger Grubbs. Richard and Susanna themselves had lost their confidence and favour for two reasons, which added to his life-long tensions:—

(a) First, with the reputation the Grubbs had gained for giving first class weddings to their daughters, Susanna had insisted they could not do less for the youngest daughter Susan on her marriage in 1843 to a member of the Church of Ireland, William Carroll. The Quaker meeting house nearly opposite their front gate was much too small for the expected guests. A fashionable wedding was arranged in the beautiful Parish Church across the river. Next year they attended the baptism of their grandson William Carroll therein.

(b) The Earl of Glengall, owner of Cahir Castle was more often away than in residence, leaving a gap in the communal and social life of the town that from time to time Richard and Susanna accepted invitations to fill.

More than 150 years association of his family with the Friends made

---

[14] *Life of James N. Richardson*, p. 9ff. Its author was brought up by his father John Grubb Richardson, and aunt, Mrs. Malcolmson, at Lisnararvey. His mother Helena (*née* Grubb) was a most beautiful woman: he gives a photograph of her in this book.

Richard reluctant to the last irrevocably to snap the ties that bound him to them. He lived to celebrate his golden wedding, and remained a Quaker to his death leaving instructions he wished to be buried among his forbears in the Quaker Burial Ground at Clonmel.

A last amusing incident, characteristic of the hilarity of Richard's family, occurred at his funeral in 1859. The Grubb organising powers were brought fully into play to muster and marshal sufficient carriages, tandems and coaches to convey all the mourners over the twelve miles hilly journey to Clonmel. To complete the requisite number, their mother's old "Cork covered car" was pulled out of the stables, cleaned and polished for some of the sons or grandsons to use. As this long and variegated cortege wound its slow way up and over the hilly gravel roads, and through the dark wood where Susannah had encountered the bandit Ryan, the old Cork car shed two or three of the bolts that held the flooring in place. The unaccustomed weight of the Grubbs it was carrying after it had been so long in idleness and discarded, more than accounted for the mishap. But the Grubbs of Cahir were never non-plussed. Rather than halt the whole procession, they kicked away the damaged splintering flooring. Careless of what the respectful or the curious halted by the roadside might think, four pairs of mud-bespattered black-suited Grubb legs could be seen, as it were headless, running along within the carriage frame and keeping pace with the horses, until the town of Clonmel was reached. "Those rollicking uncles of mine," whispered Helena Richardson in the next following coach, "Can't they resist their pranks even at a funeral?"

So originated a characteristic Grubb saying from this truly Irish funeral: "The Good Lord gave our family a sense of humour, knowing how often we should need it."[15]

From the words of a contemporary, Richard Grubb's faith may be summed up, as he went to join his fathers:—

"So long Thy power has kept me, sure it still will lead me on,
O'er moor and fen, o'er crag and torrent, till the night is gone.
Keep Thou my feet ; I do not ask to see
The distant scene: one step enough for me."

J. H. Newman (1801–1890)

---

[15] Another remarkable Grubb funeral was that of Samuel Richard Grubb, J.P. (1855–1925); Squire of Castle Grace, Clogheen, a Quaker, who wished to be buried in the highest spot of the Knockmealdown Mountains, his own land. But the bearers could trudge no further and had to deposit the heavy coffin among the heather and peat half-a-mile short of the top!

COLLATERAL TABLE "H"

RICHARD GRUBB, 1780–1859 and SUSANNA (*née* HAUGHTON) d. 1863

They had 12 children (of whom five died during their parent's lifetime): Eight sons and four daughters; and 40 grandchildren (28 of them Grubbs)

All the sons and their wives (except Augustus 2nd) were buried in the Quaker Burial Ground, Clonmel.

1.	SAMUEL	b. 1809; d. 1843	3 children
2.	BARCROFT HAUGHTON	b. 1811; d. 1879	6 sons
3.	RICHARD	b. 1812; d. 1886	11 children
4.	FREDERICK	b. 1815; d. 1891	2 daughters
5.	ALFRED	b. 1817; d. 1846	No issue
6.	AUGUSTUS	b. 1823; d. 1824, *died young*	
7.	AUGUSTUS	b. 1824; d. 1879	6 children
8.	OCTAVIUS	b. 1828; d. 1871	No issue
*1.	Sarah	b. 1808; d. 1878; m. 1833, Henry RIDGWAY of Garrygowan. Large family in Waterford to whom are a number of memorials in Waterford Cathedral.	
2.	Margaret	b. 1813; d. 1830	
3.	Helena	b. 1819; d. 1850; m. 1846, John Grubb RICHARDSON (1813–1890), of Ulster	2 children
*4.	Susan	b. 1821; m. 1843, William CARROLL of Cork. One son William; m. (2) Rev. Wm. GRAHAM, of Kettering. They had one son, Vivien James.	

*Joined the Church of Ireland.

---

1. SAMUEL. He married 1834 Anna Watson (d. 1874). He died aged 34 in a hunting accident. They lived at Cooleville, Clogheen. Three children.
   (1) RICHARD WATSON GRUBB (1835–1903); m. Frances Castle of U.S.A. They settled in America and had one son and one daughter:
      (i) FRANCIS LECKY WATSON GRUBB, b. 1879 (Named after the famous Irish historian).
      (ii) SUSAN WATSON GRUBB (1877–1903).
   Their Grubb grandchildren continued in America (*see Appendix "E"*).
   (2) SAMUEL SEYMOUR WATSON GRUBB, b. 1842; m. 1902, Mary Clarkson. No family. Historian of the family.
   (3) ELIZABETH WATSON GRUBB, 1838–1902.

2. BARCROFT HAUGHTON. He married 1834, Eliza Ridgway (1814–1892) his sister-in-law. They lived all their days in one of the Abbey Houses at Cahir. He died aged 68. They had six sons, of whom only one married:
   (1) RICHARD (1836–1909). Died aged 73.
   (2) GEORGE PENROSE RIDGWAY (1837–1870). Died aged 33.
   (3) WILFRID HAUGHTON (1839–1891). Died aged 52.
   (4) LEOPOLD (1842–1869). Died aged 27.
   (5) SAMUEL (1845–1883); m. Anne Vennell. No children.
   (6) ALFRED (1847–1885). Died aged 38.

3. RICHARD. He married, 1837, Maria Garrett (d. 1870) of Granite Hall, Dublin. He died aged 74. (See Chapters Eleven and Twelve.)

Continued on next page

132

4. **FREDERICK.** He married, 1842, Anna Haughton, his second cousin (she died 1894). After his eldest brother's death, they lived at Cooleville, Clogheen for nearly 50 years, where their two outstandingly beautiful daughters were born, the elder of whom inherited it:
   (1) ROSE FREDERICA GRUBB (1846–1919). An intrepid horsewoman.
   (2) HELENA CHRISTIAN (known as "Honey") (1860–1917). She married (i) in 1890 William Sutherland. He died 1901. (ii) in 1910, Rev. Arthur B. Graham, of Kettering. No children.

5. **ALFRED.** He married Louisa Fraser, daughter of the Rector of Clogheen. No children. He died through fever caught when bathing in the River Suir, aged 38.

6. **AUGUSTUS (1st)** Died as a baby.

7. **AUGUSTUS (2nd).** He married, 1852, Maria Elizabeth Hill of Buxton. Died aged 54. They had four sons and two daughters:
   (1) AUGUSTUS HILL (1853–1888). Unmarried. Died aged 35.
   (2) ERNEST PELHAM (1854–1905). Educated Rugby. He married, 1888, Emily Mary Lawrence (d. 1900).   Two children: (i) ENID;
      (ii) LAWRENCE ERNEST GRUBB (1892–1914). Killed in action. Educated Rugby and B.N.C. Oxford; 2nd Lieut, K.O.Y.L.I.
   (3) RAGLAN SOMERSET (1856–1901). Died aged 45.
   (4) BEAUFORT SOMERSET (1862–1927); m. 1899, E. F. Lowe.
   (5) JULIANA CARLETON, b. 1858; m. 1884, Surg.-Major T. Holmstead.
   (6) AUGUSTA, b. 1860; m. 1890 Joseph Meredith.

8. **OCTAVIUS.** He married Isabella Carroll of Cork. Died aged 43. No issue.

M

CHAPTER ELEVEN

Richard Grubb (Junior) 1812—1886

Born at Cooleville, Clogheen

Merchant and Gentleman of Cahir Abbey, Co. Tipperary

He married in 1837, Maria Garrett,
daughter of Richard Garrett, Esq., of Granite Hall, Co. Dublin.

They had seven sons and four daughters

"David ordered singers to be appointed, with instruments of musick, lifting up the voice with joy."—I Chronicles, xvi, 16.

"Sing unto the Lord a new song: play skilfully with a loud noise."—Psalm xxxiii, 3.

FOUR characteristic portraits ought to exist of Richard Grubb Junior in oils or watercolours. They would reveal the man, better than any words in the four parts of his life he enjoyed the most.

(i) A somewhat elegant well-groomed after dinner speaker, responding to a toast.

(ii) Surrounded by his seven sons and four daughters around his wife seated at the family piano, with a hymnbook in front of her.

(iii) A keen-eyed and sympathetic looking Justice of the Peace presiding over the magistrates bench, weighing up evidence in his mind.

(iv) A tall brisk man with an even taller six footer son, with moustache and side whiskers, attending Moody's Evangelistic Meetings in Belfast.

The third son of his father Richard, after whom he was called, he was born at Cooleville, Clogheen three years before his grandfather died, and three years before the Battle of Waterloo and defeat of Napoleon. The first history he learned was from his nanny who used to speak of Napoleon Bonaparte as a bogey to frighten naughty little boys into obedience.

At the "family" school at Ballitore, history particularly appealed to him, as his father before him, Classical history, European history, and Irish history. There were three Irishmen who competed in his young mind as "top of the poll". Edmund Burke, the outstanding orator and writer of the previous century, one of the old boys of his school whose tradition lingered long in that "Athens of Ireland". The second was Arthur Wellesley whose victories against the French in the Peninsular War and in Belgium won for him the title "Duke of Wellington". Several of his Haughton uncles had fought under him in Spain. The third was Admiral Nelson whose dying expectation always seemed a call to Richard personally to do his duty. Whenever he was in Dublin and could make the opportunity he would take a walk past Nelson's Pillar to salute his memory; in later years his admiration for his great victories at Trafalgar and the Nile led to his purchase and display in his dining room of two fine engravings of these battles.[1] Most schoolboys go through a period of hero-worship—if history is well taught—the influence of the hero (who never knew anything about it) can be enormous upon perspicacious youth. Such is influence, and the value of history and biography in a liberal and public school education.

His ambitions aroused, Richard developed from studying Burke's speeches an ease of speaking and writing clearly, a pride in being Irish, and a keen sense of the ridiculous, which became so charming a part of characteristic Grubb humour and wit in succeeding generations, the germs of which he had inherited from his grandmother Shackleton. Like Burke, he also developed a keen interest in poetry, painting, and music. He admired the soldierly qualities of Wellesley, and his strategic genius. He took up running and boxing (which were features of his Quaker school at Ballitore) and he became determined to win, whatever the obstacles. When the great Duke became England's Prime Minister, Richard was quite content with whatever action he took or failed to take over Irish affairs. "His not to reason why, his but to do and die"—he instinctively knew it is the leader who counts, and the right Leader deserves to be supported wholeheartedly. He never lost his boyhood spirit of hero-worship. Nelson's sea battles thrilled him as much as Wellington's victories. It was sufficient for Richard that:—

> "Not once nor twice in this brave island's story,
> The Path of Duty is the Way to Glory."

The orator, the soldier, and the sailor—they all had a direct influence upon Richard's character. With his family flair for languages he maintained his historical interests all his life.

Home from school in the holidays at Clogheen there were three other influences upon him in young manhood:—

The first was that Sunday in Clogheen at the Quaker meeting, when his hot Irish blood was stirred as he heard a Friend speaking of the experiences

---

[1] Engraved by Thos. Kelly from the drawings taken at the spot by Captain John Weir of Marines H.M.S. *Audacious*, these prints have descended through his family to Torquay, where they are now in the possession of his great grandson.

M*

of Solomon Eccles, the first Quaker minister at Clogheen. Eccles had been a prosperous teacher and passionate lover of music until his conversion to Quakerism revolutionised his life and

> "pronounced judgment and sentence against the harp and the lyre and all forms of musick. I would vain have pleaded the harmlessness of Musick, but no pleading would serve. It was nothing but vanity, and vexed the good spirit of God. Oh, it was hard for flesh and blood to give it all up, for it was not only my livelihood, but my life was in it." [2]

Like St. Paul at Athens, young Richard Grubb's spirit was stirred within him, when he heard the speaker at that meeting extol the burning of viols and virginals and other forms of music as a sacrifice for conscience sake, well pleasing to God. "That's not the God I want to follow and love," thought Richard. An innate love for singing and music was intensified. It never left him all his life.

"Why don't Quakers sing the praises of God at their Lord's Day meetings?" He asked his father. He never got a satisfactory answer. "But we sing out of doors; we whistle and we cheer. What's wrong with music and hymns in worship, like the Methody people do?" His inquisitive mind led him to study the hymns they sang in the church, and that the followers of John Wesley were singing. He got hold of a collection of hymns made by Wesley in Georgia in 1738. He discovered that Methodism was born in song. He thought their poetry first class. Then he got hold of a much larger collection of Wesley hymns published in 1780, which profoundly moved him by their meaningful English, and the methodical careful arrangement of the book. Their poetry and rhythm, in contrast to the long, stilted, and often dispiriting prose he was accustomed to hear in so many Quaker circles, gave him the same satisfaction as the latest pop-music, guitars, and 'way-out' language give modern youth today, and are sometimes supposed would also do in a revised prayerbook and liturgy. The preface by John Wesley is worth quoting; had there been a Methodist congregation anywhere near, Richard Grubb might well have joined them. Wesley through his writings had as great an influence upon his developing spiritual life as he had upon his great grandparents, Joseph and Sarah.

Wrote Wesley:—

> "For many years I have been importuned to publish such a Hymn Book as might be generally used in all our Congregations throughout Great Britain and Ireland. . . . Such a Hymn Book you have now before you. It is not so large as to be either cumbersome or expensive; and it is large enough to contain such a variety of hymns as will

---

[2] "A Musick-Lector, or the Art of Musick (that is so much vindicated in Christendome). Discoursed of by way of Dialogue". *Undated Tract by Solomon Eccles*. S.E. (Solomon Eccles) is the Quaker minister immortalized in Defoe's *Journal of the Plague*, under the name of Solomon Eagle.

not soon be worn threadbare. It is large enough to contain all the important truths of our most holy religion, whether speculative or practical; to illustrate them all, and to prove them both by Scripture and reason; and this is done in a regular order. The hymns are not carelessly jumbled together, but carefully ranged under proper heads, accordiug to the experience of real Christians. So that this book is, in effect, a little body of experimental and practical divinity.

"Since but a small part of these hymns is of my own compiling, I do not think it inconsistent with modesty to declare that I am persuaded no such Hymn Book as this has been published in the English language.

"May I be permitted to add a few words with regard to the poetry? Then I will speak to those who are judges thereof, with all freedom and unreserve. To these I will say, without offence—1. In these hymns there is no doggerel; no botches; nothing put in to patch up the rhyme; no feeble expletives. 2. There is nothing turgid or bombast, on the one hand, or low and creeping on the other. 3. There are no cant expressions; no words without meaning. We talk common sense, both in prose and verse, and use no word but in a fixed and determinate sense. 4. Here are, allow me to say, both the strength, the purity, and the elegance of the English language, and at the same time the utmost simplicity and plainness, suited to every capacity. 5. Lastly I desire men of taste to judge (these are the only competent judges) whether there is not in some of the following hymns the true spirit of Poetry, such as cannot be acquired by art and labour but must be the gift of nature. By labour a man may become a tolerable imitator of Spenser, Shakespeare, or Milton; and may heap together pretty compound epithets as pale-eyed, meek-eyed, and the like; but *unless he be born a Poet* he will never attain the genuine spirit of Poetry.

"But to return. That which is of infinitely more moment than the spirit of Poetry is the spirit of Piety. And I trust all persons of real judgment will find this breathing through the whole collection. It is in this view chiefly, that I would recommend it to every truly pious reader, as a means of raising or quickening the spirit of devotion; of confirming his faith; of enlivening his hope; and of kindling and increasing his love to God and man. When Poetry thus keeps its place, as the handmaid of Piety, it shall attain, not a poor perishable wreath, but a crown that fadeth not away."

London. Oct. 20. 1779.   John Wesley.

Language such as this delighted Richard Grubb's heart. Singing and whistling and music and poetry filled many of the spare moments of his life. His generation was the first among the Grubbs to be brought up in the country. With six brothers and four sisters he loved every minute of his time at Clogheen, feeling that in the country he belonged. He became a gentleman miller, enjoying country ways and sports, riding, walking, hunting, mixing with the neighbours, and attending the social parties and dances, with no desire to become a townsman, not however, uninfluenced by the Regency culture and dress and fashions of the reigns of George IV and William IV. He was not best pleased when his father moved the family to Cahir; he never felt called to break away on his own nor to leave home to go out to preach the gospel, as his grandmother had done, and two sons of his later were to do. The ties of family were much too strong. A picture of seven brothers, his Richardson cousins in the North of Ireland and his contemporaries, was later written by one of Richard's nephews, James Nicholson Richardson (son of Helena Grubb, Richard's sister), and in many respects must closely resemble the life, dress, and other characteristics of Richard Grubb and his six brothers at Clogheen.[3]

"My father and uncles were seven brothers, sons of James N. Richardson, and as they possessed many qualities, both physical and mental in common to a more marked degree than is usual even among brothers, I attempt a general description of these men, from thirty to forty-five years of age. I believe rarely do seven such brothers meet.

"They were all well-made, good looking, some distinctly handsome, in most cases very active and above middle height, some of them attaining to more than six feet.[4] They all had fresh complexions, brown hair, and were clean-shaven, except for the soupçon of sandy coloured side whiskers, which was then generally worn. They all had the same thick bushy eyebrows, under which gleamed large expressive dark grey eyes, and they were all bald, even as comparatively young men.

"They were all careful to wear good and expensive watches, and equally careful to wear but the simplest and slightest gold chains. They all had clear, but low and pleasant voices, of similar timbre & key, and all except one had large capable well-formed hands, somehow well kept though they seldom affected gloves. They were all ever well groomed and dressed, but never appeared to give a thought to the subject.

"They all had the faculty, in greater or less degree, of turning honestly a halfpenny into a penny, and of attaching their employees whom they usually chose with discrimination, to their persons. In most cases they had a very strong sense of duty to the public, and liked to see people comfortable around them. Most of them had a taste for building and gardening, but not one of them had a taste for music. The want of this faculty often revenges itself in a love of poetry, but with almost abnormal memories for other things, not one of them, I do believe, could have quoted eight lines from any poet.

"It has been said they were fond of money, and in a healthy sense no doubt they were; commerce was their profession. But I make bold to say that not one of them was fond of money in the sordid sense. Not one of them intentionally wronged his neighbour, and not of them ground the face of the poor.

"It was a natural instinct with each of them to develop and improve whatever they were connected with; their houses; their gardens;

[3] *James Nicholson Richardson of Bessbrook.* C. Fell-Smith, pp. 37–40.
[4] One of Richard Grubb's sons, the Rev. George Grubb, and a great-grandson, Col. A. J. Watkins Grubb, were equally outstandingly tall.

PLATE XXV

IRISH COINS AND BANK-TOKENS OF THE ANGLO-HANOVERIAN KINGS 1721–1806

GEORGE I: 1722–23. *William Wood's Coinage*

Taken across the Atlantic for use in the American Colonies

Type 1. Hibernia seated, holding the Irish Harp. *Type 2.* Leaning on Harp.

GEORGE II: *Obv.* King's Head. *Rv.* Irish Harp

GEORGE III: Half pennies

Type 1. Head with short hair, 1766–69. *Type 2.* Head with long hair, 1774–82

Ditto. First Copper Penny 1805 (Proof), and Half Pennies and Farthings

Ditto. Silver Bank Tokens, 1804–06, of Six Shillings; XXX Pence; 5 and 10 Pence

Scale: 1 *to* 1½. *facing page 138*

PLATE XXVI

IN DUBLIN AS A YOUNG MAN

" Well-groomed and dressed "

their business; their neighbourhood. Money was to them as timber, bricks, and slates, are to the architect; not the end, but the means wherewith to beautify or to erect the building on which he is engaged.

"Another trait, common to the seven brothers occurs to me. With one exception, none of them, though pressed to do so, ever accepted any post or office carrying with it a title of any kind, such as a baronetcy, M.P.-ship, Justice of the Peace, Deputy Lieutenancy. As Quakers, this is understandable."

John Grubb Richardson indeed was offered a baronetcy in 1882 by Mr. Gladstone in recognition of his fine efforts for good in Northern Ireland, his founding of Bessbrook, and his firm support of the liberal policies of Mr. Gladstone. This however was decidedly refused on the ground that any honour of this kind would detract from the feeling of satisfaction he might derive from having tried to do a little to benefit his fellow men. In his letter declining the proposed title he again urged Mr. Gladstone to adopt some means of furthering Temperance Reform.[5]

To Dublin, Richard would sometimes escort his younger sister Helena, on her way to visit her Richardson cousins in Ulster, and often times John Grubb Richardson would join them there. It was essential to go either to Cork or to the Dublin shops when you wanted to order a new suit or a dress, books, or other articles not easily obtainable locally. Dublin was renowned then, as today, for good living, entertainment, music and University study. In its heyday in the Regency and early Victorian period, it was comparable to Jerusalem of old "where all the tribes would go up"; as the most convenient centre for friends from one of Ireland's four provinces to meet friends from another. It was at a concert on one such visit to Dublin that Richard met his future wife, Maria Garrett, daughter of a retired sea-captain, Richard Garrett, living at Kingstown nearby. The music and laughter of Dublin was congenial to them both, so was their mutual Quaker background, and at the end of the Regency period, in the year that Queen Victoria ascended the throne, they were married in Dublin.

All their married life was to be spent in Cahir. First in one of the tall, rather gaunt-looking semi-detached Georgian houses, fronting the pavement, later jokingly known by their sons as "The Barracks", within fifty yards of the main gates into the Abbey, and next door to elder brother Barcroft Haughton Grubb. Later in the Abbey itself. An early purchase was a Dublin upright piano. Nothing in their lives was more momentous for the Grubb family than this "piano" purchase. Around it were spent hours and hours of music and family enjoyment. Upon it the children early learnt to play and later to entertain. They all had melodious voices, and Bach and Beethoven and the works of most of the German and Austrian composers gradually covered all "tops" of furniture

---

[5] *James Nicholson Richardson. Ibid.*, p. 19.

and chairs, until it became necessary to build on another room leading out from the smallish left-of-the-front-door sitting room, which became the music room. Their home soon became a centre for friends and relations to drop in of an evening, and to gather round the piano—in days before music halls were thought of. The children's pocket-money would be spent on the latest song to be published, or a volume of music, as a hundred years later, the newest "pop-record" has become a "must" for most young people. Musical chairs and charades, hearty and possibly over-loud singing, including hymn singing, drifted through the opened window directly on the road, and across to the little Quaker chapel nearly opposite. Not that there was any ribaldry or disturbance of the quiet night hours of the quiet little town! But such "goings-on" across the road pleased not the Friends in Cahir. Because of "its hurtful and injurious tendencies" amusements and entertainments, music and dancing, such as Richard and Maria Grubb allowed or organised in their home, savoured of the "vain and giddy world" and were "utterly at variance" with the principles of the over-strict, exclusive and small body of Quakers in Cahir. Richard and Maria were repeatedly visited by "Friends", either singly, or on a deputation from the monthly meeting, to try to persuade them "with much affectionate labour" to relinquish and remove their piano, and to cease attending balls and dances. The Hunt Balls were a popular social outlet for the Tipperary gentry, and the Earl of Glengall at Cahir Castle would turn its old mediaeval hall into a large dancing salon, where from time to time the younger Grubbs would be invited. In these "salad days" of their lives, and with their inherent love for music, and also for hymn singing (what could possibly be wrong with that?), there was but one answer to be expected of any young people to the "affectionate" (sic) visitations and deputations they received.

The Quakers at Cahir had put themselves into an impossible position in seeking to restrain liberty of conscience. As Non-conformists they stood for liberty of conscience, and freedom to follow the guidance of the Light Within. Yet here were Non-conformists seeking to enforce conformity to a rigid and unbiblical discipline. They had no option left to them, but to issue the following "Disownment" of Richard Grubb Jnr. and his wife Maria. Had they been conforming churchpeople it would have been called "excommunication".

From the Minutes of the Monthly Meeting on 28th November 1844, held at Clonmel.

> "Whereas it has been the care of the Society of Friends, or People called Quakers, to endeavour to guard its members from all amusements or entertainments of a hurtful or injurious tendency, AND the practices of music and dancing are pursuits belonging to the vain and giddy world, being utterly at variance with our principles, the Society has declared its entire disunity with them. And whereas

Richard Grubb Jnr, and Maria his wife, who had their birthright and were educated in the said Society, have introduced and encouraged the practices of Music and Dancing in their house, and have also attended those hurtful and injurious entertainments called Balls at which Music and Dancing form a chief part of the amusements, they have therefore been the subjects of much concern to the body, and have been repeatedly visited by appointment of this Meeting, and much affectionate labour used to persuade them to relinquish these things, and to convince them of their hurtful tendency.

"But the care thus extended not having produced the desired effect, as they declined to discontinue the practice of Music nor would they agree to refrain from attending Balls, WE therefore feel it our duty to testify against their conduct, and WE DO HEREBY DISOWN the said Richard Grubb Jnr, and Maria his wife to be members of our religious Society; yet we desire they may be favoured to see the inconsistency of these practices with the Christian character, and that by submitting to the visitations of Divine Love they may be led into that life of self-denial and devotedness to their Creator, which is acceptable in His sight."

Signed by William Davis (clerk). [6]

Such a minute shows Quakerism at its worst. One of the continuing Quakers in the family, the scholar and historian Isabel Grubb, M.A., of Carrick on Suir and Waterford [7], (see Collateral Table F) describes it as "one of the regrettable incidents of Quakerism". The history of the Church of England and of the Roman Catholic Church show equally "regrettable incidents" in their efforts to compel obedience. What are called "the exceptions to every rule" or the inconsistencies of life (inconsistency is not peculiar to the Grubbs) are far better left alone and ignored, than calling in the forces of compulsion and punishment in religious life. The Saviour of Mankind came not to condemn, but to show mercy.

It was inevitable that the break should come. Writes Isabel Grubb—whether applicable to past members of her own family or not—"In the South of Ireland, Friends were landowners, millers, farmers, and shopkeepers. Some were very wealthy and engaged in ostentatious luxury. A number, especially of the younger generation, were but nominal Quakers, spending their time in a round of social engagements . . . they seemed to have everything that money could purchase, the season afford, and that taste and good cooking could contribute." The new life of opulence into which the Grubbs had entered on leaving Clonmel for Clogheen, and later for Cahir, and the tensions which all his life beset Richard Grubb Senior (see last chapter), had come to a head, and found their solution in the purchase of a PIANO. Ironical it might seem that the harmonies and melodies of music should have been the outward cause

---

[6] He was Richard Grubb's first-cousin. His wife Elizabeth (third daughter of Abraham Grubb of Clonmel) was also a first-cousin (see page 85).
[7] *Quakers in Ireland.* Isabel Grubb, M.A., p. 126ff.

of the break, which had radical consequences for the Grubbs, and was to lead them out all over the world. Very different their history might have been had they not waited among the Friends until the break was forced upon them. Despite all their spirit of independence, it was not they who made the break. "I don't believe in the stark silence of Heaven, but in its music and melodies", said Richard. "Come, Mother, let's get round the piano, and praise our Maker while we've breath; we shall find peace and contentment in song and praise, in our acceptance from God of our disownment by the Friends". Maria opened the hymn book, and they sang Wesley's hymn through the opened window:—

> "Oh, for a thousand tongues to sing
> Our Great Redeemer's praise:
> The glories of our God and King,
> The triumphs of His grace.

> "Our Gracious Master and our God,
> Assist US to proclaim,
> To spread through all the earth abroad
> The Honours of Thy Name."

Five of his seven sons, and many of his grandsons and a grand-daughter were later to go out into all the world . . . China, Australia, New Zealand, America (North and South) and the Congo . . . to spread abroad their Saviour's Name.

Richard could not refrain a loud guffaw when later in life he heard that the Quakers in Ulster had introduced hymn singing and the piano into their worship about the time that Ira Sankey came from America to "sing the Gospel" with his magnificent voice. He rejoiced when General Booth (into whose family a descendant of the Anner Mill Grubbs had married) founded the Salvation Army with trumpets and drums to carry the Gospel in the open air into the back streets and slums of great cities. If there had been a Methodist congregation in Cahir, he would surely immediately have joined it. He was jubilant. Another "Richard Lionheart" had come into being. If the Grubbs had always seemed to be one step ahead of their fellow Quakers in the past, they were two steps ahead now! All things were working together for good in the purposes of God for those who had been called and marked out for His purposes in the world. Punishment and "disownment" are poor weapons of religious strategy. The Tipperary Quakers in their shortsightedness saved the Grubbs from becoming ostriches!

Yet the next four years were not easy ones for Richard, and Maria perhaps felt their disownment more than her husband.

In his marriage to the placid and broadminded Dublin girl, Maria Garrett, Richard had found the ideal partner to match his active humorous temperament, and the cost of the break from Quakerism. This break had meant a lot to Maria, whose grandfather John Garrett, a Dutchman by birth, and a Speaker among the Quakers in Dublin, had been a friend of John Wesley's, and profoundly influenced by him. Wesley described him as: "One of the most lovely old men I ever saw." The Quaker Speaker used to love to entertain the Prince of Preachers to breakfast, when he was in Dublin. But Maria all her life had loved the sound of music. Like the serving maid in the inn at Killcock, whom Wesley had been agreeably surprised "to find singing one of our hymns" while she swept the stairs,[8] she had been brought up from a child to sing them at all times and in all places—hymns handed down in her family by her grandfather.

She loved things bright and beautiful, and would always believe the Lord God Almighty made all things well, even pianos! She just couldn't understand these Tipperary Quakers, and wished she could persuade Richard to pull out from Cahir, and let them make their home in Dublin or somewhere else. She would continue teaching her children the stories of Jesus in song: little Isabella, her eldest was already six—she had called her after her own mother who had been born Isabella Alexander—and Susanna was only a year younger, named after Richard's mother Susan. It was good of Richard to agree to call their second son Alexander after her mother's family—a name that has been passed down in every generation of the Grubbs ever since; Lord Alexander of Tunis, distinguished in the Second World War sprang from the same family. Naturally they had named their eldest son after his father and grandfather, with Cambridge added as a second Christian name to distinguish him, not because there was any link with Cambridge University as yet, but because his grandmother's mother had been a Miss Cambridge before becoming Mrs Haughton. Her baby, born last year, Richard had insisted should be called after her—Maria with a second name Louise added to distinguish her. They were going to call the one she was carrying Frederick, if he was a boy, after the great German king who had dared to defy the world. She at least had her children to occupy her, difficult as the next few years must be for her husband after their disownment by the Quakers. True the outbreak of the Potato Famine throughout Ireland next year was to keep him busy with relief work, but where were they going to worship? There was no Methodist congregation in Cahir, and the Parish Church by the river down the road seemed the only alternative. At that moment her mind turned to her cousin William Alexander, and she knew within herself he was just the man whom Richard must meet, who could probably help them both in their dilemma.

Dr. William Alexander, of Trinity College Dublin, was exerting a profound influence throughout Ireland at this time by his oratory and efforts, and doing more than most to restore the Church of Ireland from the "dead" state into which it had lapsed, despite the Gospel itinerations by

[8] *Journal of the Rev. John Wesley, A.M.* Vol. ii, pp. 343, 418.

John Wesley and the Grubb ladies in the previous century. He was to become Bishop of Derry (Londonderry) and Raphoe—his episcopate lasted 29 years—and eventually he became Primate of Ireland. His wise counsel and vast learning coupled with his simplicity of life and his friendliness, and with the fine poetry and moving hymns of his gifted wife (Mrs. C. F. Alexander) all combined to make the ecclesiastically "low" Church of Ireland attractive to Richard and Maria, and encouraged their inherent love of hymns. They discovered the Church of Ireland held firmly to the authority of the Bible and the need to read and study both the Old and the New Testaments; they came to delight in the incomparable language of the Book of Common Prayer, and they found the simplicity of its church buildings and administration of the Sacraments (so different from the colourful incense-laden Catholic churches in Ireland) were meaningful aids to devotion. Richard found in Dr. and Mrs. Alexander[9] another formative influence upon his life.

Four years elapsed from her disownment by the Quakers before another child was born to Maria on October 31st 1848. The arrival of their fourth son and seventh child (he was to be followed about every two years by the second half of Richard's family of eleven children) faced his parents with the question of Baptism, and particularly Infant Baptism. Having joined the Church of Ireland (there is no record at Cahir that Richard and Maria themselves received baptism) they decided to accept the responsibility of having their younger children baptised soon after birth, and—very wisely—that their elder sons and daughters should wait until reaching an age to decide for themselves. Two years later, when their fifth son William Pike had been born, there took place the first baptism among the Grubbs since their Anabaptist days 200 years before.[10] Experts now in arranging weddings and funerals, the Grubb clan collected in the stately Cahir parish church on Sunday afternoon, October 31st, 1850 with some trepidation for the baptism service to be conducted by the Rev. Walter Giles, the vicar. Brother Frederick and Anna his wife brought over their eldest daughter Rosa from Cooleville, Clogheen; Richard and Maria brought their two little boys Percy and William; their grandparents Richard Senior and Susan and most of the family attended, and at a great "Grubb Get-together" afterwards at the Abbey.

Between 1859 and 1863 all six of Richard's elder children chose to be baptised as adults. In the wisdom of God, Harry Percy, first of the Grubbs to receive infant baptism, was also to be the first to receive

---

[9] A three-light window in Derry Cathedral commemorating the Archbishop's wife, Mrs. C. F. Alexander, represents three of her best known and loved Irish hymns, *viz.*:
Once in Royal David's city.
There is a Green Hill far away, and
The Golden Gates are lifted up.

[10] True a nephew of Richard Grubb, William Carroll, his sister's son—had been baptised in Cahir Church in 1844, the year he was 'disowned' by the Quakers.

ordination into the ministry of the Church in Ireland. His younger brother George, baptised in Cahir Church, was later to be ordained on a title as curate of Cahir, where he served five years from 1880–1885, the stay and comfort of his father in his old age.

Cahir Church came to mean much to the Grubbs under the influence of the next vicar, the Rev. John Morgan. They attended regularly; most of them taught for a while in its Sunday school. They played its organ; they assisted in youth work and the life of the parish. Its memory stayed with them, when most of them had left Cahir for ever, and perhaps particularly their stirrings of heart on the many occasions they sang around their piano, or in church, that finest Irish-composed hymn:—

"Jesus calls us. By Thy mercy,
   Saviour may we heed Thy call.
Give our lives to Thy obedience.
   Serve and Love Thee best of all."

(Mrs. C. F. Alexander)

Wherever they went, their speech now betrayed their origin. It is another paradox about the family that for the first hundred years in Ireland and among the Quakers they continued more English than Irish, and their speech savoured of Bunyan's *Pilgrim's Progress*. Now no longer Non-conformists and mixing freely with Irish people, the old plain Quaker "Yea" and "Nay" gave place to the charming Irish intonation and idioms of direct speech . . . longer as it was, though not necessarily long-winded. If Richard asked a son if he was going rowing or fishing on the River Suir, instead of a plain yes or no, he would be answered "I am for shure"; or "Going fishing, that I am"; or "Not rowing today". If Maria asked a daughter if she thought it was going to rain, she would be answered: "It will not", or "It will rain, Mama". If at times Grubbs have opened themselves to a charge of being long-winded in conversation or public preaching, they will tell you it is due to their upbringing, and Irish preference for three or four words where one would be enough!

The year 1863 faced Richard Grubb with the second moment of great decision in his life, with the death of his mother Susan. She had continued living in Cahir Abbey, and capably running the estate, as well as keeping an eye on her sons at the mills for the four years since her husband died. What was now to happen to the Abbey? Who would care to live there? The Grubb family were still feudalistic in their belief in primogeniture. The untimely death of Samuel Grubb (of Cooleville) in a hunting accident had brought Barcroft Haughton Grubb, the second son, into the succession, and in his father's will the Abbey was left to him on his mother's death. For the past 30 years he had been comfortably living in one of the "barracks"—as his six sons jokingly called their home, 50 yards down the road from Cahir Abbey main gates, where his father had installed

145

him on his marriage to Eliza Ridgway in 1834. He was increasingly immersed in the flour mills just behind his house, which were employing an increasing number of mill hands, and had no desire to change this for the running of a huge estate. Barcroft made it quite clear he had no intention of leaving his comfortable quarters for that rambling old house and its long drive, up the road. Trespassers were always fishing in the tempting bit of water running below the Abbey, with its deep black pools, and enjoying the trout that his Quaker parents had left undisturbed, and he had no interest in the extensive stabling, the horses, and the farm. He preferred his cup of tea from the kitchen range in his own home, which Eliza knew actually worked—the one in the huge stone-flagged Abbey basement kitchen was always going wrong—a new chimney needed to be built. Indeed the whole house needed modernising, his Mother hadn't bothered in her widowhood, and relied on her many servants to bring her meals to her upstairs. Besides he had no daughter, and his six sons were quite content with their work in the mills. Anyway, he said, he was not the eldest son, and under no obligation to inherit a demesne he had come to consider should never have been bought. He was fully immersed in the mills and his town and business affairs. "Let the place be let," he said, "unless brother Richard and Maria are bold enough to move over and live there."

In consequence Cahir Abbey was left unoccupied for some months, until Richard could persuade Maria they had better agree to tackle it and move over if only for the sake of their children, and the needed space it would give for the nine of them still at home. Susan their second daughter, was about to be married to her second cousin, Alexander Richardson from the north of Ireland, and Alexander their second son, had chosen an Army career, and was now in New Zealand fighting the Maoris. George the youngest was only seven, but Isabella the eldest, now 25, and Richard Cambridge (22) were keen to share the responsibility with their parents in running the place, and Maria Louise (20) and Frederick (19) urged them to take it, faced as they were with a decision what to do with their own lives.

Move over they did, and the Cahir Church registers show that until 1863, Richard signed himself as "Merchant in Cahir", but after that date as a Gentleman! As part of the "deal" Richard surrendered all his interest in the mills to his brother.

Repairs at the Abbey were quickly put in hand. The whole family threw themselves into the improvements and alterations, the painting, and re-decoration, and new pianos were installed, one in the long with-drawing room, full of beautiful Waterford glass and green and crimson china, and one in the new music room. The house rang again with laughter, and now with music.

146

PLATE XXVII

UPPER CAHIR ABBEY HOUSES

Built by Richard Grubb Senior for his younger sons between Cahir Abbey, and Lower Cahir Abbey Houses, with gardens on the other side of the main road.

To left. Cahir Abbey   *To right.* The Castle and Town

Behind. The Abbey Ruins

A photograph by W. Hubert Poole, Esq., the present Owner of the house on the left.
(Abbey Lodge)

PLATE XXVIII

RICHARD GRUBB, J.P.
As Widower and Squire of Cahir Abbey

LOWER CAHIR ABBEY HOUSES
(known as "The Barracks")

On the left: Richard's first married home; showing extension built as a music room
On the right: nearest to Cahir Castle the home of Barcroft Haughton Grubb.
The Mills behind

In the following years the Daniell family from the North of Ireland (from which family the late Bishop Knox of Manchester and his gifted sons were descended) and a host of visitors from all over Ireland came to stay. Maria rose to the occasion, and played her part to see that her eldest daughter Isabella was given as fine a wedding to Stephen Daniell in Cahir Parish Church, and afterwards at the Abbey as any of her aunts had had, or her younger sister Susan. Her husband died soon after the wedding, and she returned home, little knowing that her mission in life was to be the Grand Dame of Cahir Abbey to her widowed father, when her beloved Mother died in 1870, within seven years of moving her large family into the rambling abbey, with its huge basement kitchens. She had been an excellent wife, understanding, musical, less dominant than her predecessors to their Grubb husbands. A plain memorial in an alcove in the north wall of Cahir Church commemorates her. Richard Grubb, with 16 years of life to face as a widower, used often to ask himself, like his father before him: "Did I do right in moving into Cahir Abbey?" Already a Justice of the Peace, and with three daughters and two sons still in Cahir, he was able to face the future in the spirit of the hymn he chose to be sung at his wife's funeral—words that had been written by Richard Baxter, the Puritan Divine and Mystic who had so influenced his Baptist forefather, John Grubbe. They had but recently been adapted and published by John Gurney, another Quaker, of Norfolk:

Ye Blessed souls at rest	Ye saints, who toil below
who ran this earthly race	adore your heavenly King.
and now from sin released	and ONWARD as ye go
behold the Saviour's face.	some joyful anthem SING.
GOD'S PRAISES sound,	Take what he gives
as in His light	and PRAISE HIM still
with sweet delight	through good and ill
Ye do abound.	Who ever lives.

The song of praise and the sound of music that his beloved wife had shared with him for three and thirty years, the separation of death could not take from him. Richard was enabled through the ministry of singing and music to find peace and purpose and to bequeathe to his descendants that love of hymnody and harmony that has become so much a Grubb characteristic. Triumphantly he would hum and sing:—

My soul, bear now thy part,	So shall my days,
TRIUMPH in God above,	till life shall end,
and with a well-tuned heart	(what'e'er He send)
SING forth the songs of love;	be filled with praise.

N*

RICHARD GRUBB (JUNR.) 1812–1886 AND MARIA (*née* GARRETT) 1819–1870
(They had 11 children, all of whom survived their parents. Seven sons and four
daughters (all baptised in Cahir Church); and over 30 grandchildren (27 of them Grubbs).

1. RICHARD CAMBRIDGE	b. 1841; d. 1916	2 children
2. ALEXANDER	b. 1842; d. 1925	7 children
3. FREDERICK	b. 1844; d. 1919	11 children
4. HARRY PERCY	b. 1848; d. 1925	4 children
5. WILLIAM PIKE	b. 1850; d. 1915	3 children
6. CHARLES ALFRED	b. 1851; d. 1931	No children
7. GEORGE CARLETON	b. 1856; d. 1940	No children

1. Isabella	b. 1838; d. 1909; m. 1867, Stephen	No children
	DANIELL, son of Hugh Daniell, Esq.	
2. Susan	b. 1839; m. 1863, Alexander RICHARDSON	Large family (*a*)
	of Co. Antrim, son of Jonathan Richardson	
3. Maria Louise	b. 1842; d. 1890. Unmarried (*b*)	
4. Helena	b. 1854; d. 1938. Unmarried (*c*)	

(*a*) They spent their life at Lambeg House, Lisburn, Co. Down. Their eldest son,
Richard H. S. Richardson was chairman for many years of the Irish Keswick
Movement Conventions, and head of the family linen business in Belfast. His two
sons John (b. 1899) and Alexander (b. 1902) of Moyallon House, Co. Down,
succeeded him in the business.

(*b*) A memorial tablet was erected in her memory on the West wall of Cahir Church.

(*c*) Baptised privately, 1 February 1856. Blind most of her life. Died at Bournemouth.

    (2) For the descendants of Alexander, his second son, *see Chapter Fourteen.*
    (3) For the descendants of Frederick, his third son, *see Appendix "E"*
    (4) For the descendants of Harry Percy and for his 6th and 7th sons, *see Collateral Table "J"*

The GRUBBS in NORTHERN IRELAND are descended from:
  1. The eldest son, RICHARD CAMBRIDGE GRUBB (1841–1916), baptised 23
     July 1870 (the same day as his three eldest sisters, as adults); he married
     Harriet Richardson (d. 1930), daughter of Jonathan Richardson, Esq.,
     of Glenmore House, Co. Down. They lived at Killeaton House, Co.
     Antrim, and he joined the Richardson linen business in Belfast. They had
     two children:
     (1) Lilian b. 1871; m. Robert Henry Metge, J.P., LL.B. of Athlumney, Co.
        Meath (d. 1900), leaving two children.
     (2) RICHARD GRUBB, b. 1873, a veterinary surgeon, who married
        Helen Cameron; no children.

And from:
  5. The fifth son, WILLIAM PIKE GRUBB (1850–1915), baptised 31 October
     1850. He had the ablest business head in the family, and also joined the
     Richardson linen business in Belfast, where he was a director. He married,
     1889 Ethel Elizabeth, eldest daughter of Col. Lewis Mansergh Buchanan,
     C.B., F.R.G.S., of Edenfel, Omagh, Co. Tyrone (she died in 1910). They
     lived at Osborne Park, Belfast, and had three children:
     (1) Ethel Helena, b. 1893; m. 1921, her 2nd cousin, Joseph Alfred
        HAUGHTON, Esq., of Dublin (d. 1953). She has three daughters:
        (i) Jean, b. 1922; m. Percy BUCKLEY, 1946. Three children. They
           live in South Africa.
        (ii) Ethel, b. 1923; m. 1969, Henry WHITESIDE. They live outside
        (iii) Eleanor, b. 1932; unmarried.   [Dublin.
     (2) LEWIS WILLIAM RICHARDSON GRUBB, b. 1898. Educated at
        College La Chatelaine, Geneva. Served in World War I, 1915–1919
        with Royal Irish Rifles, R.F.C. and R.A.F.; m. 1925, Alice Kathleen,
        daughter of Thomas Alcester Hewlett, Esq., of London. They live
        in Belfast and have one son—BRYAN PIKE GRUBB, b. 1930.
     (3) RICHARD CAMBRIDGE WHITLA, b. 1899. Civil servant. Writer;
        broadcaster on landscape gardening. Educated St. Columba's College,
        Rathfarnham. Married 1925 (i) Isabel, daughter of William Hunter,
        of Fort William, Belfast. (ii) Kathleen Eunice, daughter of W. John
        Fowler, of Portadown. They have two children: (a) Karen Rosemary,
        b. 1948; (b) Richard Valentine Cambridge, b. 1950.

CHAPTER TWELVE

Richard Grubb, J.P.

Part II.   Squire of Cahir Abbey (1863–1886).   Widower (1870–1886)

AND

His Seven Sons

Missions of the Rev. GEORGE GRUBB, M.A. in Australia, and Russia, and Keswick

"Love took up the Harp of Life, and smote on all its cords with might:
Smote the chord of self, which trembling, passed in using out of sight."
—(Alfred, Lord Tennyson).

WITH his move into Cahir Abbey, a wider and fuller life of service had opened for Richard Grubb, Gentleman, the new Squire. He found himself completely in his element in the life of an Irish squire, with 750 acres of land now to look after.   Greatly as he missed his wife, he was not the man to sit back and repine and do nothing.   He would rather wear out than rust out.   His active temperament was always finding things to do, or that must be done.   He was not one to shout orders to others to do a job that he could do himself much more quickly, and probably much better.   He had now completely lost any "stand-offishness" or severity that had characterised the family in their Quaker days, and the tensions which faced his father had now resolved themselves. He had become genial and friendly with everybody, easy of approach, allowing no distinctions of education or social position or creed to become a barrier between himself and his neighbours.   There was nothing of the rich retired business man settling in a country sphere and station in life to which he was unaccustomed, about Richard Grubb.   Nor about any of his family, who were brought up by their father to know the meaning of honest work, to turn their hands to what needed to be done about the estate, to enjoy games and country pursuits, and to practise their religion.

With his disownment by the Quakers, Public Service of Queen Victoria in Her Armed Forces, and in the Professions was no longer denied his family.   Naturally Richard had soon been invited, on his removal into Cahir Abbey, to become a Justice of the Peace, not merely because of the position he occupied, but because of the man he had come to be.

He gave nearly 25 years to his work on the Tipperary Bench. Very deliberately as a result of his observations of his fellow Irishmen, and the experiences he had gained of human nature, he filled much of his time with this work, not merely the hours he spent upon the Bench. So much did he endeavour to temper justice with sympathy and understanding that it became widely known every defendant hoped for a lighter sentence if Mr. Grubb was sitting on the Bench. He never forgot his own experiences at the hands of the Quakers, and he developed his gift of trying and generally succeeding in seeing things from the opposite point of view to his own, and the reasons which had led to a man's crime or misdemeanour. There were not a few reformed characters through his efforts and influence. People felt he wanted to believe in them, that he would be quick to make every allowance if it was possible, that he disliked punishing if it could be avoided, and when all else seemed to have failed, his own innate humour often saved the situation. Two of his cousins at Clogheen, Samuel Richard (and Louis later) also served on the Bench, and with the passing of the years both his son ALEXANDER, his grandson ALEXANDER HENRY, and his great grandson ALEXANDER JAMES were to give of their time and energy and experience to the same work—in Kent on the Maidstone Bench, and in Cheshire.

But chiefly the companionship and interests of his growing family—while they remained in Cahir—filled his time. His widowed eldest daughter ISABELLA took her mother's place as the Chatelaine of the Abbey, assisted by her two sisters MARIA LOUISE (b. 1843) and HELENA (b. 1854) neither of whom ever married. They saw to it that their father, and such of their unmarried brothers still at home lacked nothing in the way of "good grub" and creature comforts. With her youngest brother GEORGE, Helena was particularly close. SUSAN the remaining sister had migrated North on her marriage to Alexander Richardson of Lambeg House, Lisburn, Co. Down, and one of her sons Richard H. S. Richardson became for many years the chairman of the Irish Keswick Convention. She was to be followed by her eldest brother RICHARD CAMBRIDGE, who married her sister-in-law Harriet Richardson in 1870, and joined the Richardson Linen Business in Belfast. Not long after, WILLIAM PIKE the fifth of Richard Grubbs' sons, said to have had the ablest business head of them all, followed suit and joined up with his elder brother and cousins in Belfast.

With the opening up of the Armed Forces and the Professions to his family, two of them had already received commissions in the Army before Maria died, and one after a brilliant university career had just been ordained into the Church of Ireland. ALEXANDER, the second son had seen service in Australia before being posted to New Zealand, to take part in the Maori War, to gain the New Zealand Medal, and to trace the landings of Captain Cook in the North Island. His letters home had thrilled his parents, and also young CHARLES, the sixth son, who followed suit, but after a much shorter Army career settled in Australia. PERCY, his fourth and perhaps cleverest son, outstanding in languages— a gift inherited from his forbears—and especially Greek, Hebrew and German, a lover of poetry and hymns, including German poetry, had begun his first curacy at Lambeg, where his elder sister Susan and her husband were living in the big house of the village. Richard and Maria had realised there was little to keep their virile and able sons in Cahir. Only Frederick and George were left at home. FREDERICK, the third son, who had been baptised as an adult and also married in Cahir Church to a local girl, Edith Going, shortly after his mother's death was given the "twin" Barrack House, empty since Richard and Maria had moved up the road into Cahir Abbey. He and Edith had another "batch" of eleven children born in this healthy home, all of them baptised in Cahir Church, five male Grubbs and six daughters, who later married into the Maynard, Stansfield, Holdcroft, McClintock and Riley families.

All seemed set for Frederick to succeed his father eventually at Cahir Abbey, until financial misfortune necessitated the sale of the Abbey after Richard's death, and Frederick migrated to California, where he died in 1919. One of his sons, also named Richard after his grandfather, a brilliant lawyer, later returned to Dublin and became one of the leading barristers in that Fair City. Several of Frederick's sons entered the Army and served in World Wars I and II, and a grandson, another Richard, was a prisoner-of-war in the hands of the Japanese, and is now settled in a commanding position in Vancouver. A youngest son is often particularly dear to his parents, and Richard Grubb saw more of GEORGE, his youngest son during the last fifteen years of his life than any of the others. He was outstandingly tall, and was only 14 when his Mother died. He gave his father companionship and also religious enthusiasms and interests fully to occupy him.

Out of the blue, it seemed, came a letter to Richard shortly after his wife's death, from his second son, ALEXANDER, about to commence a posting in Gibraltar, to say he had become engaged to the eldest daughter, Sara Mary (another Sarah, thought Richard) of the Vicar of Potters Bar, Middlesex, the Rev. H. G. Watkins, and his wealthy wife. Mrs. Watkins came from the exceedingly rich merchant banking city family of Bouse-field. "Could the Watkins family come over to Cahir Abbey to stay?" wrote Alexander; "they would like to meet all the Grubbs." Sudden emergencies were nothing new to Richard. The Grubbs always seemed to cope. "Of course," he wired back. "Name the date." The visit is recorded in one of Mrs. Watkins' diaries, in the writing of which she and

151

her daughter were almost as prolific as the Quaker Sarah Grubbs had been. It was a gift to be transmitted to her descendants.

Indeed, since the reign of the young Tudor King Edward VI, whose tutor (the former Provost of Eton) taught him diligently to keep his own daily journal (or Chronicles of the Day to Day Events at Court[1]), Journal Writing has been one of the practical results of the Protestant Reformation, and an overflowing source of knowledge and interest for the writer's future descendants, as for historians.

Came the day when the tall lithe figure of Richard Grubb, Esq., J.P., was to be seen standing on Cahir Station, with its rambler roses up the lamp-posts in full bloom, and buckets of flowers that were always kept watered and tended by the stationmaster adorning the platform, awaiting the arrival of the Dublin train. At Cahir Abbey the crested silver had been polished to perfection, the recently bought green banded Irish dinner service, with the Grubb crest painted on each piece laid on the long dining room table; under Isabella's supervision furniture and carpets had had an extra spring-clean by the plentiful staff of maids in the large house. . Such preparations are typical of nearly every Irish household large or little, to welcome back a returning son from across the seas. Hardly had the train stopped in the station, before a smartly uniformed Grubb was down on the platform to introduce the short stoutish figures of the Rev. and Mrs. Watkins, and their two vivacious daughters to his father, and the veritable Irish welcome they were to receive. Even the teams of horses were whinnying as the trunks were loaded, eager to be away and up to the Abbey.

Great travellers as the Watkins family had been all their lives, and continued to be—they used to spend six weeks every summer on the Continent —they had not been to Ireland before. During their stay at the Abbey, they were taken around, introduced to a quite bewildering number of other Grubbs, and shown the sights of the countryside, the splendour of the near-by Rock of Cashel, and the majesty of the Knockmealdown Mountains above Clogheen and Clonmel. The wedding of Alexander and Sara was fixed for the following May at Potters Bar.

For a comparison between earlier Quaker weddings of the family in Ireland[2] and at Isleworth in Middlesex, and the interests of its descriptive writing, a fairly long extract from Mrs. Watkins' diary of this church wedding at Potters Bar in Middlesex follows:—

"THE FIRST WEDDING IN THE FAMILY"

"It was the week before Christmas Day, which in the year 1870 fell on a Sunday. A family gathering was expected in our quiet vicarage, and the week was to be a busy one in preparing the decorations of the Church and other Christmas work. A case had been dispatched to

[1] *The Chronicles and Political Papers of King Edward VI.* W. K. Jordan.
[2] See pp. 75, 79, 95, 123–4, 130, 147.

Gibraltar containing tokens of remembrance from each member of the family to the one who was loved by all, shortly to become one of their number by his marriage with our eldest daughter. Monday always brought weekly letters from him, and on this particular morning they arrived with detailed arrangements as to obtaining three or four months' leave of absence, in order that the wedding might take place in May. It was expected that their first home would be in Gibraltar for the first year or so. These and other matters were discussed over the breakfast table, but in a moment ALL WAS CHANGED.

" . . . A telegram was brought in with these words—'I have a Staff appointment in Ceylon, and shall be at Southampton on Friday next. A.G.'

"So Christmas Day arrived with the most unexpected and most welcome addition to the home circle. Our dear son had also arrived from Oxford; all were rejoiced to be united again at this sacred season, and strove not to anticipate that half the globe would separate us before the following year. But the wedding must be hastened, and after a few weeks of happy intercourse at home, and local gatherings with friends and the preparation for a merry charade 'Ici on parle Francais' (which was unanimously pronounced a real success), Alexander must leave us to spend a month with his relatives in Ireland. The marriage was fixed for Tuesday, February 21st, THE LAST DAY BEFORE LENT.

"Now the preparations for this important event, and for a residence in a tropical climate occupied all our thoughts. A few days sojourn at the Langham Hotel enabled our dear Sara to take leave of many of her friends, to complete her trousseau, and to visit (as we have been accustomed to each New Year) various places of interest in London. These included a visit to the vast Albert Memorial Hall, now nearly completed, and to the Exhibition of Ancient and Modern Art at Burlington House. During our stay in London and for weeks besides, wedding presents of the most elegant and varied description had been flowing in from all quarters. One of the most unexpected and gratifying was from the Teachers and Children of our National Sunday and Infants School. One hundred and thirty-five subscribed to purchase a beautiful quarto Bible, bound in Morocco, with an emblazoned inscription, and on Wednesday, February 16th we all went to the Infants School that it might be formally presented & acknowledged in the presence of all the teachers, and a certain number of the children. A day or two later came another pleasing surprise—a presentation from 13 of the Tradesmen of the Village of an elegant electroplate salver and cake basket. Many of these have known all our children from their births, and we are privileged to live in a parish where a bond of friendly union unites all classes with their pastor and each other. . . .

"The final preparations of the Church had all to be made on the Monday, the covered way from the road to the porch lined with laurels & evergreens and carpeted. The principal part of the Christmas decorations were still remaining, but our friend Mrs. Robinson undertook to place camelias and other flowers on masse around the apse. Above the communion table were these words painted on a blue background with a border of orange blossoms— 'BLESS THEM, AND MAKE THEM A BLESSING'. The effect was lovely.

"In the vicarage tables had been put up in the drawing room for the wedding breakfast, and a profusion of exquisite camelias and other flowers sent by friends arranged for the decoration of the sittingrooms and the hall, where a device on crimson ground, framed with moss and snowdrops was hung 'God bless the Bride and Bridegroom' was hung. The numerous and beautiful presents were arranged in the Library for the inspection of visitors, who were invited to come and see them. From three until six o'clock we received a perpetual stream of guests, rich and poor—the Countess of Stratford & her three daughters, Lady Young, Mrs. Temple, and many other friends, tradesmen's wives and daughters, & a goodly sprinkling of the poor, who speak of Miss Watkins' wedding as a matter in which they take a personal interest. Their welcome little offerings are laid out among the more costly ones, pieces of embroidery or crochet, little bead mats and glass vases, but equally valued as presents with the same kindly wishes.

"The guests began to arrive at 6 p.m. Mrs. Daniell had come over from Ireland with her sister Maria Louise, who was to be one of the eight bridesmaids, for whom sky blue silk dresses and bonnets with streaming veils had been provided. Taking the place of the Bridegroom's mother, they were to stay in the vicarage a few days. Alfred and Emma Bousefield, my brother and sister-in-law, and Hugh & Mollie Huleatt with their three children, Constance and Fanny (to be bridesmaids) and little Hughie, who are sleeping at Parkfield with the Robinsons." (After other names, she adds that Richard Grubb is staying at a London hotel with two of his sons, the bridgroom and his brother William Pike and one of his nephews, Samuel Seymour Grubb (Groomsmen), and that his other sons and daughters could not manage to come over.) "They drove over on the wedding morning, not in their own carriage they had brought over from Ireland, which had broken a pole, but in a hired one, and brought the Best Man, Lt. F. W. Nind, R.A."

The Church was crowded. Nearly everyone in Potters Bar had assembled. The Watkins carriage was doing a shuttle service from the vicarage to the church, conveying guests, bridesmaids, Mrs. Watkins herself, and then Sarah Watkins on her brother Henry's arm. She was dressed in rich white poult de soie, trimmed with Brussels lace, panier of net and white satin, very long train, Brussels lace veil, & carried a wreath of bridal flowers, as did each of the 8 bridesmaids, the gift of Alexander. The Bridesmaids also carried each an ivory-bound prayerbook with hymns, the gift of the bride. 8 girls from her Sunday school class were standing on the steps of the church to receive her, dressed in white with pretty straw hats which Mrs. Watkins had bountifully provided. There were 8 groomsmen and the service was reverently and clearly conducted by the bride's father and her uncle, the Rev. Hugh Huleatt, Principal Chaplain at Woolwich.

Never was such a wedding in the long history of Grubb marriages.

PLATE XXIX

POTTERS BAR CHURCH, MIDDLESEX

Scene of the first Watkins–Grubb Wedding

Served by Rev. H. G. Watkins, M.A. (OXON), Vicar (1835–1889); and Rev. H. P. Grubb, M.A. (T.C.D.), Curate (1874–1879)

PLATE XXX

THE NEW ZEALAND MEDAL 1870

(As worn by the Bridegroom on his Wedding Day)

with the date appropriate to the period of active service of the recipient usually inserted within the wreath. Pieces with no dates, as above, are very rare. See also Plate XXXVI.

Alexander and Sarah left the reception at 4.30 p.m. under a shower of white satin slippers. As the Watkins carriage drove them away for their honeymoon at Windsor and Malvern, a party of redcoated huntsmen were waiting on the road to sound farewell upon their horns. Great was the excitement at this fanfare, and "Richard Grubb rushed down from the vicarage steps to thank them taking a flying jump over the two bottom ones. The poor were at their doors to see them go by, and some were lining the pavement as far away as Barnet to exchange a greeting, as they drove through". They went to Windsor for the first few days of their month's wedding tour. They had had a wedding fit for Royalty.

Back at Potters Bar about 20 of the invited guests took their leave; the remainder accompanied Mr. and Mrs. Watkins to attend the dinner at the Infants School for the tradesmen and their wives at 6 p.m. "The oldest inhabitant, Mrs. Cotton, was taken in by her pastor. Pleasant and cordial remarks enlivened the speeches." Back to the Vicarage went the untired relatives, themselves to sit down to another gigantic meal at the wedding tables, and a further succession of speeches. Richard Grubb, William Pike and Samuel Seymour left for London at 10.30 p.m. They paid another visit to the Watkins family the following Friday, were shown round the parish, and the site for an iron church Mr. Watkins was proposing to give to serve new houses being built at Little Heath, and then driven over to Hatfield Park for tea, the home of Lord Salisbury.

The costs of such a wedding 100 years ago are also given in the diary of Mrs. Watkins. They are illuminating:—

Account for Wedding Breakfast at 12s. 6d. each	£27 10s.
Extra for Dinner Party	£1 4s.
Bridal Cake	£5 5s.
Cooking 15s. and Waiting 19s.	£1 14s.
Total	£35 13s.

Ten times that price would be a low estimate today for such a reception. Mrs. Daniell and Miss Grubb entertained with singing after the dinner. They gave great pleasure, and had clearly learnt their lessons well on that famous piano at Cahir. "But for that piano," mused Richard Grubb, "this wedding of a soldier son of a former Quaker to a clergyman's daughter could never have taken place."

The Grubbs stayed on a few days in London, until the broken pole of their carriage was mended, and spent another day with the Watkins seeing the parish. The Kingstown Intelligencer records the rough journey they had returning to Ireland from the wedding. They well knew how rough the Channel can be. 100 years earlier John Wesley sometimes had to wait as long as a week in such weather, at either Holyhead or in Dublin before a ship could put out.

"A fierce gale all day had made the waters of Kingstown Harbour and of the Bay outside a surface of seething foam. Just beyond the East pier in the Man-of-War roads, her Majesty's ship 'Audacious' had come to anchor with top gallant masts struck, and heavy spars on deck, her massive iron-clad hull rising and falling momentarily as the heavy waves struck her bow. The storm flag was hoisted all day, and late in the day the 'Drum Storm Signal' was exhibited, a telegram announcing a gale having been received from London. The daily mail steamer 'The Connaught'—Capt Kendall in command —returning from Holyhead in the evening, experienced one of the heaviest passages in the winter. The seas off Holyhead were fearful, and the vessel was nearly one hour in gaining the open sea, the gale being a head one. The vessel however made a good passage in 5¾ hours, arriving at the Carlisle pier at 9.5 p.m., 25 passengers arriving with her. She was bringing Mr. Grubb, J.P. of Cahir Abbey, his daughters Mrs. Daniell and Miss Maria Grubb, Mr. W. P. Grubb, and Mr. S. S. Grubb. Both Holyhead and Kingstown were crowded with weather bound vessels."

Time the carriage was unloaded, it was much too late to think of starting the drive of over 100 miles back to Cahir that night, and they put up in a hotel. "It's been well worth it," said Richard, over and over again, clapping his hands (a habit of his, when he was excited and well pleased), "despite the terrible journey, I would gladly do it again!" Back in Cahir he never ceased to talk of the kindness of the Watkins family, his delight in his English daughter-in-law, and the appeal that this very Evangelical Church wedding had made upon him. His thoughts turned to his son PERCY. At the time he had not altogether approved of his desire to take Holy Orders, and remembered he had once told him he would surely starve, looking at it from a human point of view, so low were clerical stipends. True he had paid for him to have a year on the Continent, both to improve his French and German, but also to give him a breather after Trinity College, Dublin, to think things over, before rushing into ordination. Now that he was ordained, thought his father, what better than to introduce him to the Rev. and Mrs. Watkins at Potters Bar? That was the sort of parish that would suit him, where he would like to see him; Mr. Watkins had told him he was needing a curate now, with all the church extension he had to face at the Little Heath end of his parish on the Hertfordshire border near Hatfield. Rapidity of thought is an Irish characteristic, and since their sojourn in Cahir, a Grubb characteristic. The charm of Irish conversation is that it is undisciplined. Irish thought and expression are simultaneous. Irishmen, it is said, are continually surprising themselves by their own brilliance in conversation and repartee. Perhaps that is why they cannot help laughing with pleasure at their own jokes! Grubb biographical authorship reveals in many places this charming characteristic.

"Pity", reflected Richard, that Percy couldn't get over to Alexander's wedding. Anyway, William Pike (his fifth son, now living in Belfast) will certainly tell him about it when they get together; when the honey-mooners come to stay with me, I must see that they meet Percy, and interest him in P.B. (Potters Bar). So it was a month later at the end of their wedding tour when Alexander and Sara arrived at Cahir Station together a second time, the first thing Richard told them was: "You've got to go up to Belfast before you leave Ireland and see Percy." If the mountain could not be brought to Mohammed, then Mohammed must go to the mountain—that was always Richard's attitude. Obstacles mustn't stand in the way; they must be removed or surmounted! It is another charac-teristic of the successful man who gets things done. Alexander and Sara went to Ulster on leaving Cahir, and stayed with his brother Richard Cambridge and his wife, and met Percy; and within three years Percy joined the Rev. & Mrs. H. G. Watkins at P.B. This use of initials in their writing—not always immediately understandable to anyone else but themselves—is another characteristic of quick-thinking minds, who just haven't the time to write out in full every word again and again. Grubb handwriting was clear in the nineteenth century, but appears, it must be said, to have degenerated with the use of typewriters among their twentieth century descendants!

Percy spent a profitable five years at Potters Bar (1874–9), building up the work round the iron church at Little Heath that the Watkins money built for the parish. Little Heath is now a separate parish, and 60 years later the writer of this book often conducted services there. Happy years they were for both vicar and curate. Percy became like another son to Mr. and Mrs. Watkins, their own son Henry being now ordained, and their other daughter, Lilla, married (two years after Sara) to Dr. Edmund Symes Thompson. They were to have six Symes Thompson and seven Watkins Grubb grandchildren, although "Watkins" as a Christian name never appeared among the Symes Thompsons. In later years Percy (over 40 by that time) married Margaret Crichton-Stuart, a descendant of the Earl of Bute [Prime Minister in the time of George III]. The Bute family owned Cardiff Castle, much of Cardiff docks, and Mount Stuart, their home on the Island of Bute. Percy's mother-in-law came from a brilliant Huguenot family, the Labouchere family, possessed of the same French mercurial brilliance[3], very wealthy, and a real Victorian aristocrat. She became associated with the evangelical activities for the "upper classes" centering around Lord Radstock's large London home in Portman

---

[3] *Once Caught: No Escape.* Norman Grubb, M.C., pp. 15ff.

Square, and was an active and devoted Evangelical. Her grandson, Norman Percy Grubb, M.C. writes that she never really accepted an Irish clergyman as a son-in-law! The same use of family surnames as christian names—Crichton and Stuart—for his children and grandchildren appears among Percy and Margaret Grubb's descendants. All his children inherited his scholarship and flair for languages, his penmanship and writing ability and his evangelicalism and missionary interests. Three of them served as missionaries—in the Congo, in Amazonia, and in China, and throughout their lives have done more than most in developing ecumenicism and inter-denominational Christian activities. With such a heritage in their blood they have become known the world over; and are to-day the most distinguished "Grubb" descendants of Joseph and Sarah, builders of the Grubb fortune, of Samuel and Margaret, of the two Richard Grubbs, and of John, the Baptist Preacher.

To his five years' close association with the Rev. and Mrs. Watkins at Potters Bar, Percy owed his life-long interest in and work for the Church Missionary Society, of which he became for 12 years the Assistant General Secretary. He toured most of the world, [often with another C.M.S. Secretary, Eugene Stock] on its behalf (1885–1897). Mr. Watkins was a member of the C.M.S. General Committee, and Mrs. Watkins also for some years. Living conveniently close to Salisbury Square, they would drive in from Potters Bar in their coach and horses to attend the committees, in days when Fleet Street resounded with the patter (and dung) of horses and mules, and it was possible to move freely without crowds.[4]

Such is the link between the once Baptist and Quaker Grubbs from Ireland and the largest church missionary society, of which Percy's youngest son, Sir Kenneth Grubb, K.C.M.G., was later to be elected as the Society's President, and to serve for 25 continuous years. (See his biography.) He was also to serve for nearly as long a period as the Chairman of the House of Laity of the Church of England, and as Chairman of the (ecumenical) Church's Commission on International Affairs, and of nearly 50 other committees connected with church work. He served his country during World War II in the Ministry of Information, swiftly becoming Controller of Overseas Publicity, with rank equal to that of a Major-General, and was made a Companion of St. Michael and St. George for his services, and later knighted. How far reaching was his grandfather's disownment by the Quakers in 1844, and how much he owed to the Quaker blood of his ancestors can perhaps be judged by the words of an article

---

[4] The Rev. H. G. Watkins had been born within earshot of Bow Bells in the vicarage of St. Swithins and St. Mary's, London Stone—[of which for 44 years his father, another Rev. H. G. Watkins, was vicar]—and he knew the City of London very well. His father had been one of the original founding members of the Church Missionary Society in 1799, and was a great writer of somewhat long Victorian-style tracts and booklets for servant girls and others.

in the *Guardian* of July 4th, 1968 (accompanied by a cartoonist drawing) which stated:—

"If a single person can claim to be the Church of England, it's assuredly Sir Kenneth Grubb, who moves among the bishops like a sleepy whale amid codfish . . . as a chairman he is much sought after, and claims to act on a plan; but experienced ecclesiastical observers reckon he really gets by on a blend of no-nonsense piety, strategic craft and impromptu instinct."

Wise old Quaker Samuel Grubb of Clonmel and Clashleigh, Clogheen, seemed to be living again in his descendant!

Percy and Margaret Grubb had three sons, and one daughter, Dr. Violet Grubb, D.SC., of London University, who went out to China as an educational missionary attached to the Church Missionary Society, to serve as the only English teacher on the staff of a very special Chinese school for educated girls of high-ranking and aristocratic families under Miss Tseng. Later she served on the staff at Westfield before undertaking the headship of one of England's leading Girls' Public Schools (Westonbirt in Gloucestershire), a school housed in a magnificent mansion and park in the Cotswolds. This was followed by the Principalship of the Salisbury Teacher Training College, which nearly doubled its numbers during her reign. The Christian saintliness and scholarship of her Shackleton ancestors and their school work at Ballitore seemed to be resurrected in her never failing sweetness and smile, even when pursuing necessary disciplinary actions in her school work. Grubb organising ability shone forth in her administration. Her constant aim has been that each of her girls should find the basis of true character and purpose in life in the dominion and lordship of their Saviour Christ.

The long and active missionary life of Percy's elder son, Norman Percy Grubb, M.C., whose life of faith and tireless energy, coupled with the intense devotion of a sacrificial prayer-life, have made him from his army and university days at Cambridge a challenging and winsome evangelist among students and those "on the fringe of religion" both in the British Isles and in Canada and America, is well known. He was largely responsible for the foundation of 'Inter-Collegiate Christian Unions' in most of the British Universities, and all too modestly he has written of his life in his autobiography (*Once Caught: No Escape*. The Lutterworth Press 1969) to which the reader is referred. He has also written more than twenty "best-sellers" on the Christian Life. His debt to his Grubb and Shackleton ancestors stands forth on many pages. His life is comparable to the world-wide missionary labours of his uncle, the famed Keswick preacher and evangelist the Rev. George Grubb, M.A. Truly remarkable were to be his mission tours in Australia and South Africa and Ceylon, and the conversion to the Kingdom of God of literally tens of thousands of souls. Like his nephews, he became one of the world's really great men.

Richard and George Grubb were in Belfast in September 1874 to hear the farewell sermons of Percy, before leaving Ireland for Potters Bar, and to help him pack his things. They found the hoardings of the city and church notice boards placarded with posters:—"Moody will preach the Gospel; Sankey will sing the Gospel." They extended their visit to attend the meetings of these American Evangelists about whose three months' mission in Edinburgh the papers had been full. Richard was thrilled to discover the Belfast Quakers had joined with the Church and the Presbyterians in inviting them to Northern Ireland, despite all the singing they employed, and were all praying together for revival. Young George, at the impressionable age of 18, owed his conversion to Moody and his call to the sacred ministry for similar evangelism.

When crossing the Atlantic to Ireland, Moody was asked why he was coming to Britain? "For ten thousand souls", was his reply. Richard Grubb (30 years after his disownment by the Quakers) counted 1874 as another year of destiny, and rejoiced that his youngest and dearest son should be one of those "Ten Thousand", and an answer to the Ulster Quakers prayers. Richard and George supported Moody and Sankey all they could in Belfast, and George followed them to Limerick and Queenstown, absorbing their teachings, methods, and singing, content to be allowed to act as a steward at their meetings. Years later, after training at Trinity College, Dublin and ordination, and two Irish curacies, he began a life of mission preaching himself, travelling the world over, and in Australia where perhaps his greatest work for the Master was done, winning 10,000 souls and many more into the Church of God. Writes his nephew Norman Grubb, M.C., who shared his outlook and was as greatly used by God in mission work as his uncle[5]:—

> "It was the great number brought to Christ in the Church of England in New South Wales, that gave Sydney Diocese and its Archbishopric its evangelical foundations, which have lasted until today."

George Grubb never did things by halves. With his Irish wit and infectious fun, his love of music and singing, and his great height (during his curacy at Limerick to a Dr. Jacob, he won the nickname "Jacob's Ladder"), he towered head and shoulders above the average evangelist, and he possessed all the courage, aristocratic bearing, and Bible knowledge of any of his forbears or successors in God's Vineyard. He always counted Cahir Abbey as his home, even after it had been sold. That address appears under his name to the forewords to the many books

[5] *Once Caught: No Escape.* Norman Grubb, M.C., p. 33.

PLATE XXXI

The Rev. GEORGE CARLETON GRUBB, M.A. 1856–1940
Keswick Missioner and World Evangelist

of sermons and Bible readings he published.[6] That memorable Grubb piano at Cahir resounded times without number to the Sankey hymn that came to mean as much to him as to his father:—

> "Ten Thousand hearts to Jesus
> How gladly we would give
> Ten thousand lives to Jesus
> Had we so long to live.
>
> Ten thousand tongues shall praise Him,
> Ten thousand songs ascend
> To Him our blest Redeemer,
> To Him our dearest Friend."

Within ten years of his ordination George was invited to the Keswick Platform. His name occurs year after year among the distinguished list of Keswick Speakers until 1924, with the exception of patches of three or four years when he was in settled ministry in the Church of England in South Africa, or at the other side of the world on his missions. "Your life is no good," he would say, "unless each day you influence someone around you to trust more in God than when he rose in the morning." He moulded his sermons and sermon preparation on Moody, with a fund of common sense and simple directness of speech. Straight home addresses they were—perhaps containing "too much meat" for a twentieth century congregation—spontaneous utterances from his heart with many an illustration from his experiences and a fund of Irish humour. At the 1895 Keswick Convention he said he had come home from Alexandria quite alone on a cargo steamer with 9,000 cocks and hens. "Times of deep solemnity are often experienced at Keswick, but the play of genuine humour has never been felt to be out of place," writes Walter Sloan in his History of the Keswick Movement[7] "and when the huge audience thought of all those birds crowing and cackling while George Grubb was singing, something like a responsive crow passed over the tent."

Canon Hay Aitken tried to get the Rev. George Grubb, M.A., as a full time missioner for his recently formed Church of England Parochial Mission, and George acknowledges his indebtedness to him in the preface to one of his books.[8] But God had a yet wider ministry in store for him, and soon after his first appearance on the Keswick Platform in 1888 (he was always sorry his father never lived to accompany him) he was chosen by the Keswick Trustees to be Keswick Missioner for the extension of its message of Holiness around the world, and in particular to English colonists and tea-planters in Ceylon, and missionaries themselves. God

---

[6] Among them: *Christ's Full Salvation* (1890–1896), 4 editions; *Covenanted Blessings* (1893); *Unsearchable Riches* (1897) (delivered in Toronto): all printed and published by E. Marlborough & Co., London.

[7] *These Sixty Years*. The story of the Keswick Convention, by Walter B. Sloan, pp. 34–39, 44, 46, 70, 75, 79, 86, 87.

[8] *Christ's Full Salvation* (1896). E. Marlborough & Co. London.

was again picking upon the Grubb family for itinerant evangelism, as He had once called the Lady Grubbs, and in another generation was to call Norman and Kenneth and Henry Grubb, George's nephews. George himself had no children.

In July 1914, just before the start of World War I, George Grubb got back from conducting great missions in Russia (where he had the help of Pastor Adam of Esthonia as interpreter) to the Keswick Platform to tell of God's saving power in that vast land, and of great blessing to His preaching at the Russian Court, and before the Czar. The Keswick Report speaks of his messages as full of humour and full of helpfulness.

At the 1919 Missionary Meeting at Keswick, the Rev. C. W. Lack, just back from China, told how he had been led to Christ in Australia through the Rev. George Grubb's ministry 25 years before, which had led him out in faith to China with the China Inland Mission. In 1924, the beloved Baptist leader, Dr. F. W. Meyer, speaking of his recent mission in Australia said he had found the name of the Rev. George Grubb lovingly remembered in many parts of that great continent, and the manifestation of God's Power through him at the Geelong Convention in 1892, and particularly that oft-repeated saying of his—"Each must *use* the gifts God has given him, or he will *lose* his usefulness in God's service".

Archbishop Howard Mowll, former Archbishop of Sydney, in his biography tells of the tremendous influence at Cambridge upon himself and a great many undergraduates when George Grubb conducted two C.I.C.C.U. (The Cambridge Inter-Collegiate Christian Union) Missions during youth's impressionable days. [9] Let the last word lie with Dr. Eugene Stock, Secretary of the C.M.S., in a preface to one of George Grubb's many books (1891)[10]

> "This is a remarkable record of *modern miracles*. It tells of miracle after miracle of grace in the hearts of men in all conditions of life. I do not envy the man who can read unmoved the incidents on Grubb's journey from Colombo to Melbourne with the jockeys and theatrical troupe on board. . . ."

Are Evangelistic Missions worthwhile? Do the Converts last? To the scoffers from George Grubb's time to the recent great missions of the American Evangelist Billy Graham, who continue to ask such questions and to others who suggest that planning and committee work are the better way to revive and improve the church's organisation in the hope thereby of modernising the approach to the unchurched multitudes, such testimonies, and the lasting work of George Grubb and of his nephews,

[9] *Life of Howard W. K. Mowll, Archbishop of Sydney, and Primate of Australia,* by Marcus L. Loane. Hodder & Stoughton. 1960. 246 pp. This was in 1911.
[10] *What God Hath Wrought* by George Grubb. 1891 (Marlborough & Co.)

Ernest, Norman, Kenneth and Henry give the answer. Let it be broadcast far and wide. God deals with individuals. Souls are won one by one. He calls, prepares and sends forth his own chosen ones as Evangelists. Said George Grubb: "A Committee never won a single soul for Christ."

George was the last of the seven sons of Richard Grubb to leave Cahir. After his father's death in 1886, and the subsequent sale of Cahir Abbey, the great dispersal of the Grubbs into all the world was over.

Never to be forgotten was that final day when sons and daughters gathered round their father's bedside as he was passing from the great silence of little worlds to the infinite harmony and music of the divine; George led the singing of a hymn—one of Sankey's that they had sung in Belfast at the time of his conversion during the great Moody Mission— none could have been more expressive of the faith and purpose of the Grubbs. Richard tried to beat time, with that characteristic Grubb gesture of his hands, as if cheering them on:—

> "Ho, my comrades, see the signal
>   Waving in the sky;
> Re-inforcements now appearing,
>   Victory is nigh.
>
> Hold the Fort, for I am coming
>   Jesus signals still.
> Wave the answer back to Heaven,
>   By Thy grace, we will.
>
> See the glorious banner waving,
>   Hear the trumpets blow.
> In our Captain's name, we'll triumph
>   Over every foe.
>
> Fierce and long the battle rages,
>   But our help is sure,
> Onward comes our Great Commander,
>   Cheer, my brethren, cheer."

Richard's hands beat more feebly, as the Divine Hands clasped them to take him safely across the river, and he began to "hear the voice of harpers, as the voice of a great thunder, singing a new song before the Throne of Heaven, and to see the Lamb standing on (the fortress of) Mount Zion".[11] He was buried among his ancestors in the Quaker Burial Ground in Clonmel; two simple memorials inside Cahir Church commemorate his wife and himself.

[11] Revelation, xiv, 2, 3.

The Second Half of the Family of RICHARD and MARIA GRUBB (died aged 51), were born after their disownment by the Quakers in 1843. (*See also Collateral Table "I"*)

4. HARRY PERCY, their fourth son, and seventh child (1848–1925) was baptised as an infant in Cahir Church, 31 October 1850. Trinity College, Dublin. M.A. The first of the Grubbs to become a clergyman. Ordained deacon 1870 by the Bishop of Down; priest 1872. Curate of Lambeg, Co. Down, 1870–72. Christ Church, Belfast, 1872–74. Potters Bar (Diocese of London) 1874–79 (in charge of Little Heath). St. John, Moulsham near Chelmsford, 1879–83. Holy Trinity, Waterford 1883–85. He was Assistant Secretary of the Church Missionary Society, 1885–97. Vicar of Oxton, Notts, 1897–1905 and St. Paul's, Poole, Dorset. He married 1892, Margaret Crichton-Stuart, daughter of James Crichton-Stuart, Esq. of the Foreign Office; a descendant of the Marquis of Bute of Cardiff Castle, and of the Labouchere (Huguenot) family. They had three sons (educated at Marlborough) and one daughter.

(1) HAROLD CRICHTON-STUART, M.C., B.A. Unmarried, d. 1954.
(2) NORMAN PERCY, M.C., b. 2 August 1895. For full details of his long missionary and evangelistic life, see his biography: *Once Caught: No Escape* (1969). He married 1919, Pauline Studd, daughter of C. T. Studd, Esq., famous cricketer and missionary. Three children:
   (i) PAUL CAMBRIDGE, b. 1924; m. He has one son, NICHOLAS GRUBB.
   (ii) Margaret Priscilla, b. 1925.
   (iii) DANIEL STUDD, b. 1927. Ph.D. University of Michigan; Associate Professor, Indiana University of W. Pennsylvania; married, one son, DANIEL GRUBB.
(3) Violet Margaret, B.SC., D.SC. (LOND.). Missionary in China. Head mistress Westonbirt School, Glos.; Principal Salisbury Teacher Training College. Retired 1962.
(4) (Sir) KENNETH GEORGE, K.C.M.G. (1942), LL.B., Fellow of St. Peter's College, Oxford. Poet, yachtsman, traveller, missionary in S. America, linguist, author. Controller of Overseas Publicity, Ministry of Information 1941–46; Sec.-Gen. Hispanic Council, 1946–54; President, Church Missionary Society, 1943–68; Chairman House of Laity, Church Assembly, 1959–70; Kt. Bach. (1953), etc. (See his biography—*Crypts of Power* (1971). Married (i) Eileen Sylvia Knight, daughter of A. H. Knight, Esq. of Oxton (d. 1932). Two sons:
   (i) (The Rev.) MARTYN PATRICK, b. 1927. Clare College, Cambridge, B.A. 1951. Ordained 1957 deacon; 1958 priest, by Bishop of London; curate of St. Peter de Beauvoir, W. Hackney. *Industrial Missioner*, working in industry himself from 1960. Married 1951, Anne Bath, daughter of Bernard Bath, Esq., of Sevenoaks. They have three sons and one daughter:
    (a) DAVID, b. 1952. (b) Marion Eileen, b. 1954; (c) KENNETH ANDREW, b. 1957; (d) MICHAEL JOHN, b. 1960.
   (ii) FREDERICK STUART, b. 1930. Educated Haileybury and Trinity College, Cambridge. M.A. Poet and writer. Unmarried. Sir Kenneth married (ii), Nancy Mary, daughter of C. E. Arundel Esq. of Highgate, in 1935. Two children:
    (a) RICHARD KENNETH ARUNDEL, b. 1936. Unmarried.
    (b) Margaret, b. 1939; m. The Rev. Robert Jackson. Three children: Helen (b. 1962); Ruth (b. 1967); and Andrew (1964).

5. WILLIAM PIKE, their fifth son. See Collateral Table "I".
6. CHARLES ALFRED, their sixth son (1851–1931), baptised 1 February 1856; married Alice Britton, of Sydney, New South Wales, and settled in Australia.
7. GEORGE CARLETON, their seventh and their youngest son (1856–1940), baptised 1858 at Cahir, educated at Trinity College, Dublin. M.A. Ordained 1880 by the Bishop of Cashel, was curate of Cahir 1880–85 and of Limerick 1885–88. Keswick Speaker from 1888–1924, he became travelling evangelist and missioner for the Keswick Covention throughout the world from 1889. Incumbent of Christ Church, Johannesburg (Church of England in South Africa) 1925–30. He married Esther Wemyss Disney 1906. No issue, but thousands of spiritual children through his great campaigns in Australia, India, Ceylon, and U.S.A. Author of many books on his missions and of published sermons including *Unsearchable Riches*.

CHAPTER THIRTEEN

Lt.-Col. Alexander Grubb, J.P.
1842—1925

Born at Cahir. Royal Artillery, 1861–1884
Served in the Maori War; in Ceylon; Malta; Gibraltar; Co. Wicklow;
The Hartlepools and Woolwich
of
Stone Castle, Kent and Elsfield House, Maidstone.
He married Sara Mary Watkins, of Potters Bar, Middlesex

"To follow the Christ, the King;
Live pure; Speak true; Right wrong.
To follow the King; else wherefore born?"

"The Happy Voyagers"

A LEXANDER was born in County Tipperary two years before his parents were disowned by the Quakers. He grew up under the shadow of Cahir Abbey and Cahir Castle without the restrictions his father had known in a Quaker home. He chose to be baptised as an adult in Cahir Parish Church. He was the first Grubb for 200 years to serve in the Army, and was to voyage the world over—to Australia, New Zealand, Ceylon, Malta and Gibraltar in the service of Queen Victoria. Neat and tidy, an artist and diarist, methodical with all the inherited Grubb organising ability and a love of "knocking things together", of carpentry and collecting things, he might well have become a Methodist, but there were none in Cahir. He would have made a first-class teacher— an instructor in Army affairs he was—his Bible knowledge and study and disciplined life would have made him a good clergyman, like two of his brothers. God called him to serve in the Army. His service life was to be typical of that of most of Queen Victoria's officers.

Born in one of the Barracks (as the family jokingly called their first home) he was 17 when his grandfather Richard died at Cahir Abbey up the road; he had already left home and Ireland to join the Army (as so many Irishmen were doing), before his parents moved into Cahir Abbey after his grandmother's death in 1863. Childhood days were happy ones in a closely knit family circle, with two elder sisters and a brother, and then in due course, five more brothers and two more sisters; with six cousins living next door, and a number more in Clogheen and Clonmel. The Grubbs had their cricket team in one of the Abbey fields, and once a year Seniors and Juniors would turn out to play the town, as well as for other matches. He couldn't leave home without being conscious each day of the great massive turreted Cahir Castle in the centre of the town, with its Anglo-Norman keep and high walls enclosing several irregularly shaped courtyards, with cannon on the walls, looking what it has always been—a stronghold and fortress and place of defence. It had been restored in part, and was in remarkably good state of repair, one of the few of Ireland's 3,000 castles to be maintained and inhabited. The castle had belonged to the Earls of Ormonde for some hundreds of years, and dated from the twelfth century; it played its part in the Elizabethan and Cromwellian Wars, and was considered impregnable. It was besieged in vain by the Earl of Essex in 1599, and battered with his heavy guns; Oliver Cromwell had captured it without much resistance. A curtain wall followed the contour of the ground, strengthened by three strong towers and four smaller circular ones. Inside the inner court was a very strong keep.

The castle had become the home of the Butler family, with whom the Grubbs were on excellent terms, and its perfect medieval hall was sometimes used for dances, to which they would be invited. Between the Castle and his home in one of the "Barracks" ran a great, wide, and sloping street, like a parade ground, where the Grubb brothers often played as soldiers. The very word "Cahir" means a fort, usually a stone fort; its original Irish full name was *Cathair Dun lascaigh* and later *Cahir Doon laskig* which means "The Fortress of the Fish Abounding Dun" (or stream). Other fortresses had occupied this strong site by the River Suir before the castle was built; it had in the early ages been the home of "Brian of the Tributes", and was also mentioned in the Brehon Laws.[1] Alexander spent hours as a lad climbing its ramparts. Coming home to tea one day, he solemnly announced to his parents, "You don't know what I am going to be when I am a man, do you? (pause) I am going to be a soldier. I want to look after forts and castle and canon. And one day I shall own a castle of my very own, like the Butlers do". He added: "What's the good of grandfather's old Abbey ruins? They're nothing like so good". Just to be different, younger brother Percy said: "Alex, we ought to be glad we live by an abbey. It's where the monks used to read the scriptures and chant the psalms. When I'm grown up, I want to do the same, and tell the 'stories of Jesus' to people." Their mother never forgot their remarks; strangely prophetic they were. She

[1] *Irish Castles*, H. G. Leask, pp. 123, 143, 145. *Munster*, Sean Jennett, p. 219. *In Search of Ireland*, H. V. Morton. p. 71.

was wise enough to know that when a boy decides at an early age what he wants to do with his life, nine times out of ten he will reach his goal. She realised the influence of the castle and the abbey ruins on her boys. Freed from Quaker restraints their father put no obstacle in their way; both brothers achieved their aim. The influence of Cahir Castle upon young Alexander, coming so soon after his father's disownment by the Quakers and their joining the Church of Ireland, cannot be overestimated. In this way God's guidance came to him to be a soldier, and further to seek to enter the Artillery. Later, in God's providence he was to be posted to Ceylon to live in an old fort, and his main duties to study and report on the condition of the many coastal forts in that island. On his retirement from the army and in search of a permanent home for his family, this same interest in castles led him to find and buy a castle of his own—Stone Castle—in Kent, overlooking the shipping in the Thames between Dartford and Greenhythe.

Another day Alexander said to his brother: "Percy, you're right about the monks singing and reading the Bible in the old abbey. All of us Grubbs must witness for the Lord, and sing his praises; I must do that if I get into the Army". So it was that during his 24 years military service, he never let a Sunday pass without supporting the army chaplain, if he possibly could, at garrison or parade service; if there was no chaplain he often conducted divine service himself. Every Sunday afternoon he had a group of soldiers in his home in Trincomalee Fort in Ceylon for a Bible Class. Sara, his wife played the piano or harmonium, and the hymns he had learned as a boy round that notorious first piano in the family, would resound through the opened window. "Fight the good fight"—"Soldiers of Christ arise"—"I'm not ashamed to own my Lord, nor to defend His cause. . . ." These and many other hymns and choruses were not only a witness in their very words to his men, but they expressed his own ever deepening faith in the security and strength which was his through Christ. A favourite text he gave later to each of his sons at their confirmation, and passed on by him to the author of this book, exactly expressed all he owed to his ancestors, and the experience in life he had made his own for ever—

"I can do all things, through Christ which strengtheneth me."

Whatever Alexander did, he did heartily; every morning he and Sara would read a portion of the Bible together, generally the Scripture Union portion for the day. The number of marked commentaries, mostly small slim books easy to carry, that filled his homes, and were passed on to his children and grandchildren, ran into hundreds. Every evening his diary was as religiously written up, as any report he might have to send in. The purchase and packing of a piano in the days that preceded his marriage, and its dispatch to Ceylon, is referred to more than once in his diary, as also in that of Mrs. Watkins. Such forethought typified his orderly and methodical mind. He could witness to Christ, his Captain and Master, in the Army, where such witness was needed, and throughout his long life he never wavered in giving such witness wherever opportunity offered. Like-minded friends he made, and he had close affinity with his two clergymen brothers, by letters and by prayer when they were at other ends of the globe; each helped the other. Army chaplains were welcomed to his home, and received his fullest support in their work for the troops. During his Malta service, and after his retirement, organisations for the welfare of soldiers, such as "The Army Scripture Readers and Soldiers Friend Society" (many of whose prayer and praise papers are found stuck in his diaries, or inserted in his commentaries and prayerbooks, which have passed to the author of this book), and the Soldiers and Sailors Family Association (Sara in her Stone Castle Days used to raise £1,000 a year for the Dartford Branch of which she served as president and treasurer), had his fullest interest and support.

Loyal member of the Church of England as he became, and in later years a churchwarden, encouraging one of his five sons, Ernest, to seek holy orders, no matter the pay, Alexander frequently expressed his own admiration for John Wesley as the outstanding type of Army chaplain, who succeeded in bringing soldiers face to face with God. He was always proud of the high regard and affection his great-grandfather Garrett and his Clonmel ancestors Joseph and Sarah, and Samuel and Margaret entertained for the founder of Methodism; he believed that had there been a Methodist cause established in Clonmel, his ancestors might well have joined them, and he would be a Methodist. The four volumes of *Wesley's Journals* (now inherited by the author of this book) he kept near him on his bookshelves, that he might often refer to them, marking in pencil (another Grubb characteristic) passages that especially appealed to him. One such marked passage is Wesley's account of his experiences at Athlone in Ireland at the end of an Open-air Service.[2]

> "When I had given the blessing and dismissed them, no one seemed willing to go. We were standing looking at each other, when a trooper stepped out and said: 'I must speak. I was Saul. I persecuted anyone who called himself a Christian. I hated God and all his ways. I hated you. I spoke evilly of you. I was going after a woman last night, when Cpl. —— asked me to come to the Watchnight. There God struck me so that I could not stand it. I slept nothing last night, and came to you in the morning, but I could not speak to you. Now we will part no more.' His words were a fire; they kindled a flame which spread through the congregation. We praised God with one heart and voice. Then a second time I pronounced the blessing. But the people stood without motion

[2] *Journals of the Rev. John Wesley, A.M.* Vol. ii, pp. 190–192.

as before, until a dragoon stepped from his fellows and spoke up. 'I was a Pharisee from my youth, having a strict form of godliness: yet I always wanted something I had not got, I know not what, until something pushed me on to hear you. I have done so, since you were here. What I wanted was FAITH, and now God has supplied my need. I can now rejoice in God my Saviour'."

Though his youngest brother George did not start his mission preaching until Alexander had retired from the Army, he used often to write him and tell of similar witness given by converts at his meetings. Such testimonies always inspired him. He believed a Christian's first duty was to let others know what he was, to witness for his Master, and then to help others to put their trust in Him. Whether or no Cahir Castle had had a similar effect on George as on Alexander, both brothers were alike in their concern to conserve and protect the scriptural foundations of life.

It was an Army Chaplain, the Rev. Hugh Huleatt, principal chaplain at Woolwich, and his bride's uncle, by marriage, who officiated with Alexander's father-in-law, at his wedding, and gave the exhortation.[3] Afterwards in proposing the toast at the wedding breakfast in Potters Bar vicarage, he said: "The Bishop of Winchester used to say he never gave his sons-in-law that title, but he received them as his own sons, given to him not by the law, but by God." Alexander never forgot that remark, and when years later his own five sons and two daughters came to be married, he always treated their partners in the same way, and with the same affection. So close did Alexander come to his father-in-law, and all that their "low" church religion meant to them both, that he gladly continued the Grubb practice of giving every one of his children the name Watkins as a christian name, a practice his sons were to continue, and his grandsons in their turn. So the "Watkins Grubb" branch of the family began.

When the time for boarding school arrived, it was Grandpapa and Grandmamma Garrett in Dublin, whose advice decided Richard and Maria where to send Alexander. Ballitore was no longer in existence; if it had been, a Quaker school was no place for a budding soldier. Alexander's aptitude with his hands was in his favour, but he was not good at maths. The Garretts suggested the establishment of the Revd. William Stackpoole at Kingstown close to them, where they could keep an eye upon him, and where special coaching in maths was a feature of the school.

Alexander worked hard at Kingstown, and in 1858 Mr. Stackpoole could report "Alexander is doing remarkably well in his work. You need not have the slightest doubt about his success (please God) next July." It was a year before Richard (Senior) Grubb died at Cahir Abbey,

[3] The Barnet Press. Feb. 25th, 1871.

and to reassure the old man that his grandson was getting all the coaching necessary at Kingstown (Grandfather never quite approved of a Grubb not going to Ballitore where he had been), Alexander's father wrote again to his son's headmaster. The Revd. Mr. Stackpoole replied:

"My Dear Sir,
"Alexander is doing exceedingly well. He is getting on famously in the Mathematics, the chief portion of the business. The only fault I have to find with him he is working too hard. He sometimes looks done up. I will keep a close eye on him in this respect, that he does not defeat himself in the end. I am, dear Sir,
Yours very truly
W. Stackpoole.
Richard Grubb, Junior.   Kingstown.   Nov. 4, 1858."

A good headmaster knows his boys. School reports are worth preserving (as the above from the Grubb Family album), and often reflect a boy's subsequent career. Alexander always worked too hard throughout his life, yet was wiry and strong enough to escape any serious illness until old age came on. He was successful in passing into the Royal Military Academy at Woolwich in the summer of 1859, and when the news reached him on his summer holiday at Lake Windermere, his former headmaster wrote at once to congratulate him (in the somewhat stilted language of the period):

"My dear Grubb
"Allow me to wish you joy. You worked well, and have your reward. May you meet with all happiness and prosperity in your new profession is the sincere wish I have to offer to a most exemplary and—beyond all praise—a well-conducted pupil, viz Alex'er Grubb.
Your sincere friend
W. Stackpoole.   Aug. 1, '59"

Richard and Maria were well pleased and proud of their second son Next month the Grubb family's long connection with the Army was to commence, and Alexander began a constant life of travel, crossing from Dub ın to Holyhead (as he was to do many times, often thinking of John Wesley's delayed crossings in the previous century), and down to Kent, a part of the world he came to like so well as to settle there permanently in the castle of his dreams, when army days were done.

Training at the Royal Military Academy lasted two years, and on May 15, 1861 Alexander's commission as Lieutenant in the Royal Artillery was gazetted on the same day as that of His Royal Highness, the Duke of Cambridge, General Commanding-in-Chief, to be Colonel of the Royal Regiment of Artillery. Lieutenant A. Grubb was appointed to the 15th Brigade stationed at Pembroke Dock, South Wales.

He was in Kingstown again next year for the funeral of his Grandmother Garrett (1862), just before setting off on the long voyage to Australia (again the first of several of his brothers to take this trip), on his posting to Melbourne. Not a full year later on the outbreak of the Maori War in New Zealand, he was posted to the North Island, probably because he was an Irishman. It was a time when there were a great many Irishmen in the British Army, serving in all ranks. He often used to say "But for us Irishmen where would the poor old army be?" Later in old age he would love to point out that Ireland gave 250,000 of its sons to the Armed Forces in World War I. The Irishmen that he met in the Army were of two kinds, and in contact with both types he was equally happy.

(i) There were the Irishmen of English descent, like himself, who were generally Officers and Protestants.

(ii) There were Irishmen of pure Irish descent, generally Roman-Catholic and Sergeant-Majors.

Alexander went to New Zealand when he was 21, and he served with Irishmen of both types. He had been too young for the Crimean War, and the Army had retired him long before the Boer War or World War I, when his sons were to represent his family with gallantry. In his 23 years military service, the three years of campaign against the Maoris were to be his one experience of action against an enemy. He was the only Artillery Officer present at the engagement of Te Ranga (June 21st, 1864), and was in command, being mentioned in dispatches.[4] He was awarded the New Zealand Medal in 1870—medal collectors today know how few of them are in existence, and how expensive they are to buy. While in camp he filled many idle minutes with a number of beautiful water-colours, some of which in the present century have been bought by the New Zealand Government. Stamp-collecting and carpentry were two other hobbies and interests of his life, the former dating from his New Zealand days, and both hobbies that have passed down to his sons and grandsons. With so much water about their camp, the knocking together or adaption of small boats and canoes was a duty he excelled in, and reminded him of the experiences of one of his ancestors in building a somewhat larger boat at the other side of the world (*Chapter Five*). Character was being formed in the roughing of camp life and actions against the Maori during these three years.

A well-worn small fat calf-bound copy of the *Three Voyages of Captain Cook round the world*, published in 1833, running into 635 pages was upon his bookshelves in retirement, and is now in the possession of the author of this book. Whether Alexander had asked his father to send the copy out to him, or had studied it in his school days in Ireland, he read up all he could about Captain Cook and his landings in New Zealand. Strange that Capt. Cook received his commission as Lieut. (Navy) exactly one hundred years before he had received his (Army). It was stranger still that at Tauranga he should be in camp close to the

4 See Appendix "C".

Bay of Plenty, and Cape Turn-Again, Gable End Foreland, and Hicks Bay, scenes of Capt. Cook's first landing in New Zealand. He must get over to explore, if military duty and safety permitted. Though a hundred years had passed, he found the Maoris were still using their pattoo-pattoo club, about five feet in length, ribs of whale ornamented with dog-hair, and similar finely carved and ornamented canoes. They still used the black Amoca to stain their faces and their thighs, small interstices of flesh being left visible. Little wonder that one day he would need a large enough house for all the New Zealand curios that he was to take home with him. Such was the excitement and interest of the travel of Army life one hundred years ago in an age that could not conceive modern weapons of warfare, and in which hand-to-hand fighting with the Maoris savours today of the scrummages of a rugger match.

The citation in Colonel H. H. Greer's dispatch, forwarded by Lieut.-General D. A. Cameron to His Excellency Sir George Grey, K.C.B., etc., etc., on the action at Tauranga (sometimes written Te Ranga), reads:

"Lieutenant Grubb, R.A., whose coolness and excellent practice with the 6-pounder Armstrong under his command, when under fire during the action, and subsequently on the retreating Maoris when they had got beyond the reach of infantry, was admirable."

The number of Irish surnames in this dispatch suggests that it was because he was an Irishman himself that Alexander Grubb was selected as the only Artillery Officer to join the 43rd and 68th Lt. Infantry under the command of another Irishman, Col. Harry Greer, and to serve throughout the campaign of Waikato, and at Gate Pa.

Alexander Grubb's pacifist Quaker forebears might well turn in their graves in the secluded tree-lined and walled-in Quaker burial ground in distant Clonmel, did they know of their grandson's fire on the retreating Maoris. Cool and admirable as his obedience to his duties had been, the experience left an indelible mark upon him, and he was always thankful that in his subsequent military appointments he was never in action against an enemy again. New Zealand made him a life-long supporter of the Church Missionary Society, and of the work of its heroic bishops Selwyn and Patterson.

January 1866 saw Alexander back in Australia, stationed now at Sydney in New South Wales, 25 years later to be the scene of his younger brother George's remarkable evangelistic missions (*see previous chapter*), as well as the future home of another brother Charles Grubb, when he came out of the Army.

Eighteen-sixty-seven brought Alexander back to England for well-earned leave at Cahir, and to enjoy some family life in Cahir Abbey, into which his parents had moved. Much of his time was occupied with carpentry, and repair of the large outbuildings and stables, as well as many contacts with his contemporaries in the town, and at Clogheen and Clonmel. Life in this spacious home, with his sisters and all his brothers about, was what he needed after the rigours he had endured in the Colonies; it quietened his religious life, and gave him time for the commencement of his large and fine stamp collection. He had over a year's leave in Ireland before being posted from April 1st to Dec. 2nd 1868, to a nine month's Fire-Master's course, from which he emerged with a first-class certificate. Home again at Cahir for Christmas and the spring of 1869 before starting another nine month's course at Shoeburyness on Artillery Instruction. He gained another first-class certificate to serve as instructor in gunnery and artillery exercises, especially in regard to artillery stores and ammunition, and his certificate dated March 18th, 1870, signed by Lt.-Col. S. E. Gordon, chief instructor, remained one of his cherished possessions. The inherent Grubb gift of a teacher was revealing itself, and his future avenue of service in the Army. Alexander's success with men, and in his much later training of his own five sons, owed not a little to his experience of the power of praise as compared with blame. "Well done, old chap"—"That's not at all bad"—"Jolly good work", words such as these have meant much to others, and were characteristic of his descendants. Blame never inspired anybody; it rather provokes resentment and apathy. Praise, as the Grubbs knew from their personal experiences of religion, brings out the best and encourages another.

No girl in Ireland had yet won Alexander's heart. By 1870 he was at his prime at 28 years of age, with nine years behind him in the Army, but with little hope yet of promotion or increase in pay. He was at home in Cahir Abbey when his beloved mother died that year, and he began to wonder what woman would ever have him. But God was working his purposes out. His own experiences of missionary labours in New Zealand and Australia had induced in him a growing concern for missionary work, abetted by his brothers, and in the work of the Church Missionary Society. He attended the great London Anniversary meetings of that Society in the spring of 1870, and found himself in contact with two beautiful girls and their short clerical father and mother at the meetings. So the clear guidance came, at the right time, when he was ready and prepared and needing marriage. Invitations to stay at Potters Bar vicarage with the wealthy and missionary-hearted Watkins Family, and by the middle of 1870, on his posting to Gibraltar, his engagement was announced to Sara Mary Watkins, their eldest daughter.

There followed the visit of the Watkins family to Ireland (see pp. 151–2), and plans for the wedding in the following summer at Potters Bar, on the borders of Enfield Chase, 14 miles north of London. Brought up in a vicarage in affluent circumstances, the new Mrs. Sara Grubb had inherited through *both* her parents all the ability, command, presence, and missionary zeal shown by the first Mrs. Sarah Grubb (*née* Greer), the wife of Joseph Grubb, builder of the family fortunes (*see Chapter Six*). Through her father, the Rev. H. G. Watkins, M.A. (Mercers School and Worcester College, Oxford, 1808–1889), the first vicar of Potters Bar, his only living where he served 54 years (1835–1889),[5] she was descended through a very wealthy London auctioneer from the Huguenot family of *Sebastian Balicourt (1612–1701)*, who married *Marie Pierseni*, an Italian. Through her mother (*née Sara Lee Bousefield*), equally wealthy, she later traced back her descent to *Sir Richard Delabere*, a Norman knight who fought at the Battle of Hastings, and whose descendants for centuries were a leading Herefordshire family of soldiers.

A soldier, like a monk, is never his own master. The problems of seeking guidance, certainly those concerning the leading of the Inner Light, which beset ordinary mortals, and Alexander's Quaker forefathers—problems that can make a man too introspective—do not worry him. His sphere of service and duty is decided from above. The War Office decided his knowledge of artillery stores, forts, canon and ammunition singled Alexander out for duties of this nature in Ceylon in connection with the many old forts and castles on the coast of that island. Alexander was barely six months in Gibraltar when orders reached him to come back and prepare for Ceylon. Still he gained yet another six months leave with pay, sufficient time for a five week's honeymoon (or "Wedding Tour" as Mrs. Watkins, always a great lover of travel, described it in her diary), after his wedding, advanced to Shrove Tuesday, 1871. He took his bride to Windsor, the Malvern Hills, Cahir, the North of Ireland, and Derbyshire; enjoyed a further three months of dinner and evening parties and farewells to Sara's friends and relations, before the long voyage to Asia started (with all the preparations and packing involved) on June 12th, 1871. Alexander would often say of his Army life: "The War Office treated me very well"—a politer way of saying, "They never worked me overhard, and gave me an amount of leave". Mrs. Watkins' diary of their wedding (*pp. 152ff*) tells graphically of their leavetaking and 38 days voyage to Ceylon (*see* Appendix "D"). As the hooters sounded, and the great ship *Scotland* swung round into position and began majestically to sail down the Thames to the wavings of hand-

---

[5] The Rev. H. G. Watkins was a Governor of five Royal Hospitals in London; a member of the Committee of the Church Missionary Society for much of his long life, of which his father—also the Rev. H. G. Watkins, M.A., OXON. (1765–1850) (St. Edmund Hall, Oxford), Rector of St. Swithins London Stone with St. Mary Bothaw (1805–1850), had been a Founder in 1797–1800, and Committee member, and which Society they both loved. They both had an intimate knowledge and affection for the City of London, and were connected with innumerable societies and charities therein. The father wrote many tracts and booklets for the City workers, clerks and servants, and his friendship with the Earl of Stafford, builder of Potters Bar Church, led to the appointment of his only son as first vicar, after his curacy with his father. St. Swithin's church, rectory, and most of the parish were pulled down to make way for the new Cannon Street Railway Station.

kerchiefs and the tears of the women folk now parting, Alexander and Sara looked across the shipping to notice towering above on the South Bank the grandeur of a castle, as it were guarding the river and speaking of security and strength. The memory of this Second Castle in his life, as he first saw it, remained with Alexander all his days. The time would come when he was to buy and reside in Stone Castle. But meanwhile other (old Danish) forts were awaiting him at Trincomalee in Ceylon, —*Fort Frederick* and *Fort Ostenburg*, one of which was to be their first married home for the next three years—and at *Jaffna* and *Batticola*.

The six weeks voyage to Ceylon deepened yet more the love of travel inherent in both Alexander and Sara, whose parents used to take their children with them every year on the Continent, and sometimes twice a year. During their long lives they were to spend holiday after holiday travelling and climbing in Switzerland or Norway, visiting Italy, France, the Low Countries and Germany, or cruising to Corfu, Greece, Egypt, the Holy Land and Turkey. Well kept illustrated diaries (with photos or postcards stuck on alternate pages), and beautifully mounted large photographs or watercolours in leather albums were religiously prepared and kept, a source of information to those "who come after" and to the author of this book. They were always sorry they just missed meeting the great Dr. Livingstone in the flesh when they were in Egypt. Did Alexander sometimes wish that his boyhood explorations in Cahir Castle had prompted him to a similar life of exploration and travel as Livingstone? This same love of travel and exploration led one of his nephews to an extensive journey of exploration on the Upper Reaches of the Amazon, and another across the Andes from Brazil and Bolivia to the Pacific Coast, and back through Venezuela and the Spanish Main: Sir Kenneth Grubb wrote a remarkable book of these treks in his young days,[6] and he vividly describes his experiences, generally alone, in Latin America in his autobiography.

Another Grubb was also to explore these South American regions, a distant cousin of Alexander's, whose ancestor William Grubb had joined William Penn in his new Quaker Colony in Pennsylvania, and whose maternal grandparents had long been associated with the East India Company. Dr. Barbrooke Grubb, F.R.G.S. became the great pioneer of the South American Missionary Society, and for long the Superintendent of its missionaries in the Argentine, Chaco and Bolivia. As a boy, inspired by Capt. Cook's adventures in the Antipodes, he had wanted to go to New Zealand and the Pacific as an explorer of undiscovered islands. Man proposes, but God disposes. It was Alexander who was sent to New Zealand, and Barbrooke who opened up the interior of South

---

[6] *Amazon and Andes* by Kenneth G. Grubb, F.R.G.S. (1930) with 139 beautiful photographs of his own taking. See also his autobiography "*Crypts of Power*" (1971).

America and carried the Christian message to the numerous nomadic tribes of indians in the dense forests and spreading tropical plains of the Chaco, beginning his missionary life in the Falkland Islands in 1886.[7]

This was the year of his father's death, of the sale of Cahir Abbey, and of the beginning of his youngest brother George's worldwide evangelistic conventions and journeys. Alexander was then retired from the Army, and was to take the greatest personal interest in the exploits of these two relatives overseas, and later in his old age to rejoice that his eldest grandson, Henry Grubb, M.A. (Cantab.) had been accepted by the South American Missionary Society to go out to the Chaco as a missionary among those same tribes (see pp. 198–199). This was in 1922, and Henry Grubb gave all his life to South America, becoming in due course Superintendent of the Argentine Chaco Missions, and with his Irish riding experiences travelling everywhere on horseback to conduct services, preach, teach, and undertake elementary medical work as well.[8] He retired in 1959 and died 1964.

On arrival at Colombo Alexander and Sara spent their first week in Ceylon at *Galle Face*, the military headquarters, 72 miles south by stagecoach, and attended a ball in their honour given by the Ceylon Rifles on July 29th, a delightful British introduction to the quite new life they were now to live for three and a half years. They also attended the *Colombo races*, which Alexander described "as very stupid", met the Bishop (to whom they had introductions from Mr. Watkins at Potters Bar), and engaged four native servants (bandies) to accompany them across the island to *Trincomalee* on the south-east coast, where they were posted. They had first a four hour train journey through beautiful Alpine scenery to *Kandy*, where they bought three bullock-carts, stayed awhile, and then commenced a week's trek through the jungle with their bandies, their piano, and all their luggage. Alexander himself walked most of the way, and always attributed his affection in later years for Switzerland and the Alps to the beauties of similar scenery in Ceylon in this most impressionable part of his life. Their route took them via *Matale* (where they stayed at the Rest House) and *Dambool*, where they visited the famous Buddhist temple, cut out of the solid rock, reputed to be 2000 years old, and surmounted by a 35 feet high figure of the Buddha. To a young artillery officer, shrewd and observant, the long salvage work and its costings on the Suez Canal, and the amazing and ancient construction of this Buddhist temple, were of tremendous interest. They travelled through the forests and jungles about 16 miles in seven hours each day, with many rests, and arrived tired out at Trincomalee

[7] *Barbrooke Grubb: Pathfinder* by N. J. Davidson. (1924). Gives some account of his life and missionary labours. See also his own book: *A Church in the Wilds*.
[8] See *The Land between the Rivers* by Henry C. Grubb, M.A.

PLATE XXXII

TRINCOMALEE, CEYLON, 1872

An original painting by Lt. Alexander Grubb, R.A.

PLATE XXXIII

ALEXANDER and SARA GRUBB.

At Fort Frederick, Trincomalee, Ceylon, 1875; with their two eldest children

At Llandudno 1878, on holiday with Rev. and Mrs. H. G. Watkins, M.A. (*Oxon*), H. G. Watkins (brother), and Dr. and Mrs. Symes Thompson (sister), and Harry S. Thompson.

to take up their new appointment in lavish quarters allocated to them in Fort Frederick, close to and overlooking the magnificent natural harbour, and another old Danish fort, known as Fort Ostenburg, which was used for gunnery practice out to sea.

From their respective diaries and letters to Mrs. Watkins an interesting picture emerges of their three-and-a-half years at Trincomalee, largely to be occupied for Alex in travel through the jungles, on horseback, but often on foot, wading or swimming rivers, to inspect abandoned forts, and make reports on the old guns, projectiles, etc., lying about in the Ceylon Command.

Trincomalee 1871
Fort Frederick overlooking Fort Ostenburg, and the
natural harbours.

Their eldest child, a daughter, named after her mother, was born in the December of the year of their arrival. She kept the name Grubb all her life, marrying an Irish cousin (another descendant of Joseph and Samuel Grubb of Clonmel), the owner of Ardmayle House, near Cashel, *see Chapter Fourteen, p. 199.* Alexander Henry Watkins, the eldest of their five sons, was also born at Trincomalee (in 1873). Alex had his Sunday Bible class, often took a Sunday service, in the absence of the commanding officer, and there was a sufficient social life to occupy them. Periods of leave were spent at Colombo, often staying with the bishop who became a close friend and baptised their son.

At the end of his tour Alexander received a dispatch to convey to him the thanks of the Secretary of State for War "on the very able reports he had submitted and the great trouble down to the smallest detail he had taken". It was as Captain Grubb, R.A., accompanied by Mrs. Grubb and two children and nurse, that they left this lovely island in January 1875 on his promotion to a new appointment in Malta. They sailed on the *Oxfordshire*—with no home leave intervening, and arrived at Valetta, the great British Port of Malta, in February, where they were to live for the next two years, and where their second son, Herbert Watkins was born the same year (1875).

Life in the great bastion of Malta was very much the same for the British garrison there as in Gibraltar or anywhere else overseas; in this British stronghold in the Mediterranean it has not changed all that much today. Alexander's duties were largely as Quartermaster and he and Sara rented a house, No. 2, Strada Seconda in Floriana, just outside the walls of Valetta. They seem to have been popular with the Governor and Lady Staubenzee from the number of dinner parties and balls they attended at St. George's palace, and Alexander acted at times as A.D.C. Alexander did not a little for the wives and families of the soldiers quartered in the island, especially at Christmas time in organising parties and socials; they themselves enjoyed the social life of this very hospitable island, accepted many invitations and entertained largely themselves judging from the size of their home and their very "elegant furniture", which was put up for auction in a two-day sale and advertised widely by Mr. A. S. Santucii, on their departure from the island. Again it was a citadel and a fortress in which Alexander's service was spent, deepening those religious experiences, begun in Fort Frederick or maybe even earlier by the influence of Cahir Castle, of a serene trust and security in God, his Hope and Strength, whom he proved "a very present help in trouble". Another "favourite" hymn in the Grubb repertoire of favourite hymns dates from this period, the translation from Martin Luther's "A Safe Stronghold"—

> God is a stronghold and a tower
> A help that never faileth,
> A covering shield, a sword of power
> When Satan's host assaileth.
> Man's night of dark despair,
> When storm clouds fill the air
> Is God's Triumphant hour,
> The noon-day of His power.
> Our safe Stronghold for ever.

Back "home" to Ireland for his next appointment returned "the

Happy Voyager" and Mrs. Grubb and three children in 1877, to take up his new duties as Adjutant of the Wicklow Artillery Militia, stationed in the capital town of one of Ireland's most beautiful counties, a close rival indeed of County Tipperary some 70 miles away. Wicklow lies on the coast but thirty miles south of Dublin, a quaint attractive town of some 3,000 people with "The Black Castle" standing majestically on the headland above the town, built by the Fitzgeralds, and today one of Ireland's many ruins. For centuries this castle had stood exposed to the frequent raids of the O'Byrnes and O'Tooles who had their fastnesses in the Dublin mountains, and around nearby Glenmalule. The county town looks out from its position on the side of a hill towards the sea which sweeps in on the north to form a good safe harbour. Behind the three miles of shingly beach is a long grassy spit of land, known as the *Murrough*, a fine stretch of sward used by Captain Grubb (as by his predecessors) as a parade ground, and shooting site. Behind the Murrough again and separated by it from the sea, is a fairly wide creek, which became in early days an excellent harbour of refuge for the Vikings Sea-rovers, and gave the town its name . . . Vykynlo or Vikings Loch, Wickynlo, shortened to Wicklow. This early stronghold of the Danes rang another bell in Alexander's mind. His family had always told him the Grubbs were descended from the Danes, and were once Danish princes. In Ceylon his job had been to report on old fortresses built by the Danes, including one by a possible distant relative, Capt. Eric Grubbe. He was indeed "coming home", in this Irish posting to Wicklow.

Again it was to be a very large house, judged by modern standards of a captain's pay, that Alexander and Sara Grubb took, about a mile outside Wicklow town on the road to Rathdrum and the Wicklow Mountains, known then, as today, as Marlton House. It was a typical square whitewashed three storey house, standing in well wooded grounds with wellingtonias and rhododendrons in abundance, about a quarter mile above the road, approached by an ascending winding drive opening out from large wrought-iron gates. Now owned (as are so many Irish estates) by a German family, open fields lie all about it, and run down into Wicklow itself. Here the next two "Grubb sons" were born, Ernest in 1877, the father of the author of this book, who became a clergyman, and Walter, the first of two sons who became sailors, in 1879. They were both christened in the fine copula-covered Church of Ireland church in the town, beyond the Franciscan Priory ruins.

These years in Wicklow were perhaps their happiest. There were no riots or disturbances to mar their peace; Sinn Fein outbursts were as much of the future, as the O'Byrne and O'Toole raids were of the past. Dublin was always a delight to visit. His father at Cahir Abbey often sent up his carriage and horses to bring the family down to County

Tipperary, and was a frequent visitor; so was his youngest brother George. Alex got up to Belfast several times a year to see his brothers and sister living there. His military duties were not onerous. His job was to assist in the conversion of the Wicklow Rifles into Artillery, and most of his duty consisted in training recruits, parade ground work on the Murrough beside the sea, and office work. A healthy and congenial life for any soldier, and for an Irishman in particular. In July 1880 the *Irish Times* published the following report:

"The Wicklow Artillery assembled on the 18th inst for annual training, marching in strength to the Murrough, 11 officers and 300 other ranks. The increase of pay, change of drills, and improvement in clothing has given an impetus to recruiting, and the diversity of drills in which the men are instructed on the Murrough daily, gives great satisfaction. To carry out the new drills they have four large guns . . . the instructors are indefatigable in their exertions, and show great patience in teaching the men, who vie with one another by close attention to their new duties. The steadiness of the regiment, and the phsyique and soldier-like bearing of the men on parade, bears comparison with the Regular Army. They have attained that state of efficiency at which any militia regiment might feel proud to arrive. The officers attending the training are: Colonel Gunner Cunninghame: Major Bayley: Capts. Hoey, Howard, Brooke, and Welch. Lieutenants Cunninghame, Howard, and Kennedy. Surgeon-Major Blew. Adjutant Alexander Grubb, Captain R.A."

"Inspiring leadership; instruction that banishes boredom and monotony; enthusiastic initiatives that bring out the best in his men; increases in pay and improvements in clothing . . ." their Irish adjutant, Capt. Grubb, R.A. could feel well pleased with such a report on his activities.

Typical of Alexander Grubb's power of oratory is another report on the Wicklow Artillery Militia in the *Irish Times* some months later:

"ON TUESDAY AFTERNOON the Permanent Staff and men of the above Corps paraded at Head Quarters in review order, and marched to the Murrough headed by the band of the regiment to witness the presentation of a silver medal to Trumpet-Major Sprent of the permanent staff for long service and good conduct. The presentation was made by Capt. A. Grubb Royal Artillery, the Adjutant of the Regiment, who spoke in eulogistic terms of this non-commissioned officer's past conduct, to whom after a term of 18 years service with an irreproachable character, Her Majesty had been pleased to award this honourable distinction of her approbation. Fastening the medal on the breast of the Trumpet-Major, Capt. Grubb called upon all present to emulate his conduct informing them they would always find good conduct duly appreciated by Her Majesty, and pointing out that there were now three of his staff with this honourable distinction."

The last intake of recruits—83 of them—were due for passing out by April 1881. The completion of their training meant the completion of Alexander's appointment in Wicklow, and he was placed on the supernumerary list. It was becoming obvious his days in the Army were numbered, and Sara was already thinking ahead of his retirement, and where they should settle, and whether in Ireland or not. They could remain where they were at Marlton House; father-in-law Richard had already offered them one of the "barracks" at Cahir, where Alexander had been born. Guidance for the future took six months to come; with no other door opening they were glad to remain where they were and to enjoy an Irish summer. The elder children were already at Dame School in Wicklow; their musical evenings were filling a gap in the social life of this Irish town (like his parents' before him at Cahir over their famous piano); Irish lyrics and ballads were learnt and passed around, as well as the better known songs of the period—"I'll sing the songs of Araby"—"Our hands have met but not our hearts", and the like, in days when television and pop-music and cinemas were unknown, and a community made its own entertainment.

Autumn had descended upon the lovely Wicklow hills, where Alexander and Sara had long since discovered the joys—and the effort and exercise— of climbing: joys, effort, and the glorious sense of achievement that for the rest of their lives they were annually to enjoy and re-discover on their holidays in the Swiss mountains. The leaves were falling at Cahir Abbey where his youngest brother George, his training at Trinity College Dublin completed (he had often spent long weekends with them at Wicklow from Dublin), had returned home to live after his ordination as curate of Cahir. Then "out of the blue" came the announcement of Alexander's appointment as Major (vice J. B. Richardson, one of his cousins) gazetted on November 15th, 1881, and a new and temporary appointment as Adjutant of the Durham Artillery Militia in the North-east of England at Hartlepool—a job very similar to that he had successfully completed in his four years at Wicklow. Alexander was keen to continue his army life: Sara not so keen to go to Hartlepool with five small children, and all the domestic upsets of a move from so comfortable and commodious a home. Such is Army life, its officers constantly on the move. To Hartlepool they went. It meant goodbye to Ireland, the land of his fathers, for ever.

"Lodgings for Militia"—a cutting stuck in an obscure place in the family album, behind a three column account of one of the carnival balls they had attended in Malta (when Sara went dressed as Rebecca, and Alexander had typically preferred his uniform to any "dressing up"), is the sole record of their year at Hartlepool. It reads:

"PERSONS DESIROUS of having militia men as lodgers during the ensuing Preliminary Drill and Training, are requested to send their names and addresses, and the number of men they can accommodate, to the Quarter Master at the Barracks, Hartlepool, not

181

P

later than April 10. Lodgings will be held under the same liability as billets under the Army Act 1881: they will be held exclusively for Militiamen. The sum of 4d per night will be paid for each man. Recruits Drill will commence April 17, 1882."

ALEX GRUBB. Major. Royal Artillery.
The Barracks. Adjutant. Durham Artillery Militia.
Hartlepool. 26th March 1882.

After the fascination of life among the forts of Ceylon, the social life in the bastion and stronghold of Malta, the peace and happiness of Wicklow, it is no surprise that Sara Grubb at any rate had no inclination to retain memories of their year in a north-country seaport town, whose landladies were content to let lodgings at 4d a night. They both rejoiced when Alex was given command of his own battery of artillery at Woolwich next year. It was his one and only command, and his retirement from the Army came in 1884 with the rank of Lieutenant-Colonel. Was it undistinguished military service? May be, but typical of that of a great mass of officers in a peace-time Army of vastly greater numbers than prospects of national need or promotion warranted. Alexander was 42 years old at retirement; he had spent 23 years of his life on the Army pay-roll. He was to live another 42 years as a retired Lieutenant-Colonel. Such is Army life today, as then, leaving its officers in the prime of life to look for new work and occupation, not only to augment their pension, but to fill their time with satisfying employment that they may continue to render the service that they are capable by all their experience and training to offer to their fellow men. For many people life only begins at 40!

Does an officer in such a position, sit down and quietly wait for a job to offer? Does he start looking for something, however seemingly unsuitable, to while the time away and bring him in an income? The second alternative was intolerable to Alexander. Fortunately he was comfortably off, and financially needed not to increase his pension. Farming, teaching, ordination, as two of his brothers had done—and this meant a period of training—these were possibilities he made up his mind he was too old to commence, well as he might have turned his hand to any of them. Sara would hear none of it. Alexander had served his country; now it was time for him to relax as a country gentleman, and devote himself to his family and his hobbies. They consulted Richard Grubb and both the Rev. and Mrs. Watkins. They had not been faced with so cruel a choice, and could only advise "Wait and see". They could continue living in another barrack-looking and rather ugly house, called Marlborough Lodge at Old Charlton, close to Woolwich and Blackheath, which they had secured in 1883 and where their youngest two children, Reginald and Elsie were born. Besides their elder children were now at day school in the neighbourhood—May at Blackheath High

School for Girls, and the elder three boys at Kidbrook House Preparatory School. To move anywhere meant upsetting their education, and the education of their children was surely now their first concern. So it was that they spent the first five years of retirement living where they were, and any thoughts of a return to Ireland were out. The guidance was clear. No new door had opened. "Put the children first".

Ever eager to learn, to discover, to find out, to see things for themselves, Alexander and Sara had both decided that the very best possible education must be given to all their children—seven of them—and for the boys that meant boarding school. In the officer's mess at Woolwich, Alexander had been made well aware of the numerous brochures offering special terms for the education of sons of officers at the fairly recently established Wellington College in Berkshire. This public school had been founded by public subscription in 1859 as a memorial to a fellow Irishman, Arthur Wellesley, first Duke of Wellington, and the Prince Consort had devoted to the scheme much of his amazing capacity for detailed plans, viewing it in some measure as a counterpart to the many military academies in Germany. This was enough for Alexander, with his own Irish and Germanic blood. He had never been at public school himself; the old Grubb family school at Ballitore had long been closed, and it would have been out of the question to consider sending his boys back to Ireland, with that horrid crossing from Holyhead to Dublin. To Wellington they should go.

Wellington College had made rapid progress under its first headmaster, Dr. E. W. Benson (later to be Bishop of Truro and Archbishop of Canterbury), stern and severe as his discipline had been. Dr. Wickham, another classical scholar like his predecessor (later to become Dean of Lincoln), accepted Alexander's eldest son in 1886, and the next two in 1888 and '89 (first of many occasions later when there were to be three, and even four Grubbs at the school at the same time). An outbreak of diphtheria, due to defective drainage, had led the school to be transferred to Malvern for a time, and rumours of continuing insanitary conditions and laxity under Wickham's mastership had led to a drop in numbers. Ernest Watkins Grubb, their third son, whom Alexander had already sent as a boarder to Temple Grove, East Sheen (1885–1889), where he gained the school prize for French, was perhaps their cleverest son and won a scholarship to Wellington, worth in those days £50 a year for so long as he remained at college. The three of them were placed in the Combermere dormitory under the tutorship of the Rev. H. W. McKenzie, became in due course school prefects, won their share of school prizes, while Ernest played cricket for the School first XI for two years, and won his cap. Ernest continued under the third Headmaster, Dr. Bertram Pollock (appointed when only 29 from the staff of Marlborough College, and later to be

Bishop of Norwich) who reimposed the strictest disciplines of the first Headmaster Dr. Benson, and prepared E. W. Grubb for confirmation. Parents became proud again to have sons at Wellington, and later as Old Wellingtonians.[9] Alexander and Sara ever considered their choice of this school fully justified, and a "guided" choice from God.

In the rigid disciplines and roughing of Wellington, as in the classical scholarship of its headmasters, and in its teaching of modern languages, French and German, and history and boxing, a close comparison exists with Ballitore Quaker School in Co. Kildare, which had been the "Grubb school" of the previous century. The school lists of Ballitore show that for 70 years from the first entry of a Clonmel Grubb (Samuel) in 1762, until 1832 when the school finally closed, there were 14 Grubbs educated there. At Wellington, which became the "Watkins Grubb" school from 1886 with the arrival of Alexander's three sons, followed by their sons and grandsons, the registers for a similar period of 70 years reveal the names of 12 Grubbs, and six more since 1956, a number which includes four "Castle Grace" Grubbs from Co. Tipperary.

Another school in which Alexander also took the greatest interest in his 40 years of retirement, and to whose governing body he was to devote much of his time, was the Royal School for Officers' Daughters at Bath. He served as a governor for over 30 years, and as the chairman of governors for exactly 25. At a later date his second son, Herbert succeeded him, and sent his own daughter Elaine there. The Grubbs hardly ever missed a Speech day. Many were the speeches Alexander had to make, and the occasions when Sara distributed the prizes. To have resided permanently among retired officers in a town such as Bath or Cheltenham was not, however, Alexander's idea of retirement at all.

Seven years Col. and Mrs. Grubb lived at Marlborough Lodge, Old Charlton. Needing space and grounds for their growing family, they were on the look out for a larger home, and used sometimes to drive down the river and call at Stone Castle, ever the Castle of their dreams. The certain guidance came in 1890, when after the marriage of William Ross, the only son of the owners of the Castle, Mr. and Mrs. William Munro Ross, to Maud Bevan, the eldest daughter of Thomas Bevan, Esq., D.L., J.P. owner of the adjacent Stone Park, the Castle was put on the market, and its owners returned to Scotland. Their dream of twenty years before on starting their long voyage to Ceylon found fulfilment in its purchase; a purchase to be as momentous in the lives of their children as Cahir Castle years ago had been to Alexander.

Stone Castle is a large spacious turreted building overlooking the Thames between Dartford and Greenhythe, standing in acres of parkland

[9] *A Twentieth Century Bishop.* Bertram Pollock, D.D., K.C.V.O., Late Bishop of Norwich, p. 5.

PLATE XXXIV

STONE CASTLE

Overlooking the Thames

PLATE XXXV

THE RIVER THAMES AND THE *ARETHUSA*

Looking across their fields and wood from Stone Castle

woods, and fields on chalky soil. It resembled Cahir Abbey internally in size, awkward corners, and huge kitchen quarters; also in its large stabling around a flagged courtyard, and many unnecessary outbuildings. Of the original Norman twelfth century castle only the great massive square tower, the dungeons below, some fine lancet windows, and a perfect stone circular staircase remained; the rest had been modernised in character earlier in the century. Known as *Estanes* in Norman times, it was a Manor House in the Middle Ages, when *Sir John de Northwood* answered for the "Manor of Stone Castle" in the twentieth year of King Edward III.[10] *Richard Benevant* died siezed of the Castle of Stone in 1459, and his son Nicholas in 1516; later it passed to the *Champley*, *Carew* and *Atkins* families. The Castle lay close to the ancient *Watling Street*, and above the landing place of *King Sweyn, father of Canute*, the first Danish Conqueror of England. Nearby at Greenhythe (The "Greenhaven of Kent") lay anchored the *Arethusa* and *Worcester*, used as training ships for young boys (particularly orphans) for naval service.

Life for Alexander and Sara and their family at Stone Castle was typical of that in most large country houses, whether in England or Ireland. They attended Stone Parish Church on Sundays, and found in their Rector and his family close friends. They entertained, they pulled their weight in local organisations, the Dartford Volunteers, the Dartford and district Horticultural Society, the Conservative Clubs, the Primrose League, the Soldiers Friend Society, etc., etc., all of which at one time or another turned to them for service as Chairman or President. They took the greatest interest in the boys being trained for the Navy on the *Arethusa* and *Worcester*, frequently entertained their officers who had no small influence upon their youngest two sons, and allowed the boys the use of a paddock for exercises. They were active in furthering the War effort during the Boer War, speaking in factory buildings, church halls, smoking concerts, the Dartford men's working club, on South Africa, quoting from the letters from their eldest son, a combatant in the balloons section, and a lucid and regular writer of letters to his parents. Thanking Col. Grubb after one such occasion, the speaker said it seemed as if he wished he was out there himself, so eagerly had he summed up the situation and course of events. Always once, and sometimes twice a year, they would make up a party of their friends and as many of their growing or grown children as might be available for a month in Switzerland in the mountains, and there was scarcely a hotel proprietor in mountain village or lakeside resort who did not welcome them back again and again. Were there no chaplain on the Sundays in their resort Alexander would conduct divine service. Perhaps Zermatt

---

[10] In the list for the levy of 40 shillings on every knight's fee for making a knight of Edward the Black Prince. See further *Hasteds History of Kent*.

and the Riffel Alp above it gave them most pleasure, and they were consistent in support of the Colonial and Continental Church Society in its work for British speaking tourists.

Preparation for such holidays—grand tours they might almost be called—was equally as enjoyable as the holiday itself. The study of maps, of timetables, of mountain routes—for they rarely stayed more than a few days in each centre, and the menfolk would walk and climb, and the ladies drive or entrain to the next hotel. Their diaries make fascinating reading, and their photographic skill commendable. Their heredity from the Shackletons and Watkins family as well as from the Bousefields made it essential that each of their children accompanying them on such a holiday should be made to write his or her own diary of the tour. Said his youngest son Reginald to the author of this book "It was not that we always wanted the labour of diary writing each evening—we had to; it was a law of the Medes and Persians that every evening on returning from an expedition to our hotel (we were generally out all day with a flask and picnic lunch) we went upstairs to our rooms for a bath and for diary writing before dinner. We could be forgiven if we were a little late down for the meal, so long as our diary was written up of the days events, and ready to be read out and laughed over afterwards."

Most of these Grubb diaries on the everyday happenings of a tour carried coloured postcards or an illustration in black and white on opposite pages to the writing, and (except for Sara's) are nearly as clear to read today as when they were written. The writer of this book like his father and mother, has done the same ever since, and well over a hundred of such old diaries have come into his possession. No picture of the Watkins Grubbs on holiday would be complete without the alpenstock in their hand, an old cap on the head, a rucksack upon their shoulders, setting out to "climb every mountain"; the higher they ascended into the fresh keen Swiss air, the nearer heaven they found themselves. They were always fortunate to have a large and sufficient staff of servants and retainers to look after home, gardens, and animals in their absence. Such training of his family through foreign travel, through first class schools, and through the learning of foreign languages had its effect upon those who came after. The best school education in the world needs the supplement of the home.

Alexander and Sara Grubb had every cause to be proud of all their sons, to whose interests and families their lives were to be devoted and fully occupied from Stone days onwards. Their eldest two, Alexander Henry (called Lexie) and Herbert, brought up in an Army home and an Army school, naturally followed their father into the Army, the one into the Royal Engineers, the other into the Border Regiment. Both were to win the C.M.G. and D.S.O. for distinguished services in World War I, to their parents' greatest delight. In the Boer War Lexie was mentioned in dispatches for his service in balloons, and first class map-reading. He served in the Salonika Campaign, and as Director of Signals A.H.Q. 1917–1919, ending his Army service as Chief Engineer British Army on the Rhine, 1924–1927. Herbert was commissioned in 1896 and also saw service in South Africa, and for a great many years in India and Burma and Ireland. He served in France 1914–1918, an Instructor at the Staff College, Camberley in 1920, and commanded the Border Regiment in 1923 until his retirement in 1925 as Lieut.-Colonel. He was the last British officer to leave Ireland, the land of his fathers, on the evacuation of all British troops. Both Lexie and Herbert had sons who followed them in an Army career with distinction.

Ernest, the third son, born in Ireland at Wicklow, a cricketer, ruggerplayer and in the Classical VIth, went up to New College, Oxford, through the influence of Dr. Pollock his headmaster, Canon Murray his rector at Stone, and of his two clerical uncle's Percy and George, and took holy orders after training at Leeds Clergy School. He served curacies in Leeds, and South Croydon, and had been but four years in his first living—the country benefice of *Shepherdswell* (or *Sibertswold*) near Dover, with a promising career in the church before him, before his untimely death after an emergency operation for acute appendicitis (1914).

The move to Stone Castle had had the greatest effect upon his life, and that of his two younger brothers. Like their predecessor's only son at Stone Castle, he also fell in love with a daughter of the Bevan's at Stone Park, whose lands adjoined the Castle. They had first met tobogganing in the snow in the Park. But Pauline Bevan's father who had unsuccessfully stood for Parliament in the Liberal cause, had built up an extensive and valuable business in cement alongside the Thames (now the Port of London Authority) and had just retired from office as High Sheriff of Kent, was a strong believer in liberal thought and Biblical criticism, and held Darwin's view of the descent of man from monkeys. He disliked all and sundry who held to what he regarded as old-fashioned Bible teaching, and Col. Grubb in particular with his positive and conservative Irish evangelical and Bible views. He refused his consent to the marriage of any daughter of his to a clergyman, or to a young Grubb, and threatened to cut her off with a penny in his will, if she married him.

Ernest remained sure of his calling. Pauline, after her mother's death (she was Emma Bayes, of Kimberley, Norfolk) had to serve her father as chatelaine of Stone Park (she was the only unmarried daughter), and as his companion on his many visits to the south of France, Paris,

187

and Italy. Both put the call of duty before love, and waited seven years or more for their union after Thomas Bevan's death in 1907.

Upon Walter and Reginald the effect of Stone Castle above the shipping in the Thames was obvious. They heard and obeyed the call of the sea. After training at Osborne and Dartmouth, and on the *Britannia*, they sailed the High Seas in a number of ships, the one rising to the rank of Lieut.-Commander at the beginning of World War I on board H.M.S. *Creçy*, and gave his life for his country; the other to the rank of Captain, serving in World War II in charge of Naval Operations in Bermuda.

Eighteen-ninety-six saw their silver wedding celebrations at the Hotel Metropole. All their family, except for Walter their fourth son, a young midshipman serving on his first ship, the H.M.S. *Trafalgar* at Alexandretta were present, together with Percy and George Grubb and their wives, bridesmaids from Potters Bar days and many others. Walter was the artist of the family, and with his eldest brother Lexie, the most lucid and prolific letter writer among them. His letter of congratulations to his parents (he was aged 17) is worth recording, typical of his father's style and ability of expression:

H.M.S. Trafalgar.

Feb. 15th, 1896. Alexandretta.

My dearest Father and Mother,

You cannot think what immense pleasure it gives me to think that next Friday is your silver wedding. I do wish I could do more than write to congratulate you on that glorious day from this desert little place many many miles away. I shall very well be able to imagine what an extremely happy family gathering there will be in London on that day of joy and thankfulness. I sincerely hope that God will be kind enough to allow us all to take part in your golden wedding 25 years to come. I received both your letters this morning by the French mail. Thank you for them very much.

I am glad to hear how full our wood is of rabbits still, and also that the cats are better at catching traps than rabbits. I am glad to hear Regie is getting on well at Littlejohns; it is curious his great friend is a foreign prince. I hope he will not start talking Siamese to me when I come home! We have played four hockey matches since last I wrote, all of which we won handsomely, and we are now crack ship at hockey at Alexandretta.

A great many midshipmen and assistant engineers have been ordered to England from the fleet, and they left in the Arethusa for Port Said last Sunday evening. They had to go at 15 knots all the way to catch the steamer. Howell, the senior A.E. and Kirkness our senior midshipman both went home. They are the two best men in our hockey team. I do not know how we shall get on without them, and we have not played a match since they left. We have had some heavy rain in the last few days, but no bad squally weather.

The Forte left Malta the day before yesterday to relieve the Arethusa, which has been here five months. A French gun-boat, the Fauçon arrived a few days back to relieve the Cosmos. The Russian Squadron was here for four days, and then sailed for the Piraeus. The American Cruiser Minneapolis came in a few days ago, and left last night. She is the fastest cruiser in the world, and on her trials steamed over 23 knots. She has a very light armament. We exercised landing parties the other day: on counting up we found we could march 1000 men ashore, not counting boat crews. We did some quiet coaling last Monday, only 67 tons an hour. We are waiting for the Ramilles to beat our last one, before we make another record.

Hoping that everything will be an immense success.

Believe me, Your loving son.

WALTER B. WATKINS GRUBB.

Not a bad letter for a midshipman of only 17. It reflects credit on naval education at the time. Alas his hopes to be spared to keep his parents Golden Wedding anniversary were not to be fulfilled. He was to be one of the early casualties of World War I, drowning in the sinking of his submarine, H.M.S. *Creçy* a month after war was declared. He had been married but three months, and left an unborn son, who bears his father's name, and is now a poultry farmer in Sussex.

Excavations for chalk under their extensive grounds at Stone Castle led Alexander and Sara Grubb to make the last move of their lives. Financially much the better off through the sale of their castle, they bought a mid-Kent country house and estate of some 30 acres at Hollingbourne, near Maidstone, then known as Elsfield House, situated on the main London–Canterbury Road. (On its next sale after their deaths it was turned into a country club known until this day as "Great Danes" and extensively patronised). This three-storied rectangular house, with a wing added on one side, and a long drawingroom built out on the other, somewhat ugly looking, reminded Alexander of the "Barracks" at Cahir where he had been born. With its ten bedrooms and five large sitting-rooms it was more than ample to contain their profusion of curios and Victoriana, and to house married sons and daughters and grandchildren, when they came to stay. Tennis and croquet on the well kept lawns, a profusion of rare shrubs and cacti and other scarce plants, a large walled-in garden, and faithful retainers, Skinner the butler, and Murray, the lady's maid and housekeeper, remain among the author's childhood memories.

Alexander served as a Justice of the Peace (on the Bearsted Bench) for many years, as his father in Ireland before him, and both his son and his grandson after him, "running the second mile" in making the after-care of prisoners particularly his own. He paid frequent visits to the Maidstone convict prison and to Borstal, and later received a personal letter of thanks from the Home Secretary (Mr. Shortt) for this especial service as Chairman of the Board of Visitors. He became churchwarden for many years of Leeds Church, nearby, and on terms of personal friendship with Archbishop and Mrs. Davidson at Canterbury.

Two last outstanding occasions of joy and pride must be recorded. The one in 1908 at King Edward VII's Levee for Officers at St. James' Palace, when Lieutenant-Colonel Grubb, J.P. was summoned to attend with his four sons—Captain A. H. Watkins Grubb, D.S.O., R.E. Headquarters Staff; Captain H. Watkins Grubb, the Border Regiment; Lieutenant W. B. Watkins Grubb, R.N. and Lieutenant R. Watkins Grubb, R.N. While Sara Grubb in the same year (as in 1900 in Queen Victoria's reign) and again in 1909 and 1910 presented each of her daughters and daughters-in-law to the King and Queen Alexandra at Buckingham Palace following their marriages.

The other was their Golden Wedding celebrations in 1921 at the Langham Hotel, when his brother George offered their thanksgivings to the Lord who had called, led and blessed them from Irish days to that hour. All their surviving children and their wives, the two widowed Mrs. Grubbs, and their two eldest grandsons Henry and Cedric were present. Within four years they were to meet again at their funerals, in 1925 within a few months of one another in Leeds Parish Church. The Church stands at the top of a steep hill overlooking Elsfield, in the churchyard of which they lie buried.

The vicar paid this tribute:

> "If ever there was a kindly gentleman, a Christian man, one who never wavered from the path of duty, it was Colonel Grubb.
> "One of the important duties of a clergyman is to visit the sick in his parish. I know not how often I have visited him these past four years of his illness at Elsfield House. It was a great many. The same thing invariably happened. Before I got a chance to sit down, the Colonel would say: 'Can we have a word of prayer?' After we had prayed he always asked after members of our congregation. I often thought as I mounted those great wide stairs to his bedroom of that text—'They went into an Upper Room, and continued with one accord with prayer and supplication'. I single out the Colonel's prayer life, above all his distinguished army services and his concern for others in this area as something all who follow after should covet. If ever there was a man ready to die it was Alexander Grubb."

His sons chose the hymn with which both services ended—

" . . . Now upon the Eternal Shore
land the voyagers at last."

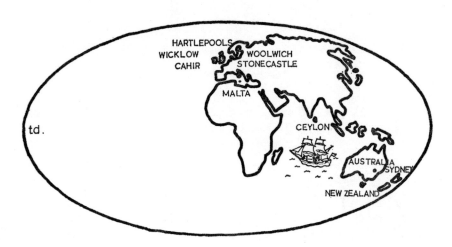

The map shows how extensive and widespread their voyages and journeyings in this finite world of time and space had been; fitting prelude for these experienced and happy voyagers as they set out on the long last journey to the Land of Pure Delight, there to see their Master face to face.

From earth's wide bounds, from ocean's farthest coast
Through gates of pearl stream in the countless host,
Singing to Father, Son, and Holy Ghost.
Hallelujah.   Hallelujah.

Or—as his father and brother George with their infectious Irish enthusiasm would have concluded the hymn adding a third "Hallelujah" and a Hoorah!

[11] A stained glass window in Leeds Church commemorates Alexander and Sara Grubb, placed by his sons alongside another given by their parents in memory of Ernest and Walter Grubb, their sons.

191

The Watkins Grubb Descendants

1873–1971

"Followers of them who through faith and patience inherit the Promises."
—Hebrews, vi, 12

ALEXANDER GRUBB (1842–1925) and SARA (née WATKINS), of
STONE CASTLE, KENT, had SEVEN CHILDREN, five sons and
two daughters; and 15 grandchildren

1. ALEXANDER HENRY WATKINS 1873–1933   1 son
2. HERBERT WATKINS   1875–1934   3 children (2 sons)
3. ERNEST WATKINS   1877–1914   3 sons
4. WALTER BOUSFIELD WATKINS 1879–1914   1 son
5. REGINALD WATKINS   1883–1954   2 daughters

Their two daughters were:

1. SARA MARY WATKINS (always called "MAY" to distinguish her
   from her Mother) 1871–1938; 4 children, 3 sons—also GRUBBS,
   as she married her second cousin, LOUIS HENRY GRUBB, D.L.,
   J.P., (1865–1929) on Jan. 18th, 1899 in Stone Church, followed
   by a big reception at Stone Castle. (*See Collateral Table "G"*.)
2. ELSIE MARIA WATKINS, 1886–1959; m. 1911 from Elsfield
   House, Hollingbourne, to Dryden Donkin, Esq.; 1 son (b. 1930).

1. *Col. ALEXANDER HENRY WATKINS GRUBB, C.M.G., D.S.O.,
   Order of the Redeemer* (Greece), J.P. their eldest son.

Born in Ceylon, and named after his father and his Watkins grandfather,
Lexie (as he was called to distinguish him from his father), was the first
of some 18 Grubbs to be educated at Wellington College, in Berkshire.
At his preparatory school at Kidbrooke House, Blackheath, the headmaster (The Rev. Edward W. Snell, F.R.A.S.) reported: "He has been an
obedient, industrious, & scrupulously honest boy, possessed of much
intelligence and an excellent memory, in every way a young gentleman."

From the Combermere Dormitory at Wellington, under the Rev. H. W.
McKenzie, he passed 11th out of 80 into the Royal Military Academy
in 1889, and was awarded the Pollock Medal in 1892 as the most distinguished cadet of the season. He also gained the prize for Fortifications
and for Military Topography, preparing him for the greatest work of
his life in balloons (the forts of the air) and map-reading. Castles and

forts and travel were "in his blood". Commissioned in 1892 he concentrated on the construction and flying of balloons, as well as point-to-point horse racing for the Royal Engineers. He was an excellent letter-writer to his parents, clear in explanation and description (another inherited trait), and was continually advising them about his horses "Sunset", "Moonlight", "Giddy-Girl" and some dozen others, as well as his balloon racing. In Brussels in 1907 at the 9th Annual Conference of the Permanent International Commission on Aeronautics, he accompanied the Hon. C. S. Rolls in his balloon "The Britannia" in the International Balloon Race, finishing third, and earthing near Sanguinet, Arachon, in the Gironde, having covered 800 kilometres (550 miles) in 25 hours, no mean achievement. He served in balloons in the Boer War, gaining the D.S.O. and narrowly escaping with his life, as well as the Queen's Medal (South African War, 1899–1902) and the King's Medal, and was appointed to the headquarter staff at Pretoria with the rank of captain. From the letters he wrote his parents twice a week from South Africa a book might have been written upon the movements in that War. He was appointed to supervise the photographic section of the Military School of Ballooning, and lectured widely on the subject, his style reminiscent of modern day reports on Apollo 13, and travel to the Moon. Lecturing to the boys at Wellington, he urged them not to think of him as a Bally-Lunatic (balloonatic), and with a prophet's eye foretold the conquest of the Moon. Appointed Major in 1912, Bt.-Lt. Colonel in 1916, he served in the Salonika campaign as Director of Signals (A.H.Q.) 1917–19, commanded the Royal Engineers at Aldershot in 1922, and ended his army career as Chief Engineer, British Army on the Rhine, 1924–1927. He inherited Elsfield House on his parents death, where he lived six years until his early death at the age of 60, serving as a Justice of the Peace (like his father before him), on the Maidstone Bench. He married 1908, Frances Marie Cox, of California; they had one son:

Lt.-Colonel ALEXANDER JAMES WATKINS GRUBB, J.P., b. 1909. Educated Wellington College (1922–1927) and R.M.A. Prize Cadet. Commissioned in the Royal Artillery (like his grandfather), he served in India and Ceylon. B.M.R.A. 36th Ind. Division 1943. B.L.A. Holland and Germany, 1944–45. Retired as Lt.-Col. 1950. Appointed J.P. for Cheshire 1956 and High Sheriff 1972. He married 1936, Margaret, dau. of R. W. Dale, Esq., of Cherry Hill, Malpas, Cheshire; they have two sons:

  (i) ALEXANDER RICHARD WATKINS GRUBB, b. 1941. Educated Wellington College. m. 1968, Jane, dau. of Major Reginald Waugh-Harris of Pontesford, Shropshire, and has one son: CHARLES RICHARD WAUGH WATKINS, b. 1969.

  (ii) PETER JAMES WATKINS, b. 1944. Educated Wellington; m. 1967, Julia, dau. of Norman Longe, Esq., o.b.e., of Gorey, Co. Wexford, Eire.

2. *Lt.-Col. HERBERT WATKINS GRUBB, C.M.G., D.S.O., Officier Merite Agricole* (France), their second son.

Born in Malta, and educated at Wellington College, as were his two sons, and his grandson; (all of them in the Cumbermere Dormitory, as were his 2 brothers and 4 nephews), Militia (King's Regmt) 1895, Herbert was commissioned in the Border Regiment 1896, in which he served throughout his 30 years army service, and commanded in 1923–1925. He served with distinction in South Africa, in India and Burma, and in France during World War I. He was an instructor at the Staff College, and retired as Lt.-Col. in 1925. He married 1909, Eva Noel Mears (d. 1971), dau. of Capt. Arthur Mears, M.S.C., and succeeded his father as a Governor of the Royal School for Officer's Daughters at Bath. He had the distinction of being the last uniformed British officer to take the salute in Ireland before Southern Ireland became a Republic. He died 1934, aged 58, leaving two sons and one daughter—

ELAINE WATKINS GRUBB, b. 1910. Educated Royal School for Officers' Daughters, Bath. Unmarried. Commissioner Girl Guides.

(The Rev.) PHILIP HERBERT WATKINS GRUBB, M.A. (Oxon.), b. 1912. Educated at St. Peter's College, and Wescott House, Cambridge. Curate, St. Mary's, Portsea 1936–43; Rector of Bedhampton, Hants. 1943–53; Shillingstone, Dorset 1953–1965; Barford St. Martin, Wilts. 1965–70. Director of Samaritans in Salisbury Diocese, and Custos of Hospital of St. John, Heytesbury, Wilts. He married 1942, Audrey Gwendoline, dau. of Brig.-General Sir Julian Young, C.B., C.M.G., D.S.O. Their daughter JUDITH MARY, b. 1947. Educated at the Grove, Hindhead, Surrey. Worked at Dr. Barnardo's. London Hospital 1967–70, S.E.N.; m. 1970 Iain David Fraser. Their son Iain was born 1971.

(Major) MICHAEL WATKINS GRUBB, b. 1920. R.M.C. Sandhurst. Border Regt. 1939. He served in France, North Africa, Italy, Holland in World War II, and took part in the parachute landings at Arnhem in 1944. Instructor R.M.A. Sandhurst, 1946–49. He served in Malaya and Germany, and made a thorough exploration of the site of his ancestors' castle and properties in the Hartz Mountain. Retired 1960 with the rank of Major. From 1962 serving with Howard Rotavator Co. Ltd. (Agric. Machinery Manufacturers). He married 1948, Elizabeth Bois, dau of Edgar C. Canter, Esq. They have two children:

(i) MARTIN JOHN WATKINS GRUBB, b. 1949. Bristol University. He won an Army University Cadetship. Commissioned Light Infantry, 1967. Serving in Northern Ireland (Belfast) 1971.

(ii) ROSEMARY DIANA WATKINS, b. 1951. Bruton School for Girls, Som. Student Nurse, St. Thomas' Hospital, London, 1969–72.

PLATE XXXVI

Walter   Herbert   Alec Grubb Lexie   Regie.
Feb. 1908

IN THE SERVICE OF THE KING
At St. James' Palace Leveè.   Feb. 1908

PLATE XXXVII

ALEXANDER and SARA GRUBB, 1905
In the Swiss Alps above Zermatt, with their son—ERNEST

3. *The Rev. ERNEST WATKINS GRUBB, M.A. (Oxon)*; their third son.

Born 8th February, 1877 at Marlton House, Wicklow. At the age of eight he was sent as a boarder to Temple Grove School, East Sheen, where he won the prize for French (1888), and a scholarship to Wellington College of £50 per annum. At his confirmation at the school in 1892, he received from his headmaster, Dr. E. G. Wickham (formerly Fellow and Tutor of New College, Oxford, whose influence led him to the same Oxford college), a copy of S. Thomas-a-Kempis *Imitation of Christ*; his heavily underlined passages therein reveal something of the Grubb character he inherited, and which in a short life he strove to make his own:

"Be grateful for the smallest gifts of God . . . so will you be counted worthy to receive greater. Let the smallest thing in your eyes have the value of the greatest, even that which might appear trifling. Do not concern yourself with other people's matters; keep your eye on yourself first. Let nothing stand in your way of spiritual improvement. You have the time and opportunity now. Why put it off until tomorrow? Always bestir yourself and say 'Now is the time to be up and doing. It is easy to lose through neglect that which has taken much labour to secure. The happiness of man consists not in possessing temporal things in abundance, but in being satisfied with having enough'."

A framed copy of the words of St. John Chrysostom always hung in his study: "*A little thing is a little thing, but faithfulness in little things is a very great thing*".

Under the headmastership of Dr. Bertram Pollock (1894–1910), later the great Bishop of Norwich, Ernest became school prefect and head of the school, and developed his love of cricket. He was in the school XI for two years, 1895–96. Through the influence of his two clerical headmasters, and of his uncle George Grubb and of the Rector of Stone, (Canon Murray) he heeded the call to be ordained, and went up to New College, Oxford (under Dr. E. W. Spooner, whose "Spoonerisms" he would try to emulate in his Irish humerous way), and to Leeds Clergy School (1900). He was ordained by the Bishop of Ripon to a curacy at St. Matthew, Holbeck, Leeds (1901–1905), followed by a second curacy at St. Peter's, South Croydon, in the Diocese of Canterbury (1905–10), until Dr. Randall Davidson, the Archbishop of Canterbury appointed him to the country benefice of Sibertsworld (or Shepherdswell) between Canterbury and Dover in 1910. He loved climbing, and accompanied his parents for some 20 years in succession on their annual climbing holidays in Switzerland, often officiating as the holiday (C.C.C.S.) chaplain at the resorts where they stayed. He ascended many of Switzerlands highest peaks, and always hoped to reach the top of the Matterhorn. The Riffel Alp, above Zermatt, the Reider Alp, Wengen and Murren were particularly favourite centres; there was hardly a Swiss guide he did not know by name in such centres, and he was an easy mixer with the climbing fraternities. Perseverance, patience, climbing, attention to detail, and the lucid writing of copious diaries and journals—the Grubb seed of his heredity had burst forth to full flower in the manhood of Ernest. As a clergyman he was a faithful pastor, and he also conducted several missions under his Archbishop's parochial missions organisation; his sermon notes, written in full hand, ran into thousands. He died October 2nd, 1914, aged 37, under an emergency operation for appendicitis, performed by lamplight on the kitchen table, and is buried at Shepherdswell. He married, 1907, MARY PAULINE, youngest daughter of Thomas Bevan, Esq., D.L., J.P., of Stone Park, Kent. She was a good musician, and a keen traveller on the Continent, and on her widowhood returned to the same house in Birdhurst Road, South Croydon, to which she was married. She was elected *Presiding Member for the Mother's Union* for the Archdeaconry of Croydon for many years, and was a Diocesan Speaker. She died at Cullompton Vicarage in Devonshire (where she had spent the war years with her eldest son) in 1946, and was buried at Shepherdswell beside her husband. They had three sons:

(The Rev.) GEOFFREY BEVAN WATKINS GRUBB, M.A. (Oxon.) F.R.N.S., b. 1908. Educated at Wellington and New College, Oxford like his father (2nd cl. Theol. 1931) and Lond. Coll. of Div., he was ordained by Dr. Winnington-Ingram, Bishop of London (who had a great influence on his life), in St. Paul's Cathedral 1933, as Tutor of the new Oak Hill Theological College, London, and curate of St. Paul, Winchmore Hill, w. St. Peter Grange Park (1933–37). He moved to Devonshire as Vicar of Cullompton (1937–46), and later Officiating Chaplain to the Forces and Surrogate. He was elected Proctor in Convocation for the Diocese of Exeter in the Convocation of Canterbury 1945–50. Vicar of St. James' Tunbridge Wells and Chaplain Pembury Grange 1946–52. Rector of Cranfield (Diocese of St. Albans) and Chaplain Royal College of Aeronautics at Cranfield 1952–1957. Rector of Spaxton with Charlynch, Somerset, 1957–1965. Permission to Officiate Diocese of Exeter since 1965. He married ANNA KATHLEEN, elder daughter of the Principal of Oak Hill College, Prebendary H. W. Hinde, M.A. (formerly Vicar of Islington), and Mrs. Hinde in 1934. Two children:

(i) SARAH MARY WATKINS, b. June 25th, 1939; m. 1960, Harold Smith, Esq. of Bridgwater. Two children: Timothy Richard and Anne Pauline Patricia.

(ii) DAVID HERBERT WATKINS GRUBB, b. Feb. 9th, 1941. Educated St. George's School, Harpenden, and Culham Teacher Training Coll., Abingdon. Schoolmaster at Torquay 1965–71. Head of English Dept., Calverhay School, Bath from 1971; m. Mrs. Beverly (*née* Brenner) Strong, M.A., of Indiana, U.S.A. 1969. They have a daughter (1970) Clare Elizabeth Watkins Grubb.

(Major) RALPH ERNEST WATKINS GRUBB, M.A. (Cantab.), F.R.I.C.A., F.L.A.S., b. April 12th, 1911. Educated Wellington College and Trinity College, Cambridge. Barrister (Inner Temple), 1936. Joined Inns of Court Regt. Cavalry), 1936. Transferred Intelligence Corps, 1942. Major 1945. G.S.O.2 (Intell.) Palestine 1945–46. East Sussex County Councillor from 1954. Land Agent and Farmer. High Sheriff of Sussex 1972; m. 1944, CAROLINE ELIZABETH MABEL ARBUTHNOT (J.P. Sussex from 1944), younger daughter of W. Rierson Arbuthnot, Esq., of Old Plaw Hatch, East Grinstead. They have three daughters and one son:

   (i) PATRICIA CAROLINE WATKINS GRUBB, b. 1947.
   (ii) ANTHONY ARBUTHNOT WATKINS GRUBB, b. 1950. Educated at Wellington.
   (iii) JOANNA PAULINE WATKINS GRUBB, b. 1952.
   (iv) OLIVIA ELIZABETH WATKINS GRUBB, b. 1955.

BERNARD ARTHUR WATKINS GRUBB. Their third son, b. July 14th, 1914, three months before his father's death. Educated at Crowthorne Towers and Wellington College. Died at school of meningitis, 1929.

4. *Lieut.-Commander WALTER BOUSEFIELD WATKINS GRUBB, R.N.*, their fourth son.

Born 1879, in Ireland at Marlton House, Wicklow. Educated H.M.S. *Britannia.* Midshipman H.M.S. *Trafalgar.* Awarded King Edward VII Coronation Medal 1902, when in command of H.M.S. *Hornet.* Lieut.-Commander H.M.S. *Crecy*, 1914. Lost in action in the North Sea, September 22nd, 1914. (Commemorated with his brother Ernest, who died three weeks later, by a beautiful stained glass window in Leeds Parish Church, Maidstone, erected by his parents). He married, July 1914, MARGUERITE, only daughter of Dr. and Mrs. Dunbar of Crowborough, Sussex. They had one son: WALTER BOUSEFIELD WATKINS GRUBB, b. 1915. Educated Charterhouse; m. 1951, AUDRY CUTTILL (daughter of Admiral Horsey, C.B.). Poultry farmer in Sussex.

5. *Captain REGINALD WATKINS GRUBB, R.N.*, their fifth son.

Born 1883. Educated Temple Grove School, East Sheen (1891–94) and Osborne and Dartmouth. Midshipman on H.M.S. *Marvel.* He was awarded the order of St. Anne of Russia (with swords) for distinguished service in the Battle of Jutland, when he was in command of H.M.S. *Marvel.* He had a long naval career, ending i/c Shipping in Bermuda. He married (i) ZOE KATHLEEN, daughter of Capt. Bertram Wilson Gwynne, R.N. They had one daughter:

YVONNE WATKINS GRUBB (1909–1971). Unmarried. Dress designer.

He married (ii) ETHEL BENDEL. They had one daughter:

SONIA WATKINS GRUBB, b. 1925. Unmarried. Nurse in United States.

HISTORY HAS A HABIT OF REPEATING ITSELF . . .

Appropriately this chapter on the Watkins Grubb descendants of the Grubbs of Tipperary ends with the return to the Land of her forefathers of the eldest child of Alexander and Sara Grubb, who was also the eldest granddaughter of Richard and Maria Grubb of Cahir Abbey. Like Anne von Grubbe (*Annie Winthrop, see chapter two*) 400 years before her, she came if not to Castle Grace itself, to marry a descendant of the Grubbs of Castle Grace in County Tipperary—the High Sheriff of the County—her father's second cousin, Louis Grubb, who had already made a name for himself in introducing and developing the motor-car into Ireland.

LOUIS HENRY GRUBB, D.L., J.P., M.A. (*Oxon*), 1865–1929, of Ardmayle House, near Cashel. (*See Collateral Table "G"*). Was the grandson of SAMUEL and DEBORAH GRUBB (1787–1859) of Clashleigh and Castle Grace, Clogheen, the younger brother of RICHARD GRUBB, 1780–1859, of Cooleville and Cahir Abbey, the great grandfather of his wife.

SARA MARY WATKINS GRUBB (called *May* to distinguish her from her mother) was born in Ceylon at Fort Frederick, Trincomalee, in 1871 within a year of her parents' marriage, baptised by the chaplain of H.M.S. *Glasgow*, flagship to Admiral Cockburn, and educated at Blackheath High School for Girls. She returned to live in Ireland on her marriage in 1899 from Stone Castle to her second cousin—(such marriages were frequent in Quaker days)—thus retaining the name of Grubb.

After a long honeymoon in Egypt and Palestine, May was presented at the last Court of Queen Victoria by her mother on May 11th, 1900. She became President of the Cashel, Emly, Waterford and Lismore branches of the Mother's Union (Church of Ireland), and of the Cashel Red Cross Society and was indefatiguable in all good works. She possessed all the Grubb spirit of vivacity and charm, and played a full part at Ardmayle in church and county life. On leaving Ireland in 1921 during the Sinn Fein riots, for Bournemouth, the Ardmayle Select Vestry in a farewell minute spoke of Mr. and Mrs. Louis Grubb as "Pillars of the Church in Ireland"—foremost in every good cause. Their hearts remained in Ireland, even when their lovely home, Ardmayle, was burnt to the ground. They devoted themselves to rousing interest and support in the Bournemouth area for the South American Missionary Society. They had four children, three sons, and one daughter:

PETRONELLE DOROTHY MAY, b. 1908, who died in 1919 of typhoid.

Their eldest son—*HENRY CECIL GRUBB*, M.A. (1899–1964). Educated at Rugby and Trinity College, Cambridge, he became a Missionary in

South America, and later Superintendent of the CHACO Missions of the South American Missionary Society, 1922–1959. Extremely modest, a fine musician, and an expert on languages, he literally maintained the mission during the War years, and never spared himself in riding vast distances to open new stations among the Chaco indians, to heal the sick, and to teach and preach. (See further: Sir Kenneth Grubb's autobiography *Crypts of Power*.) He was married in 1950 to a fellow missionary, OLIVE LEAKE (sister of the present bishop of Paraguay), at Brimscombe Church, Glos. (by his cousins the Revs. Geoffrey and Philip Watkins Grubb). No children. Author of *The land beyond the Rivers*.

CEDRIC ALEXANDER GRUBB—their second son, b. 1902. Educated at Rugby, he was for nearly 40 years a farmer in South Africa (1921–1959) until he returned to Ireland. He married AILSA MARJORIE CAMPBELL and lives at Kiltynan, near Fethard, Co. Tipperary. They have one son:

> PATRICK LOUIS CEDRIC GRUBB, B.A., PH.D. Educated Cape Town University (B.A.); St. Andrew's University (PH.D.). Geologist in Australia, and later Professor University of Rhodesia, Salisbury. He married 1969, FRANCES LYNN RICHARDSON of Perth, Western Australia.

SAMUEL LOUIS GRUBB, M.A. (Oxon.), their third son, b. 1905. Educated Rugby, and Wadham College, Oxford, he returned to County Tipperary after his mother's death, and his marriage to PHYLLIS AMERY, daughter of Walter Hutton, Esq., Painter and Artist of Bournemouth in 1937. He farms at Beechmount, Fethard, and has collected or inherited much of the information concerning the Grubbs of Tipperary (freely made available to the author), on which this book is based. They have two sons and two daughters:

> (i) CLODAGH MAUREEN PETRONELL, b. 1938. Educated Bishop Foy School, Waterford and Trinity College, Dublin, B.A., H.DIP.ED., School Teacher in Finland, who married a fellow student at T.C.D., John McCormick, B.A., PH.D., now Lecturer in French at Trinity College. Dr. and Mrs. McCormick have four daughters—Julie, Rose, Sylvia and Tua (twins), 1965.

> (ii) PETRONELLA AMY MARY, b. 1941. Educated Bishop Foy School, Waterford and Alexandra College, Dublin N.F.F. Worked in Australia, and married 1968, Peter Clifton-Brown (nephew of the late Speaker of the House of Commons). They have one son, John, b. 1969.

> (iii) LOUIS MICHAEL GRUBB, B.A., M.SC., b. 1944. Educated Bishop Foy School, Waterford and Trinity College, Dublin. He is an Agricultural Research Chemist in Co. Leitrim, working on reclamation of Irish land.

> (iv) BRYAN CHARLES HENRY GRUBB, b. 1952. Educated Newtown School, Waterford and University College, Dublin. Architect.

As a Soldier, Puritan, and a Baptist, the first Grubb came to Ireland in 1656 to take over and live in one of its 3,000 castles. There he dedicated the remainder of his life to the ways of peace. He became a Quaker. His descendants remained Quakers for 200 years, some of them to this day. They became farmers, millers, merchants, shopkeepers, country gentlemen. Later they served as justices of the peace, high sheriffs of County Tipperary, barristers, professors, teachers, clergymen, soldiers and sailors. The last British officer to leave Ireland on its becoming a Republic was one of his descendants. They have gone into all the world in the service of their Monarch, and of the King of Kings. Like Abraham and Ishmael of old, told to leave their homes, and travel to a country that God would show them, for the past 100 years the Grubbs have been on the move, striking out new paths, avoiding the "ruts" of life, hopefully travelling into the future. Statistically from the landing at Waterford of John and Mary Grubb and their five children in 1656, there have sprung 352 Grubbs, of whom records given in this book are available, and probably three to four hundred more in America, Canada and Australia. With their descendants in the female line, his offspring have "multiplied as the stars of the heavens, and as the sand which is upon the sea-shore" (Genesis 22, 18); their prayer must surely be that "through them all the nations of the earth shall be blessed".

> "Long as our life shall last
> TEACH US THY WAY.
> Where 'er our lot be cast
> TEACH US THY WAY.
> Until the race is won,
> Until the journey's done,
> Until the crown is won,
> LORD, TEACH US THY WAY."

> *The Sure Traveller,*
> *Though he alight sometimes*
> *Still Goeth on.*
> *George Herbert.*

YOU ASK ME WHY . . . ?

You ask me why I see no charm nor glory
  In this world's pleasures, or its wealth and fame?
And why I love the Galilean story
  Of ONE WHO DIED upon a Cross of Shame?

IT IS BECAUSE . . .

It is because I see a distant morning
  When stand God's sons around His glorious Throne—
I see bright crowns their furrowed brows adorning:[1]
  And I too long to hear my Lord's 'WELL-DONE'.

[1] *See p.* 137.

ADDENDA

(Later births into the family after 1971, marriages, deaths, and corrections may be added here)

BIRTHS
1971   Susan Joy Watkins Grubb, daughter of A. R. Watkins Grubb (p. 193).
Camilla Lucy Watkins Grubb, daughter of P. J. Watkins Grubb (p. 193).

APPENDICES

THE DIFFICULTIES OF TRAVEL IN THE YEARS 1760–1790

Being extracts from the Journals of John Wesley, A.M.[1]

and of

Mrs. Sarah Grubb (*née* Tuke; Wife of Robert Grubb)

I

Sailing from Dublin to Holyhead, and on horseback to Bristol
(five days).

(Whereas today it is possible to fly from Dublin to Bristol in under an hour, and the sea crossing of St. George's Channel takes under four hours, delays and hazards due to contrary winds often delayed the traveller in the 18th century by six or seven days.)

1760. At the end of his Irish tour John Wesley records in his Journal:

Mon. Aug. 18. (He was in Cork.) "Being advised from Dublin that Captain Dansey (with whom I desired to sail) would sail on the 19th or 20th, we took horse early; and it was well we did; for our seven and thirty Irish miles, so called, were little less than seventy English(!). I preached at a Friend's house soon after three, and then procuring a fresh horse, about the size of a jack-ass, I rode on with more ease than state, and reached Clonmell between five and six in the evening. I took my usual stand near the barrack-gate, and had abundantly more than my usual congregation, as it was the Assize week, so that the town was extremely full of gentry, as well as common people.

Tues. 19. We had many light showers, which cooled the air and laid the dust. We dined at Kilkenny, noble in ruins: I see no such remains of magnificence in the kingdom. The late Duke of Ormonde's house, on the top of a rock, hanging over the river, the ancient cathedral, and what is left of many grand buildings, yield a melancholy pleasure. We lodged at Castle-dermot, and reached Dublin on

Wednesday 20; but Captain Dansey was not to sail this week. I then enquired for a Chester ship, & found one that was expected to sail on Friday morning: but on *Friday morning* the Captain sent us word he must wait for General Montague. So in the afternoon I rode over to the Skirries, where the packet lay: but before I came thither, the wind which was fair before, shifted to the east and blew a storm. I saw the hand of God, and, after resting awhile, rode cheerfully back to Dublin. It being the watch-night I came just in time to spend a comfortable hour with the congregation. *Oh how good it is to have no choice of our own, but to leave all things to the will of God!*

Sat. 23. The Captain of the Chester ship sent word that the General would not go, and he would sail the next morning. So we have one

[1] *The Journal of the Rev. John Wesley, A.M.,* Vol. iii. pp. 9–14.

day more to spend in Ireland. Let us live this day as if it were our last.

Sun. 24. At seven I took leave of my friends, and about noon embarked in the *Nonpareil* for Chester. We had about forty or fifty passengers on board, half of whom were cabin passengers. I was afraid we should have an uneasy time in the midst of such a crowd of gentry. We sailed out with a fair wind, but at four in the afternoon it failed, and left us in a dead calm. I then made the gentlemen an offer of preaching, which they thankfully accepted. While I was preaching, the wind sprung up fair; but the next day we were becalmed again. In the afternoon they desired me to give them another sermon: and again the wind sprung up while I was speaking, and continued till, about noon on—

Tuesday 26, we landed at Parkgate. Being in haste I would not stay for my own horse, which I found could not land till low water. So I bought one, and having hired another, set forward without delay. We reached Whitchurch that evening.

Wed. 27. We breakfasted at Newport, where finding our horses beginning to fail, we thought it best to take the Birmingham road, that if they should fail us altogether, we might stay among our friends. But they would go no further than Wolverhampton: so we hired fresh horses there, and immediately set out for Worcester. But one of them soon after fell, and gave me such a shock (though I did not quit my seat) that I was seized with a violent bleeding of the nose, which nothing we could apply would stop. So we were obliged to go at foot pace for two miles, and then stay at Broadwater. (? Broadway.)

Thurs. 28. Soon after we set out, the other horse fell lame. An honest man at Worcester found this was owing to a bad shoe. A smith cured this by a new shoe; but at the same time, by paring the hoof too close, he effectually lamed the other foot, so that we had hard work to reach Gloucester. After resting here awhile we pushed on to Newport; where I took a chaise, and we reached Bristol before eleven. I spent the following two days with the Preachers, who had been waiting for me all the week: and their love and unanimity was such as soon made me forget all my labour.

Mon. Sept. 1st. I set out for Cornwall. . . ." So the constant journeyings of the intrepid Evangelist continued. Time off he took none.

II

Continental Travel

From Munster Province in Ireland to Munster in Germany 1787

"Our difficulties in the way of travel began when we left Holland. After gliding along in Treckschutes upon their quiet waters, we got into waggons in Germany, the best public conveyances the country afforded. The roads being extremely bad, we were jolted along to a degree not easy to suppose. For want of imperfectly knowing the language, we were imposed upon, and induced to take our passage in the post waggon to Munster, understanding that we should have it to ourselves, arrive seasonably at our lodgings the two nights of the journey, and have time enough to rest.

"But instead of these things, after they got our money, a Cappuchin Friar and a very ill-looking man were put in with us. We were kept in this situation with two meals wanting through a dark rainy night (the wet coming in upon us), till three o'clock next morning; after two hours rest we were summoned again, and without stopping to take any meals, save our dinner, we travelled on until we arrived about one o'clock next day at the gates of Munster, a fortified city. Here we had to wait for an entrance more than half-an-hour, and then find our lodgings among a strange people, whose principal object seemed to be to get from us what they could. This is a hint of the manner in which we got along, and I mention it to show the inconveniences strangers are subjected to, and how different the fare of these countries is from England and Ireland; at the same time an acknowledgement of providential care is abundantly due from us. Our minds during this trial extraordinary of body and spirits were remarkably sustained with cheerful tranquility, and an abundant desire to comfort one another. We were also preserved at the time from suffering in our health, and found that part of two days rest in Munster recruited us finely.

"Our stay in Munster was very satisfactory, finding it to be a place of considerable openness. One man in particular, a Professor of languages in the University, received us with brotherly affection and joy: we had a very satisfactory conversation with him, and he was glad to receive some of our books, some of which he intended to put into the public library. He told us of a relation of his in another part of Germany, where we have not been, who is fully convinced of our principles, but who has not dared openly to avow them, and he said that there are many such known to him in other parts. We have since found this to be the case. A serious young nobleman, intending to take a tour of England and a pupil of his, was desirous of being recommended to some Friend in London. Many other opportunities occurred of casting books into the hands of serious people, and in our imperfect way of intimating to them such Truths as at that time we were possessed of. From Munster we came by way of Warrendorf, Padderborn, etc., through Westphalia to Pyrmont, which we reached on the 23rd of the 7th month. Here our minds were much comforted in the belief that there is a Seed in these parts, which however hidden from the world, and the main churches that profess the Christian name, are pressing after an establishment on the right foundations. Nevertheless, there have been seasons when Satan did not fail to suggest to the weakness of my mind that we were running in vain. . . . We received accounts of our brother Joseph Grubb being in a very declining state of health, and being in partnership with my Robert Grubb, and the care of the business forbidden to our brother, my husband thought it his duty to offer him all the relief he could, which meant our return home. We have travelled 2500 miles on this tour . . we were detained in Amsterdam longer than we expected, owing to the printing of some extracts from Hugh Trimford's writings, with an addition from Mary Brook on *Silent Waiting* which we have translated into French. . . ." [2]

Sarah Grubb also writes of the long sea voyage from Holyhead to Dublin, which owing to contrary winds took five days.

[2] *Some Account of the Life and Religious Labours of Sarah Grubb.* Printed for R. Jackson, No 20 Meath Street, Dublin. MDCCXCII. (1792), pp. 205–212.

The WHITEBOYS in County Tipperary,
and
LIGHT DRAGOONS and FOOT RGMTS. stationed in Clonmel, 1786

(Extracts from the Journals (a) of the Rev. John Wesley, A.M. for 1762;
(b) of John Grubb (1766–1841) for 1786–87)[1]

(a) *Monday, 14 June, 1762.*

"I rode to Cork. Here I procured an exact account of the late commotions. About the beginning of December last a few men met by night near Nenagh in the County of Tipperary and threw down the fences of some commons which had been lately enclosed. Near the same time others met in the Counties of Cork, Tipperary, and Waterford. As no one offered to suppress them or hinder them, they increased in number continually. They called themselves *Whiteboys*, wearing white cockades and white linen frocks (i.e., their farming overalls). In February there were five or six parties of them, two or three hundred in each, who moved up and down, chiefly by night; but for what end did not appear. Only they levelled a few fences, dug up some grounds (i.e., at the entrance or gates to fields), & hamstrung some cattle, perhaps fifty or sixty in all.

"One body of them came into Cloheen (i.e. Clogheen) of about 500 foot, and two hundred horse. They moved as exactly as regular troops, and appeared to be thoroughly disciplined. They now sent letters to several gentlemen, threatening to pull down their houses. They compelled everyone they met to take an oath to be true to Queen Sive (whatever that meant), and to the Whiteboys; not to reveal their secrets, and to join them when called upon.

"It was supposed eight or ten thousand were now actually risen, many of them well-armed: and that a far greater number were ready to rise whenever they should be called upon. Those who refused to swear they threatened to bury alive. Two or three they did bury up to the neck, and left them: where they must quickly have perished, had they not been found by some travelling by. At length towards Easter a body of troops, chiefly light horse, were sent against them. Many were apprehended and committed to gaol; the rest of them disappeared."

———

(b) *Eighth month, 1786.*

26th, 7th Day. "One Company of the 1st or Royal Scotch Foot marched for Carrick, and one Troop of 8th Light Dragoons came here from Clogheen on Account of the Disturbance occasioned by the White Boys."

---

1 These extracts from the Journal of John Grubb (eldest son of Benjamin Grubb, *Collateral Table F*) for the year 1786, are printed by kind permission of Mrs. M. E. Grubb of Ross-on-Wye, one of his descendants by marriage. They show the reason for so many troops being stationed in Clonmel, the County Capital.

27th, 1st Day. "This day some Whiteboys assembled at Rose Green for to swear the People. Parson Hare of Cashel came there with some of the Army, and desired them to disperse, & they not complying, he ordered the soldiers to fire, which killed two and wounded several."

28th, 2nd Day. "One Company of 1st Foot, which marched for Carrick last 7th Day, coming back with two Whiteboys were attacked by a great number of people, who pelted them with Stones, which obliged the Army to fire, which killed one Boy, and wounded several. The light Horse returned to Clogheen."

Ninth Month, 1786.

1st, 6th Day. "Major General Lutterel (who is appointed to be Commander-in-Chief of the Province of Munster, to subdue the White Boys) sent fourteen of 'em to Gaol from Cashel: they were escorted by some light Infantry, lately sent down from Dublin. Parson Hare came to town in custody of the High Sheriff, for shooting a man who gave him some opposition when valuing some Tythes."

2nd, 7th Day. "The Light Company of the 1st marched for Carrick, and that of the 26th came to remain in their place, also one troop of the 8th light Dragoons from Clogheen. The Army posted up a proclamation of General Lutterel's to caution the Whiteboys from assembling."

3rd, 1st Day. "The Army were ready all day to receive the White Boys, but they did not come. General Lutterel arrived in Town from Cashel, & proceded to Curraghmore. The Light Horse went back to Clogheen."

9th, 7th Day. "The Light Companies of the 48th & 62nd Regiments came to Town from Tipperary."

10th, 1st Day. "The Army, which arrived yesterday, marched off early this morning for Dublin. The Judges came to Town. Sergt. Toler comes as an Assistant Judge to try the Whiteboys."

11th, 2nd Day. "The Assizes began: not much business done. I took a little walk by Gallows Hill."

12th, 3rd Day. "I was in Court about an hour, hearing the trial of Francis Oldis and Saml Hacket for murder: they were both acquitted. 4 persons were found guilty of robbery."

14th, 5th Day. "Eight Whiteboys were found guilty, of whom the Captain was capitally convicted."

15th, 6th Day. "Parson Hare was tried and acquitted."

16th, 7th Day. "A Man who had been discharged this Assizes went last Night & broke a Man's Houses near Ardfinan, & attempted to rob it, but was taken & brought to Town this morning, & sent into Court immediately, tried, found guilty, and recd sentence of Death, with seven others, one of whom is the Captain of the Whiteboys. The Judges left Town."

19th, 3rd Day. "I saw two Men going to be hung: one of 'em the man for robbing last 6th Day night; the other a young man about 20 years of age for robbing & attempting to murder a man near Carrick; they seemed very much composed, & behaved in a penitent manner."

23rd, 7th Day. "There were two Whiteboys whipped thro' the Street, but it was done in a very slight manner."

26th, 3rd Day. "Two troops of the 8th Light Dragoons came here to stay a few weeks."

27th, 4th Day. "The Light Company of the 20th Regt., which came here on acct of the Whiteboys, marched this morning for Dublin. Capt Mitchell was sworn Major."

30th, 7th Day. "Two Whiteboys were whipped through the Town, guarded by two companies of the 1st Regt Foot, and one troop of the 8th Light Dragoons."

14th, 7th Day. "There was one Whiteboy whipped thro' the town, which was better done than any of the former, & he roared at a great rate."

20th, 6th Day. "Two Troops of the 9th of Buff Dragoons came to remain in place of the Light Horse, who went away a few days ago."

Eleventh Month, 1786

24th, 6th Day. "Two Companies of the 1st Regt. Foot, and one Troop of the Buff Dragoons came to town to assist in guarding the Whiteboy who is to be hung tomorrow, for fear the People might attempt to rescue him. There was a small Bull-Baiting in the street near Sam Davis's."

25th, 7th Day. "John O'Flaherty, Captain of the Whiteboys, was hung this day about 12 o'clock, for firing a gun at a Gentleman of the name of Mannin, & taking some fire arms from him. He was guarded by three Companies of the 1st Regt, & two Troops of the Buff Dragoons: the High Sheriff with another troop remained in Town, riding up and down the Streets with their swords drawn, to deter the people from rising; they were so much exasperated at his being hung, but all remained quiet. He did not appear at all affected, when going out, but looked as well as anyone there, had his hair nicely powdered, and was well dressed; he was kept up nearly an hour."

If history is said to repeat itself, particularly Irish history, some comparison between the stationing of far greater numbers of British troops in Northern Ireland from 1969 to meet the threats and murders by a comparable number of discontented Irishmen, may be worked out.

THE NEW ZEALAND MEDAL

(PLATE XXIX)

In 1869 a medal was struck for presentation to officers and men who served in the Maori Wars in New Zealand between 1845–47, and 1860–66.

The causes of these two wars were the acquisition of Maori land by the incoming settlers (known as *pakehas* = white men), the absence of proof of the price paid before the coming of the first Governor Capt. William Hobson, R.N. in 1840, and the Treaty of Waitanga whereby New Zealand became a Crown Colony, and the natural reluctance of the inhabitants of these Pacific Islands, 1300 miles from Australia, to be dispossessed of their remaining ancestral lands [uncultivated and swamps as much of it was], whether by the New Zealand Company or by the Crown, for resale to incoming settlers at a very much higher price than they had paid the Maoris. Adam Smith wrote truly, "Plenty of cheap land has been one secret of British Colonial prosperity".

It was a situation parallel to that in Ireland after the Cromwellian Settlement, and the influx of English (Puritan) settlers like John Grubb into the best of Irish lands and castles, with the dispossession of the original Irish owners.

Ireland, through such men as Sir George Grey, K.C.B. (1812–1898), twice Governor of New Zealand, (who had been brought up in Dublin, and after training at the Royal Military College, Sandhurst, spent the first six years of his army life in the 83rd Foot Regiment, serving in Ireland and learning its deep-seated problems), Sir E. F. Bowen, K.C.B., his successor as Governor, who was born in Ireland in 1821, the black-bearded Irish Protestant Edward Stafford, one of New Zealand's earliest Prime Ministers, and Irish officers and men serving in the Maori Wars, made a decisive contribution in settling New Zealanders, white and brown, on the road to prosperity in a happy and progressive British Colony.

The *obverse* of the New Zealand Medal carries a profile of Queen Victoria (which appears on no other Campaign medal save that for Abyssinia) facing left; her crowned head heavily veiled. The Prince Consort died in 1861. Inscription—*Victoria D: G : Britt : Reg : F : D.* *Reverse*—A Laurel Wreath with inscription—*Virtus Honor.* This is a reference to the honourable way the wars were conducted, and to the gallantry of three Maori chieftains in bringing water under English gunfire to succour British wounded officers at Gate Pa. Both faces of the medal are the work of J. S. and A. B. Wyon.

The ribbon consists of two stripes of deep blue, with a central width of red. The clasp comprises a plain ball, from which project straight arms chased with the designs of fern fronds, so prolific in beautiful New Zealand. No other British medal uses this arrangement. There were no bars; the date struck in the centre of the reverse of most (but not all) medals serving this purpose. Each different date for the years 1845–46–47—1860–61–62–63–64–65–66 was struck by a separate die.

Alexander Grubb wore this medal at his wedding in 1871, and at King Edward VII's Leveé. (*Plate XXXVI*).

THE "MAORI WAR" IN NEW ZEALAND, 1864

The Engagement at Te Ranga (Tauranga)

The following dispatches were published in the *New Zealand Gazette* on Saturday.

Head Quarters,
Auckland.
June 30, 1864.

Sir

I have the honour to forward for your Excellency's information a second and more detailed report from Colonel Greer of the recent action at Tauranga.

The valour and discipline of the troops, and the ability of their Commander were conspicuously displayed on this occasion. The 43rd and 68th Light Infantry on whom the brunt of the engagement fell, behaved in a manner worthy of the high reputation of these distinguished regiments. The conduct of the Colonial Forces also reflects the greatest credit upon them.

The enemy appear to have fought with the most determined courage. I have & & &

D. A. CAMERON. Lieut.-General, K.C.B.
Commanding Her Majesty's Forces in New Zealand.
His Excellency Sir George Grey, K.C.B. & &.[1]

June 27, 1864.   Camp.
Te Papa.[2]

Sir

I have the honour to state for the information of the Lieutenant-General commanding in New Zealand that I have little to add to the report which I sent on the 21st instant, beyond to bring to his notice those who more particularly distinguished themselves.

About $10\frac{1}{2}$ o'clock the troops were so disposed in front and on both flanks that retreat without heavy loss seemed impossible for the Maoris.

About $12\frac{1}{2}$ o'clock, having reinforced skirmishers with 2 Companies of the 68th, and cautioned the men to reserve their fire (which they did in the most steady manner), the Advance was sounded, and the men moved forward as if on parade.

To the dash, determination, and steadiness with which the attack was made, the success which followed is due.

From the fact that the attack was made in Light Infantry order, and from the Maoris having waited for the charge, and making a desperate

---

[1] Sir George Grey, K.C.B. was Governor of New Zealand 1845–52, and 1861–68.
[2] *Te Papa*, close to the present town of Tauranga, and still standing today carefully preserved, was the Mission Station of Archdeacon and Mrs. Alfred Brown, two of the first Missionaries to New Zealand sent out by the Church Missionary Society. *Pa* is the Maori and Colonial name for a fenced encampment, or fort.

hand-to-hand resistance, more opportunity was offered of showing *individual gallantry* than might occur in more extensive operations. The attack was so simultaneous, and all did their duty so well, that it is difficult to make selections.

I beg however to bring the following to the favourable notice of the Lieutenant-General Commanding:

(Here follows a list of 28 names & their exploits—a selection only is given here.)

Major Synge, 43rd Light Infantry, commanding the line of skirmishers, who had his horse shot under him in 2 places, when close to the rifle pits.

Major Colville, 43rd Light Infantry, who gallantly led the left of the line of skirmishers into the rifle pits, himself being one of the first in.

Major Shuttleworth, 68th Light Infantry, who commanded the support, consisting of the 68th Light Infantry and 1st Waikato Militia, and brought them up in the most soldierlike manner, and rushed on the pits at a critical moment.

Captain Trent, Acting Field Officer, 68th Light Infantry, who fell severely wounded when leading two companies of the 68th into the left of the rifle-pits, and continued cheering on the men until the pits were taken.

Captain Smith, 43rd Light Infantry, who is reported to have been first into the right of the line of rifle-pits, and whose gallant conduct was so conspicuous. I have forwarded evidence with a view to his *being recommended for the Victoria Cross.* He was wounded severely in two places.

Captain Casement, 68th Light Infantry
Captain Berners, 43rd Light Infantry
⎫ Both severely wounded in two ⎬ places in front of their com- ⎭ panies.

Captain Seymour, 68th Light Infantry, who took Captain Trent's place, when that officer fell, and led into the left of the rifle-pits in the most gallant manner.

Lieutenant Stuart, 68th Light Infantry, who was one of the first into the left line of rifle-pits, and had a personal conflict with a Maori armed with an Enfield rifle and bayonet, and by whom he was slightly wounded, but succeeded in cutting him down with his sword.

Captain the Honourable A. Harris, 43rd Light Infantry, who was detached to the right in command of two companies of the 43rd to enfilade the enemy's position and afterwards brought the companies at a critical moment to assist in the assault.

Captain Moore, who commanded the 1st Waikato Militia. He led his men up to the rifle-pits, & shared in the assault.

Lieutenant Acting Adjutant Hammick, 43rd Light Infantry, who performed his duty with great coolness & courage under a heavy fire.

Lieutenant Grubb, R.A.,[3] whose coolness and excellent practice with the 6-pounder Armstrong under his command when under fire during

[3] The number of Irish surnames in this Dispatch suggests that it was because he was an Irishman that Alexander Grubb was selected as the only Artillery officer to join the 43rd and 68th Lt. Infantry.

the action, and subsequently on the retreating Maoris when they had got beyond the reach of infantry, was admirable.

Surgeon-Major Best, 68th Light Infantry, Principal Medical Officer, who performed his duty assiduously under fire, paying the greatest attention and care to the wounded.

I can say the same for:

Assistant-Surgeons Henry, 43rd; Applin, 68th, and *O'Connell, Staff.* The former was particularly brought to my notice by Major Synge, commanding 43rd Light Infantry.

Lieutenant & Adjutant Covey, 68th Light Infantry; Field Adjutant and Ensign Palmer, 68th Light Infantry, acting as my Orderly Officers, who performed their duty coolly and gallantly, affording me valuable assistance. Lieutenant Covey having been sent on a message by me to Major Shuttleworth when he was on the point of attacking, went with the supports, and was dragged into a rifle pit by a Maori, who thrust his spear through his clothes.

Ensign Palmer was struck in the neck by a musket ball and knocked from his horse insensible when riding beside me; when he recovered and had his wound dressed, he performed his duty during the rest of the day.

Sergeant-Major Tudor, 68th Light Infantry; Sergeant-Major Daniels, 43rd Light Infantry; Acting Sergeant-Major Lilley, 70th Regiment of the 1st Waikato Militia, who distinguished themselves in several personal conflicts with the enemy in the rifle-pits.

No 2198 Sergeant Murray, 68th Light Infantry, whose gallantry & prowess were so distinguished, I have thought him worthy of being recommended for the Victoria Cross, & have forwarded evidence.

No 2832 Corporal J. Byrne, V.C., 68th Light Infantry, who when the order to charge was given, was the first man of his company into the rifle pits. A Maori whom he transfixed with his bayonet, seized his rifle with one hand, and holding it firm with the bayonet through him, endeavoured to cut him down with his tomahawk—his life was saved by Sergeant Murray.

During the engagement several reports were forwarded to me that a large body of natives was coming down by the Wairoa[4] to attack the Camp, Te Papa, at low water, which on that day was 3.30 o'clock. The information was given by friendly natives. I was back in camp by 2.30 o'clock, and Artillery, Mounted Defence Force, and reinforcements of Infantry were following me. I found that every necessary arrangement had been made by Lieutenant-Colonel Harrington, 1st Waikato Militia, who was in command of the Camp during my absence.

I beg to bring to the notice of the Lieutenant-General commanding the readiness with which Captain Phillimore H.M.S. "Ess", senior naval officer at this station, and Commander Swan, H.M.S. "Harrier", responded immediately to my request (which I sent on finding the Maoris) that they would land all their available force for the protection of the Camp.

[4] *The Wairoa River* was but a mile up the Harbour from Tauranga at the northern end of the Bay of Plenty.

I have since ascertained that the report of the natives coming down to attack Te Papa was true, but that the result of the affair at Te Ranga disarranged their plans. For nearly an hour previous to the assault I had seen a Maori reinforcement coming down from the woods, yelling and firing their guns, and when the advance was sounded they were not more than 500 yards from the rifle-pits.

I beg further to add that while in command here I have only endeavoured to carry out the instructions given me by the Lieut.-General commanding, and if I have had any success, it is to the foresight of those instructions, and the good discipline and courage of the troops under my command that it is to be attributed.

On Wednesday morning I sent a strong patrol under Major Colville 43rd Light Infantry, to bury the dead, and fill in the rifle-pits, which they themselves dug the morning before. The patrol returned the same afternoon without having seen anything further of the hostile natives, nor have any since been observed in the neighbourhood.

In addition to the number buried in the rifle-pits, fifteen of the wounded prisoners have died since they were brought in. I am sending up eight wounded, and eleven unwounded prisoners by the 'Alexandra', and nine are detained for further treatment in the Hospital at this station, making a total of 151 Maoris accounted for. Enclosed are lists of the arms captured from the enemy, and handed to the Military Store Department, and returns of the killed and wounded of the Forces under my command.

I have, &&&

H. H. Greer. Colonel.
Commanding Tauranga District.

Archdeacon Brown's report to the Church Missionary Society on the actions at Tauranga and the Gate Pa, as a result of which streams of the blood of British and Maori christains, some of them from his own Mission, such as Wiremu Taratoa one of his school teachers, had left an indelible stain upon the Society's Mission Compound, inspired his friend, the Rev. H. W. Fox, the 19th Century Poet of the Society, to add another verse to one of the finest and popular missionary hymns used by the C.M.S. at their great London meetings and at Farewells to recruits, that begins "I HEAR TEN THOUSAND VOICES SINGING THEIR PRAISES TO THE LORD ON HIGH."

It runs—

> Fair are New Zealand's wooded mountains,
>   deep glens, blue lakes, and dizzy steeps:
> But sweeter than the murmuring fountains
>   ascends the praise from Maori lips—
> BY BLOOD did Jesus come to save us,
>   so DEEPLY STAINED WITH BROTHER'S BLOOD:
> Our hearts we'll give to Him, who gave us
>   deliverance in the fiery flood.

Maori Chivalry after their Victory at the Gate Pa

The Engagement at Te Ranga avenged the British defeat two months earlier, at the Gate *pa* but four miles from Tauranga, when Lt.-General Cameron, Commander of Her Majesty's Forces in New Zealand, himself had come with reinforcements from Auckland to direct the British strategy in the North Island. Having had reports around Christmas that east coast Maoris from the Tauranga district were infiltrating the forests to ambuscade his troops, and assist their kinsmen on the west coast in the Waikato Campaign, the General had decided the best way to hasten victory in Waikato was to send a military force to Tauranga, to stop the campaign spreading. Before the end of January 1864 two detachments of the 43rd and the 68th Regiments, newly arrived reinforcements from Australia, Lt. Alexander Grubb, R.A. with them, and some of the Waikato Militia—about 700 men in all, were sent from Auckland under the command of Colonel Greer, an Irishman.

The Maoris—there were only about 250 of them—occupied a *pa* about seven miles from Tauranga township, and hopefully awaited the British attack. But Greer did not move. New to New Zealand conditions of warfare, and unaware of the strength of the Maoris, he hesitated to attack their strongly entrenched *pa*, and preferred to await reinforcements. His troops set up their tents and marquees around Archdeacon Brown's C.M.S. Mission station at Te Papa, close to Tauranga township on *pakeha* (i.e., non-Maori) land.

The Maoris were disappointed. With their characteristic sense of fun they sent a message to Col. Greer that they had built a road from Tauranga to their *pa*, so that his troops would not be too tired to fight when they arrived! Still Greer remained at Te Papa.

By April 1864 the Maoris had built a new *pa*, a formidable redoubt or fort on the crown of a ridge overlooking and only two miles from Tauranga Harbour, with a smaller *pa* on its left flank, together with trenches, rifle-pits and underground shelters. It stood by the gate in the fencing which separated *pakeha land* (i.e. Tauranga C.M.S. Mission station—land belonging to the whites) from Maori land, and became known as the Gate *pa*.

Not until April 21st did General Cameron arrive with 500 more troops and a naval brigade of 400 men from Her Majesty's warships *Miranda*, *Ess*, and *Falcon*, anchored in the harbour. He should have found victory an easy matter. His troops now outnumbered the Maoris by six or seven to one. But strange and unexpected things happen in warfare!

On the night of April 28th after a week's delay, the Commander-in-Chief sent Col. Greer and 700 men, mostly of the 68th Regiment, to take up positions in the darkness behind Gate *pa*. At daybreak next morning the bugles sounded the attack with a heavy artillery barrage, but it was not until about 4 o'clock in the afternoon Gen. Cameron considered a wide enough breach had been made to admit a storming party. This consisted of 150 seamen and marines, a moveable column of 150 men of various regiments, followed by a reserve of another 300 men of the 43rd Regiment, and the rest of the naval brigade. When the assault began, Col. Greer and the 68th were ordered to move in with intensive rifle fire to prevent the Maoris escaping.

"It was an extraordinary battle.[5] The storming parties rushed into the breach made in the left angle of the *pa*, and in fierce hand-to-hand fighting there were many casualties—the Maoris' tomahawks and musket-butts against the sailors' cutlasses and the soldiers bayonets. The Maoris were driven out of the greater part of the *pa*; so far the assault had been successful. But they could not get away. Rather than face the hail of bullets from the 68th Regiment under Col. Greer, they rushed back again into the *pa*.

"This was the turning point of the battle of Gate *pa*. The seamen and marines, unused to this kind of warfare and confused by the intricate lines of the *pa's* trenches and underground shelters and rifle pits, suddenly heard the warcries and saw the returning Maori warriors—and a woman among them—brandishing their tomahawks and leaping to attack them in the strong rays of the setting sun. 'They're coming down upon us in thousands', cried one of the sailors. Confronted in the sun's glare by what they took to be a mass-attack by fresh Maori warriors, the sailors and marines turned and fled from the *pa*, leaving their wounded comrades and dead where they lay. Capt. Hamilton of the *Ess*, in charge of the Reserves, tried desperately to stem the retreat, but he was shot while trying to rally his men. The whole British forces fled ignominiously back to their ships and Te papa." Lt. Alexander Grubb was on the southern side of the Gate *Pa*, and knew nothing of the Maori victory until later, after they had silently evacuated the *Pa* under the cover of darkness.

But where was General Cameron, the officer commanding the operations? Had he been present, the muddle and consequent British flight might never have occurred. Why did he put sailors, and not his seasoned troops into the front line of the attack? "I am at a loss to explain this repulse", he wrote to the Governor, Sir George Grey, "and the bad relations between them were intensified. Later Cameron accused Grey of having personally ordered Col. Greer not to attack the Maoris in the February or March; the consequence of such neglect, he said, was that the Maoris were left free to construct their formidable Gate *pa*. Cameron was replaced by General Sir Trevor Chute as C.-in.-C in the following year, and ended his days as Commandant of the Royal Military College, Sandhurst.[6] He retained the support of the War Office against Grey."[7]

* * * * * * *

On the evening before the attack on Gate *pa*, Archdeacon and Mrs. Brown had entertained to supper as many of the officers encamped at Te papa as could be spared from their duties, after which a Communion service was held for the troops before the battle. The next night only one of the officers entertained was still alive. The casualties were 46 killed, and 122 wounded, and about 20 Maoris.

[5]*The Strangest War* (1962). Edgar Holt, Ch. 20, from which admirable account much of this description is condensed.
[6]For the difficulties confronting a Colonial Governor and the Commander-in-Chief of the armed forces, *see Life of Sir George Grey (1812–1898)*. J. Rutherford, PH.D., pp. 504, 528–538, 570–575. For a criticism of General Cameron, *see The Strangest War*, E. Holt, pp. 196–227, who quotes a scathing comment from Archdeacon Hadfield—"There can be no doubt the men of the assaulting party at Gate *pa* were a lot of arrant cowards. The explanation may be that both officers and men had lost confidence in old Cameron, who seems to be a nervous old woman in uniform".

The chivalry with which three Maoris, a half-caste woman Heni Pare (as good a shot as any man), Wiremu Taratoa, and Te Ipu treated British wounded at Gate *pa* "liveth for evermore". The severely wounded young captain Booth in his pain was crying out for water; his British comrades had fled. There was no water obtainable in any of the Maori *pas*. It could only be obtained from a near-by brook which ran down into the Harbour of Tauranga, and this meant taking cans and going out at the risk of their lives under the fire of Col. Greer's troops, with whom Lt. Grubb was serving. "They won't shoot a woman. I will go", said Heni Pare. Wiremu Taratoa, had already gone. Te Ipu slipped out twice with two cans. If other Maoris also went, they did not live to return. So was the thirst and agony of the wounded quenched by these heroic Maoris. It was later found that not a watch, nor a ring, nor a coin had been stolen from the dead or wounded.

Wiremu (William) Taratoa had been baptised as a boy by Bishop George Augustus Selwyn, old Etonian and Cambridge rowing blue, first Bishop of New Zealand (1841–1868) and one of the famous and colourful men in New Zealand history. He had been curate of Windsor and a tutor at Eton until at the age of 32, with the cries of his Etonian friends "Floreat Etona"[8] ringing in his ears, he pulled himself away from ease and prospects in Victorian England on his 13,000 mile voyage, to proclaim the gospel of the Saviour of all mankind in once cannibal islands of the Pacific. Wiremu was one of his first converts, and later trained as a teacher in the bishop's school in Auckland, and taught in the Mission school at Tauranga. Two months later he was himself killed in the Engagement at Te Ranga, and on his body was found a copy of the Maori rules for warfare that he had faithfully kept, with the text—

> "If thine enemy hunger, feed him,
> If he thirst, give him drink. . . ."

A stained glass window to these three brave Maoris was later erected in Lichfield Cathedral.[9]

Alexander Grubb never spoke much of his New Zealand experiences, where he encountered noble *and* ignoble men, both white and brown. How often did he wonder if he had done right to leave Ireland and Cahir Abbey to join the army? Had it been "the admirable fire from his 6-pounder Armstrong on the retreating Maoris" (to quote Col. Greer's citation in Dispatches) that had killed the heroic and christian William Taratoa? He would never know. Such are the agonies and hazards of warfare, when christian is fighting christian, and both sides are praying to the "One God and Father of All Mankind", believing that He must be on *their* side. The strength of the Quakers, as the Grubbs once knew and have always since recognised, has been their total renunciation of war. Had the Quakers not "disowned" his father and mother in the year of his birth, Alexander asked himself if he would ever have become a soldier? Once trained and started on a career, he knew it was too late to turn back But increased a thousandfold was his determination to do all he could in his army life to proclaim the everlasting gospel to all ranks, and to give his open witness to his Saviour. He became a life-long supporter of the work of the Church Missionary Society.

⁷Sir George Grey was born in the same year as Alexander Grubb's father, and outlived him by ten years. Both of them had the same experience of Irish and Dublin life, but Grey had the easy opportunity of entering the army (his father had risen therein to high rank, and died under the Duke of Wellington in the Peninsular War), denied to Richard Grubb Junr., who remained a Quaker in his impressionable years, until disowned. Grey also after six years in Ireland *took the initiative* in applying to the Royal Geographical Society to go on exploration to North-western Australia, which led to an appointment as British Resident in the King George Sound, and at the age of 28 (in 1841) to be Governor of South Australia. His life illustrates the truth of the words: "Once to every man and nation comes the moment to decide". Throughout his two Governorships of New Zealand he never forgot his six years Irish experiences of ill-clad, poor, and discontented people, eking out a miserable existence on patches of land in cabins and hovels, their ancestral lands and farms occupied by English immigrants after the Cromwellian Settlement of Ireland. He was determined this should not happen to the Maoris, and this helps to explain his constant disagreements with General Cameron, who conceived it his duty to suppress utterly the defiant Maoris, and open all parts of the islands to English settlers and traders.

⁸Wiremu Taratoa was brought up in the Bay of Islands, where bishop Selwyn was allowed by the Church Missionary Society the use of its Mission Station at Waimate as his first home and centre. It may be that Wiremu was the Maori boy who first taught the language to the young bishop on his 90-day journey out, so that he was soon able to preach his first sermon in Maori after landing; and who also taught him the navigation of the difficult New Zealand coast line in the north island. The captain of a merchant vessel once remarked, "it almost made him a Christian to see the bishop bring his schooner into harbour".

⁹Eton did flourish in New Zealand during Bishop Selwyn's episcopate. He wrote to his brother in 1861 that three Old Etonian bishops in New Zealand had had the great pleasure of consecrating a fourth Eton man, J. C. Patterson, as missionary bishop in the South Pacific. The three Eton bishops were Selwyn himself, C. J. Abraham, bishop of Wellington, and E. Hobhouse, bishop of Nelson. G. A. Selwyn was one of New Zealand's greatest mid-century figures, a bishop who was a politican as well as pastor, and for a time "the best-hated" man in New Zealand because of his fearless championship of Maori rights. Described as the "beau ideal" of bishops through his strong and handsome features, in 1868 he was urged by Lord Derby, England's prime minister, and by the archibshop of Canterbury to become bishop of Lichfield. He declined to leave his beloved New Zealand, until the Queen herself sent for him to stay at Windsor, and he obeyed Her royal command. One of his first acts at Lichfield was to have a memorial window erected in his cathedral to Wilemu Taratoa and the other Maoris, based on II Samuel, xxiii, 15–17, showing King David being brought longed-for water by three of his mighty men, who broke through the host of the Philistines, but declining to drink it, because of the jeopardy with which they had hazarded their lives. Bishop Selwyn was the only non-combatant to be awarded the New Zealand Medal.

¹⁰Major Gustavus Von Tempsky, once a Prussian officer, a flamboyant soldier of fortune and the picturesque company commander of the Forest Rangers, had fought in guerilla wars in Mexico, and among the Mosquito Indians in Central America, and was very much at home in swift hand-to-hand actions in the New Zealand bush. He was of striking appearance, with his forage cap perched on a mass of long dark curly hair extending almost to his shoulders, his drab uniform enlightened by a bright red silk sash. For all his swagger he was a dangerous opponent, skilled in guerrilla tactics, and of great courage. The bowie knife, with a blade ten to twelve inches long was his favourite weapon, and his men were taught how to use it and especially how to throw it. In bush warfare he was unrivalled. He was killed in the second attack on the Maori stronghold or *pa* of *Te Ngutuotemanu* on September 7, 1868, and his body burnt on a funeral pyre, so greatly did the Maoris fear him.

(See *The Strangest War*, pp. 144, 195, 228, 243; *A History of New Zealand*. A. Read. p. 123.)

PLATE XXXVIII

GOVERNORS OF NEW ZEALAND
THE BISHOP; AND OFFICERS WHO SERVED
IN THE MAORI WARS

One of a Collection of Photographs formed by the New Zealand Government at the end of the nineteenth century. *Ex Libris Alexander Grubb.*

| *Row 1* | General Sir Duncan Cameron, K.C.B., C-in-C. New Zealand Forces (*See note 6*) | Sir George Grey, K.C.B. Governor of New Zealand (*See note 7*) | Col. Sir Thomas Gore-Browne, K.C.B. Governor of New Zealand 1854–1861 | Cap. Peter Cracroft, R.N. H.M.S. *Niger* |

Col A. J. Russell   Sir George Bowen, K.C.B.   Major-General
Governor of New Zealand 1868   F. Mould

Row 2 (3rd from left): General Sir Trevor Chute, C.-in-C. 1865   Col. Greer

Row 4. (2nd from left): The Bishop of New Zealand   Major Gustavus Von Tempsky
(Rt. Rev. George Augustus Selwyn)   (*See note 10*)
(*See notes 8 and 9*)

Row 5 (3rd from left):   Alexander Grubb (Lt.-Col.)

THE BUILDING OF THE SUEZ CANAL
and
36 DAY VOYAGE TO CEYLON FROM LONDON DOCKS. 1871

(From the Diary of Mrs. Watkins of Potters Bar, and the letters of Lieutenant and Mrs. Alexander Grubb on board s.s. *Scotland* and from Ceylon)

Alexander and Sara " . . . secured the best cabins on the steamer 'Scotland' a large fine vessel lying in the East India Docks. Stores of preserved meats, jam & all other things for household use, a suitable amount of light clothing for a hot climate, as well as china, glass, lamps, cutlery, etc, had all been packed by Sparkes of Oxford Street in one vast barrel, so carefully that not a single article was broken on the voyage or its transport by bearers through Ceylon. Mrs. Birch, who had had 20 years experience in India, and was strongly recommended by (Uncle) Hugh Huleatt (C.F.) was engaged to go with them as servant and later as nannie. Their piano by Collard was also already on board, when after a week or two postponements of the sailing, the telegram reached us at Potters Bar on the morning of *June 12th* (*1871*), that they are to be on board the same afternoon."

They had a great send-off. The Watkins Family, joined at the Docks by Sara's brother Henry Watkins who had managed to get down from Oxford, rowed out to the "Scotland", anchored in the river, to see the last of them. "We found Uncle Hugh and Aunt Milly Hulleat had come on board from Woolwich, and Mr. and Mrs. Birch, who had nicely arranged their cabin. As the next one was unoccupied, Alex was able to use it as a dressingroom. Not being a favourite season for a voyage to India, there were no other lady passengers. We took tea together with fresh milk provided for us, and they found the provisions very good throughout the voyage. The parting was very sad. I cannot speak of it."

"The voyage to Ceylon was scheduled to take 30 days. The 'Scotland' burnt 30 tons of coal a day. It was thought this would be quick time on one of the fastest vessels, but it actually took 38 days. They passed Cape St. Vincent and the beautiful south coast of Portugal, which we ourselves have never visited, and then Cape Trafalgar. They thought of Nelson whom Alex has always admired so much. They spent an afternoon in Gibraltar, and Sara rode on horseback through the galleries. Then they both drove to Europa Point, and Alex showed Sara the fortifications of the Rock, and where their new home might have been, had he continued in his appointment there, instead of being posted to Ceylon. They sent me a letter from Gibraltar.

"*June 21st.* They passed a range of snowy peaks—the Sierra Nevada. On this day seven years ago Alexander was under a shower of Maori bullets, when his life was mercifully preserved.

219

"*Sunday, June 25th*. They passed Cape Bona. At morning service there were 20 sailors; 5 officers; 5 passengers, including Alex and Sara and Mrs. Birch. Next day they passed the Island of Pantellaria, and then saw the lights of Malta. They had a day in Malta (little knowing then that within a few years they would be making their 2nd home there).

"*Friday, June 30th*. They landed at Port Said. Wretched place, Alexander described it in a letter to me. 'Its hotels, cafes, shops and bazaars crowded with 6000 people, mostly Levantines and Greeks. Its wooden houses like brown paper, that would burn from end to end in 10 minutes.'

"*Sunday, July 2nd*. They had a morning service on board, lying at anchor in the Bitter Lake, & Alexander wrote us this interesting account of the works on the Canal they were sailing through:

THE BUILDING OF THE SUEZ CANAL

" 'The Suez Canal Company have been 14 years at work upon this gigantic labour—a canal 100 miles long, and to be 100 yards wide at the waters edge, and 25 feet deep in the middle, with no locks or bridges. The progress increases as we moved along what seemed to be a wide river, with villages upon its banks, and smoky funnels and white sails on its surface. The hydraulic machines groan and snort and rattle their chains as they work. They are of enormous size. Each of them seems to be pouring forth a volume of mud, although it is very hard to believe that all of them together can lift out and throw over the banks enough to make any appreciable difference between yesterday and today. The sand dredged from below is carried out to sea in barges, or taken further inland right away from the canal. We are told that the expenses are £200,000 a month, and that the work has already absorbed £8 million sterling.'"

Alexander's own diary continues "Ismalia is a pretty oasis halfway along the canal, which here enters Lake Timsah, known as the Crocodile Lake. Here the Arabs and their camels, and the jackals of the desert are alongside the steamboats, and the whirling lathes and resounding forge-hammers of the Company's workshops . . . the tall poles of the electric telegraph, and the hot rails of the railway. A cool and sweet draught of Nile water may be had from a fresh water canal, which comes all the way here from Cairo. It then branches out north and south along the whole extent of the salt-water canal.

"At Chaloof about 15,000 men (approx.) were at work. They laboured very hard, running up the hill, 'like the soldiers of the old Duke of York,' with baskets of sand upon their heads, and then running down again to refill their baskets, and repeat the process. In contrast to these simple carriers of sand and beasts of burden, which reminded me of Moses and the Book of Exodus, and of the Lord's people of old having to make bricks in Egypt, the mighty power of steam toils and puffs as it hurls up bulks of heavy clay. Perhaps only in Egypt does one see human and animal power exerted in such close competition with steam power. The labourers are sent here from all parts of Egypt. They must come, and have no option to refuse such labour, but they are paid 2 to 3 francs a day. Prices of food and labour have risen very much since the canal was begun. Fish is plentiful. The salt water canal seems to abound in fish. . . .

"The Expedition for the Survey of Sinai left a few days ago. Dr. Livingstone arriving next week. Pity we shall not be here to meet him."

Continued Mrs. Watkins in her diary—"The voyagers reached Aden half-dead with the heat. The temperature was 95 degrees in their cabin. Suez to Aden is 1,300 miles. There was tremendous surf when they landed at Colombo on the 20th July, and Captain Betty came out in the Royal Artillery boat to take them ashore. They were eight days overdue, owing to the delays in the Canal.

"*Friday, July 21st.* They reached Galle Face, 72 miles in the Stage Coach, where they proceeded to their quarters.

"*Sunday, July 23rd.* They attended divine service at the Garrison Church. Mr. Kelly the chaplain preached a good sermon. They sent off home letters.

"*Monday, July 24th.* They left cards on Lady Hercules Robinson. Nearly all the officers and their wives called. They were invited to many dinner and croquet parties. [1] There was a ball, given by the Ceylon Rifles on July 29th.

"*September 12th.* They left Colombo by train for Kandy through beautiful mountain scenery and stayed at the Queens Hotel. Their bandies arrived.

"*September 14th.* They started their seven days' trek across Ceylon. Mrs. Birch, servants, and three bullock bandies went ahead. They followed in a carriage and horses they bought off an officer returning from Trincomalee. They travelled about 16 miles in seven hours each day through the Jungle.

"*September 16th.* Mrs. Birch started at 5. Alex and Sara at 7. Lovely scenery until 10 o'clcock. They detoured to *Dambool* to visit a wonderful Buddhist Temple in the solid rock, 2000 years old. A colossal figure of *the Buddha*, 35 feet high, reclines from the rock. They stayed at the Guest House.

"*September 17th to 21st.* Continuation of their journey through the jungle, and on the Thursday they arrived at Trincomalee, and were received by Capt. and Mrs. Meardon. They moved into their new quarters —a large and long bungalow in Fort Frederick on Friday the 22nd. Alex sent us a carefully drawn sketch. It has a large sittingroom, 36 x 24 feet opening onto a long verandah, outside of which are trees and shrubs and grass, and then the road. They have three bedrooms, and a dressing room for Alex, and boudoir for Sara. They have their own stable and coach house, and a nice garden, and a well with lifting apparatus.

"*September 29th.* The Flagship *Forte* arrived. Alex called on Admiral Cockburn, who proved a most kind friend.

"*Sunday, October 1st.* No clergyman. Capt. Meardon conducted Service parade. *The eclipse of the sun* was seen to great advantage. Stars became visible, and a sudden spark of light like the sunrise on the Rigi was observed.

"*December 13th.* Great anxiety about the illness of the Prince of Wales. Alex received a telegram telling him to be ready to fire 31 minute guns."

---

[1]Croquet rather than tennis seems to have been the popular game; there are frequent references to their games in Ceylon in their diaries and throughout their lives. Tennis is never mentioned until the next century, after their move to Elsfield House, Kent.

As o'er each CONTINENT AND ISLAND
  The dawn leads on another day,
The voice of prayer is never silent,
  Nor dies the strain of praise away.

We thank Thee, that Thy Church unsleeping
  While earth rolls onward into light,
THROUGH ALL THE WORLD her watch is keeping
  And rests not now by day or night.

The sun, that bids us rest, is waking
  OUR BRETHREN 'NEATH THE WESTERN SKY,
And hour by hour fresh lips are making
  God's Wondrous Doings heard on high.

John Ellerton, 1826–1893.

IRISH GRUBBS IN AMERICA & CANADA

Further knowledge is necessary to paint a full picture and trace back the origins of the many Grubbs settled in America and Canada. Within the confines of this book the following Grubbs are known to have emigrated from Ireland and founded families in the States or in Canada.

1. *WILLIAM GRUBB*. About 1708, with William Penn to Pennsylvania. He was a grandson of the first John Grubbe, the Anabaptist Preacher of Ravensthorpe, who came to Ireland in 1656, and the eldest surviving son of Samuel and Rebecca (née Thrasher) Grubb, of Annaghs Castle. He had three sons.

(See Collateral Table "B")

2. *THOMAS GRUBB*, b. 1783. Son of George Grubb, Clothier in Clonmel, and a Great-grandson of John & Anne Grubb of Meylers Park and Woodhouse. It was his great-grandfather who went to America to build a trading ship.

(See Collateral Table "C")

3. *ROBERT GRUBB* (1790–1882). The fourth son of Samuel and Margaret (née Shackleton) Grubb (Chapter vii), and a second cousin of Thomas Grubb (above). After his clandestine marriage to his young sister-in-law Anna Fayle, they emigrated, and with their three children settled in British Columbia. The descendants of his two sons, Samuel (b. 1813) and Thomas Henry (b. 1817) have become prominent Canadian citizens.

(See Collateral Table "E")

4. *RICHARD GRUBB* (1835–1903). Great-nephew of the above, and eldest son of Samuel and Anna (née Watson) Grubb, of Cooleville, (who was killed in a hunting accident), and grandson of Richard Grubb of Cahir Abbey. He married an American, Frances Castle in 1876, and his son FRANCIS LECKY WATSON GRUBB (b. 1879) and his sons constituted the senior branch of the "Grubb of Tipperary" family.

(See Collateral Table "H")

5. *FREDERICK GRUBB* (1844–1919). First-cousin of the above, and third son of Richard and Maria (née Garrett) Grubb of Cahir Abbey. He was baptised as an adult in Cahir Church in 1863, where he was also married in 1871 to a local girl, Edith Going, and where all their eleven children were baptised. An accountant and miller, he lived in one of the Abbey Houses, and looked after the Abbey estate for his father, until its sale, they all left Cahir for California, where some of his family remain until this day. *(See Collateral Table "I".)* His wife died in 1905. There were five sons, and six daughters:

(i) William b. and d. 1875.

(ii) FREDERICK ERNEST, b. 1878. Certified Public Accountant. Educated Trinity Hall, Cambridge. He married 1906 *Hilda* (d. 1954), *dau. of Robert McClintock*, of Dunmore, Carrigart, Co. Donegal. They had three sons.

(1) *ROBERT GOING GRUBB*, b. 1906. He was married twice:
   (a) 1933 to *Dorothy Herrington*. They had one daughter—Roberta Lynn Grubb, b. 1938, m. Joel C. Uranga (U.S. Army) of Texas. They have one daughter.
   (b) 1955 to *Toni Elizabeth Kendall* of British Columbia. They have one daughter. Mary Ann Grubb, b. 1956.

(2) *FREDERICK ERNEST GRUBB (Junr.)*, b. 1910. He became a Commander in the Royal Canadian Navy; married 1941, *Carolyn King, dau. of Edward Burneat Robb*, of Moncton, New Brunswick, Canada. They have three sons:
   (i) RICHARD EDWARD GRUBB, b. 1941.
   (ii) DAVID McCLINTOCK GRUBB, b. 1944.
   (iii) JOHN BURNYEAT GRUBB, b. 1953.

(3) *RICHARD HENRY ALEXANDER GRUBB*, b. 1912. The Black Watch and 93rd Argyll and Sutherland Highlanders. He married twice:
   (a) *Lily Elizabeth Simpson* of Colchester (1931), and has one daughter, Patricia Grubb, b. 1932 R.C.A.F.
   (b) *Peggie Dackombe* of Faversham, Kent (1949) and has two sons and a second daughter:
      (i) *MICHAEL JOHN GRUBB*, b. 1952.
      (ii) *PATRICK ALEXANDER GRUBB*, b. 1954; and
      (iii) Maureen McClintock Grubb, b. 1950.

(iii) RICHARD, b. 1880, Barrister-at-Law. Trinity College, Dublin. He married twice:
   (a) 1910 to *Vera, dau. of Robert McClintock* of Dunmore, Carrigart, Co. Donegal (his sister-in-law). She died 1930. They had one daughter: Vera Grubb, b. 1913.
   (b) 1931 to *Theodora Augusta Todd* of New York. Two children:
      (i) *THEODORE CURTIS TODD GRUBB*, b. 1932. Educated University of California; m. 1952 *Maryanne de Malville;* one son:
      RICHARD GRUBB, b. 1954.
      (ii) Maria Caroline Roosevelt Grubb, b. 1936. She married 1957 James Harvey Denny of Santa Barbara, California.

(iv) REGINALD, b. 1882. Married 1913, *Edna Temperance, dau. of Joseph Riley*, of Virginia, U.S.A. He died 1957. No children.

(v) GEORGE CAMBRIDGE, b. 1888. Civil Engineer. Educated University of California; m. 1919, *Elizabeth Stanley, dau. of Blayney Maynard, Esq.* of Harsley Hall, Yorks, and had one son and one daughter:

(1) GEORGE CAMBRIDGE GRUBB, b. 1923. Civil Engineer. Educated Cornell University, New York, and Stanford University, California. He married in 1944, *Sylvia, dau. of Herman Work*, U.S. Army, of Virginia; they have three sons and two daughters:

   (i) DAVID GEORGE GRUBB, b. 1943.

   (ii) MICHAEL MAYNARD GRUBB, b. 1950

   (iii) PETER HERMAN GRUBB, b. 1957.

   Virginia Mary Grubb, b. 1948.

   Deborah Grubb, b. 1953.

(2) Elizabeth Stanley Maynard Grubb, b. 1927; m. 1950, Gerald Wayne Hedden. They have one son and one daughter.

The six daughters of Frederick and Edith Grubb, with the families into which four of them married are:

(vi) Maria Garrett, their eldest child, born 1872; m. 1904, William Alexander ARMFIELD, son of Tyrus Alexander Armfield, of Missouri, U.S.A. (d. 1944). She died 1957 having had one son (deceased) and two daughters.

(vii) Edith, their second child, born 1873; m. 1908, Professor Herbert STANSFIELD, son of Frederick Stansfield, of Whalley, Cheshire; they have one son.

(viii) Matilda Hardinge, their third child, born 1874; m. 1899 John Thomas HOLDCROFT of Co. Monaghan and California (died 1943); they have one daughter.

(ix) Ethel Ernestine, their fifth child, born 1877; m. 1905, Professor Alfred STANSFIELD, youngest son of Frederick Stansfield, of Whalley, Cheshire (d. 1944). She died 1942; two daughters.

(x) Olive Muriel, their ninth child, b. 1883. School Teacher.

(xi) Florence Claudia, their tenth child, b. 1885. Registered Nurse, of Walnut Creek, California.

   Frederick and Edith Grubb had 14 grandchildren, and 21 great-grandchildren.

6. NORMAN and PAULINE GRUBB. (*See* p. 164.) In 1957 they went to take charge of the U.S.A. and Canadian Headquarters of their two Missions—the W.E.C. and C.L.C. (World-Wide Evangelisation Crusade and Christian Literature Crusade).

Their home is at Fort Washington, with its 30-roomed mansion, built in imitation of a Scottish castle, with 70 acres of parkland. [1]

HISTORY has a strange way of repeating itself.

CASTLES influence character.

GRUBB CHARACTER has led these widely known and much-travelled Grubbs, BACK TO A CASTLE.

[1]Norman Grubb writes of their Castle in his Autobiography *Once Caught: No Escape* 1969), pp. 141ff.

ADDENDA II

(For the insertion of details of American and Canadian Grubbs)

BUT THIS I KNOW

by a great Irish Hymnwriter

I cannot tell how Christ will win the nations,
   How He will claim His earthly heritage.
How satisfy the needs and aspirations
   Of EAST AND WEST, of sinner and of sage.

BUT THIS I KNOW . . . All flesh shall see His glory,
   And He will reap the Harvest He has sown,
And some glad day His sun shall shine in splendour
   When He the Saviour, Saviour of the World, is known.

I cannot tell how all the lands shall worship,
   When at His bidding every storm is stilled
   Or who can say how great the jubilation
   When all the hearts of men with love are filled.

BUT THIS I KNOW . . . the skies will thrill with rapture,
   And myriad myriad human voices sing,
And earth to Heaven, and Heaven to earth will answer. . . .
   AT LAST THE SAVIOUR, Saviour of the World, IS KING

W. Y. Fullerton, 1857–1932.

227

to the

ENGLISH CIVIL WAR Provincial and Parliamentary Coins

illustrated on Plate VII *facing page 32*

Charles I Half-crown Exeter or Truro Mint 1644	Sixpence mintmark Anchor 1640	Shilling m.m. Triangle 1640	Half-crown m.m. (P) Issued by the Parliament 1643–4
Charles I Half-crown Shrewsbury Mint 1642	Crown Oxford Mint 1644	Newark XXX Pence (= half-crown)	Three-Pence (York)

Rv.: Relig Prot: Leg Ang: Liber Par

Half-Groat	Charles I Half-crown Oxford Mint 1644	Charles I (Irish) Ormonde Half-crown	Newark XII Pence (= shilling)
Penny	Penny		

Nec Aspera Terrent

The earliest Motto of the Grubb Family from their German days.

Difficulties neither daunt nor deter them

BIBLIOGRAPHY

GENERAL

A History of Ireland. (1936). Professor Edmund Curtis. Methuen.
Boutells Heraldry. (1966). C. W. Scott-Giles and J. P. Brooke Little F.S.A. F. Warne.
Encyclopaedia of Ireland (1968). Allan Figgis, Dublin.
England before and after Wesley. (1938). J. Wesley Bready, PH.D. Hodder & Stoughton.
The Geraldines, 1169-1601: An experiment in Irish Government. (1951). Brian Fitzgerald. Staples Press.
German Thalers, 1700–1800. (1965). T. S. Davenport. Spink & Sons.
The Golden Hive. (1966). Eleanor Fairburn. Heinemann. London.
Henry VIII. (1946). Francis Hackett. Reprint Society.
Henry VIII and the Reformation. (1964). Dr. H. Maynard Smith. Macmillan.
In Search of Ireland. (1961). H. V. Morton. Methuen.
Irish Castles. (1951). Harold G. Leask. Dundalgan Press.
Irish Families: Their Names, Arms, and Origins (1957). Edward MacLysaght, D.LITT. Hodges, Figgis & Co., Ltd., Dublin.
Irish Miles. (1947) Frank O'Connor. Macmillan.
Medal Collector. S. C. Johnson, M.A., D.SC., F.R.E.S. H. Jenkins & Co.
Munster. (1957). Sean Jeanett. Faber and Faber.
Seventeenth Century Tokens. (1858). W. Boyne, F.S.A. J. R. Smith, Soho Square.
Shield and Crest. (1960). Julian Franklyn. MacGibbon & Kee.
Short History of the English People. (1920). J. R. Green. Macmillan.
The History of Ireland in the XVIIIth Century. 5 Vols. Lecky.
The Spirit of English History. (1943). A. L. Rouse. Cape.
The Spirit of Ireland. (1953). Lynn Doyle. Batsford.
The Stranger in Ireland. (1954). C. Maxwell. Jonathan Cape.
The Suir from its Source to the Sea. L. N. McCrath. Clonmel Press.
Worship. (1936). Evelyn Underhill. Nisbet.

NEW ZEALAND

A History of New Zealand (1961). Keith Sinclair. Oxford University Press.
Brown Frontier (1967). C. W. Vennell. Bailey Bros. and Swinfen, Auckland.
Sir George Grey, K.C.B., 1812-1898. A Study in Colonial Government. (1961). J. Rutherford, PH.D., Professor of History at Auckland University, New Zealand. Cassells.
The Story of New Zealand. (1957). A. H. Reed. Phoenix House Ltd., London. (With 80 Plates and Illustrations.)
The Strangest War. The Story of the Maori Wars 1860–1872. (1962). Edgar Holt. Putnams.
Murder by Court Martial. (1967). Zoe Lambe. Robert Hale, London.

BIBLIOGRAPHY AND SPECIALISED

Amazon and Andes. (1930). Kenneth Grubb, F.R.G.S. Methuen.
Barbrooke Grubb. Pathfinder. (1924). Norman Davidson. Seely & Co.
Life of Edward Grubb, 1854–1939. (1946). James Dudley. Jas. Clarke & Co.
The Land Between the Rivers (1960). Henry C. Grubb, M.A.
Crypts of Power (1971). Autobiography of Sir Kenneth Grubb, K.C.M.G. Hodder & Stoughton.
Once Caught; No Escape. (1969). Autobiography of Norman Grubb, M.C. Lutterworth Press.
George Grubb, M.A. Collected Sermons. (Out of Print.)
Sarah Grubb: Some Account of her life, and extracts from her letters, etc. (1792). R. Jackson, Dublin.
James Nicholson Richardson of Bessbrook. (1925). C. Smith. Longman Green.
History of My Ancestors. Elizabeth Laverick. (Published privately).
Memories of Edmund Symes Thompson, F.R.C.P.. (1908). By his Wife.
The Diaries of Edward Pease, Father of English Railways. (1907). Sir A. E. Pease. Headley Bros.
Making of William Penn. (1930). M. R. Brailsford. Longmans.
In the steps of George Borrow. (1951). E. Bigland. Rich & Cowan.
My Clonmel Scrapbook. (1907). Edited by James White. E. Downey of Waterford.
History of Clonmel. (1907). Rev. W. P. Burke. Harvey & Co. for the Clonmel Library Committee.
Journals of John Wesley, A.M. 4 Volumes.
Richard Baxter: An Autobiography. (1931). J. M. Dent.
Serious Call to a Devout and Holy Life. (1906 edition). William Law. A.M. Methuen.
These Sixty Years: Story of the Keswick Convention. (1934). W. B. Sloan. Pickering and Inglis.
Twentieth Century Bishop: Rt. Rev. Bertram Pollock, K.C.V.O., D.D. Bishop of Norwich (1942). Skeffington.
Biography of Rt. Rev. Howard W. K. Mowll. Primate of Australia. (1960). Archbishop Marcus Loane. Hodder & Stoughton.
Diary of a Dean. W. R. Inge, K.C.V.O., D.D.
Dwight L. Moody, His Life and Twenty Sermons. W. R. Moody. Morgan & Scott.
History of the English General Baptists in the 17th Century. Adam Taylor (1818).
The Leadbeater Papers; Annals of Ballitore; and Letters from Edmund Burke (2 Volumes). (1862). Mary Leadbeater. Bell & Daldry.
Quakers in Peace and War (1923). M. E. Hurst. Swarthmore Press.
Quakers in Ireland. (1927). Isabel Grubb. Swarthmore Press.
Quaker Homespuns, 1653–1683. (1932). Isabel Grubb. H. R. Allenson Ltd.
Later Periods of Quakerism. Rufus M. Jones.
The White Seahorse. (1964). Eleanor Fairburn. Heinemann. London.
Athenae Oxoniensis. Printed for Tho. Bennet at the Half Moon in St. Paul's Churchyard. MDCXCI.

M.SS., Journals & Diaries, etc. now in possession of S. L. Grubb, Esq.,
    of Beechmount, Festhard.
    Ditto.   in the Friends Y.M. Library, Eustace Street, Dublin.
    Ditto.   of Colonel Alexander and Mrs. Sara Grubb.
    Ditto.   of Mrs. Watkins, formerly of Potters Bar Vicarage.
    Ditto.   of John Grubb, for 1786–7. Kindly lent by Mrs. M. Grubb.
Journal of the Friends Historical Society. 1918. Vols. XVI & XVI.
Peterborough Marriage Licences. Diocesan Registry, Peterborough.
Parish Registers of Cahir, Co. Tipperary, and of Ravensthorpe, Northants.
Burke's Landed Gentry of Ireland and *Kelly's County Directories.*
Victoria History of the Counties of England. Vol. VII. Wiltshire.
Wellington College Registers.

THE GRUBB REGISTER

(omitting those who died young)

FAMILIES CONNECTED BY MARRIAGE WITH THE GRUBB FAMILY

A

Alcock, *Eliza*, 86
Alexander, *Isabella*, 143
Allan, *Hannah*, 70, 75
Andrews, *Thomas*, 115
Arbuthnot, *Caroline Elizabeth*, 197
Armfield, *William Alexander*, 225
Arundel, *Nancy Mary*, 164

B

Balicourt, *Sebastian*, 174
Banfield, *Susannah*, 85
Barrington, *Charles*, 115
Bath, *Anne*, 164
Bayes, *Emma*, 188
Bell, *William*, 85
Bevan, *Mary Pauline*, 187, 196
Binney, *Alice Hannah*, 115
Bois, *Elizabeth*, 194
Boles, *Margaret*, 50
Bousefield, *Sarah Lee*, 174
Brenner, *Beverly*, 196
Britton, *Alice*, 164
Brown, *Sydney*, 85
Buchanan, *Ethel Elizabeth*, 148
Buckley, *Percy*, 148
Burlingham, *Elizabeth*, 100
Butler, *Eme or Elice*, 15, 25

C

Cameron, *Helen*, 148
Cambridge, *Miss*, 143
Campbell, *Ailsa Marjorie*, 199
Cannon, *James*, 40
Carlisle, *Frank*, 86
Carroll, *Isabella*, 133
Carroll, *William*, 132
Carleton, *Rachel*, 88
Castle, *Frances*, 132, 223
Chancery, *John*, 40
Chaytor, *Susannah*, 50
Chaytor, *Thomas*, 50
Clarkson, *Mary*, 132
Clibborn, *John Brarclay*, 70

Clifton-Brown, *Peter*, 199
Cook, *Joan*, 88
Coomber, *Mollie*, 101
Cox, *Frances Marie*, 193
Crichton-Stuart, *Margaret*, 157, 164

D

Dacombe, *Peggie*, 224
Dale, *Margaret*, 193
Daniell, *Stephen*, 147, 148
Davis, *Deborah*, 85, 100, 115
Davis, *Francis*, 85, 100
Davis, *Samuel*, 100
Davis, *William*, 85, 141
De La Bere (*Sir Richard*), 174
Denny, *James Harvey*, 224
Disney, *Esther Wemyss*, 164
Dunbar, *Marguerite*, 197

E

Evans, *Andrew*, 101

F

Fayle, *Anna*, 85, 223
Fayle, *Eleanor*, 50
Fayle, *Robert*, 71, 85
Fayle, *Thomas*, 85
Fowler, *Kathleen Eunice*, 148
Frame, *Sarah*, 101
Fraser, *Iain David*, 194
Fraser, *Louisa*, 133

G

Garrett, *Maria*, 132*ff*, 221
Going, *Edith*, 151, 223–225
Graham, *Rev. Arthur*, 132
Graham, *Rev. Wm.*, 133
Greer, *Sarah*, 50, 51*ff*
Gregg, *Dominick*, 70
Gripper, *Elizabeth*, 100
Gwynne, *Zoe Kathleen*, 197

GENERAL INDEX

A

ABBOT, Henry, 26
Abyssinia, 37, 210
Acton, Miss, 62
Adam, *Pastor*, 162
Aden, 221
Aeronautics, 193, 196
Aeronautics: Royal College of, 196
Africa (North), 194
Africa (South), 148, 159, 161, 164, 185, 187, 193–194, 199
Aitken, Canon Hay, 161
Albert Memorial Hall, 153
Alcock, Rev. Alexander, M.A., 86
Aldershot, 193
Alexander Family, 143
Alexander, Mrs. C. F. 77, 144 and *n*
Alexander, Isabella, 143
Alexander, Lord, of Tunis, 143
Alexander, W., *Bishop of Derry and Raphoe*, 143–144
Alexandretta, 188
Alexandria, 161
Allan, Hannah, 70, 75
Alps, 176
Amazonia, 24*n*, 158, 175
America, 13*n*, 14*n*, 24, 38, 43–50, 45 (*Map*) 59, 75, 82, 97, 103–104, 132, 142, 159, 189, 197, 218, 223–225
America (Central), 218
America (South), 24*n*, 40, 142, 164,
American War of Independence, 103
Amersham (Bucks.), 20*n*
Amoca, 172
Amsterdam, 20, 206
Anabaptists, 2, 15, 19–22, 30–33, 65, 144, 223
Andes, 24*n*, 175
Ancorns Creek, 44
Anglia, East, 96, 100
Anglo-Hanoverians, 6, 56, 90, 91 (*Plate iv*)
Anglo-Normans, 2, 115, 166, 174, 185

Annaghs Castle (*or Annis*), 2, 9 (*Map*), 27, 36–40, 53 (*Plate ix*), 223
Anner House, 82
Anner Mills (*Anners*), 51, 63*n*, 66, 70, 75, 82, 94–95, 100, 104, 120, 142
Annersley, Francis, 43–45, 48
Antipodes, 175
Antrim, Co., 148
Arabs, 220
Arachon, 193
Ardmayle, 39*n*, 115, 177, 198
Arethusa, H.M.S., 185, 188, 189
Argentine, 24*n*, 175–176, 199
Argyll & Sutherland Highlanders, 224
Army, 146, 149–152, 159, 165, 168, 170–173, 187, 192–194
Army Scripture Readers, 168
Arnhem, 194
Artists, 165, 188, 189
Ashby St. Legers, 13–14
Asia, 174
Ascent of Mary, 96
Assizes, 62, 63, 204, 208
Astronomy, 86, 98
Asylum, 84
Atkins Family, 185
Athlone, 168
Atlantic Ocean, 44–47, 160
Auckland, N.Z., 211, 215, 217
Audacious, H.M.S., 135*n*, 156
Augustine, 118
Augustinian Monks of Cahir Abbey, 126
Australia, 88*n*, 149, 151, 159–160, 162, 164–5, 170, 172, 173, 199, 210, 218*n*

B

BACH, 139
Balicourt, Sebastian, 174

R

RADCLIFFE, JOAN, 12, 18, 25
Radcliffe, Sir Richard, 12, 18
Radstock, Lord, 157
Ramillies, H.M.S., 189
Raphoe, 144
rapparees, 34, 39. (*See also high-*
wayman)
Rathcormuck, 61
Rathdrum, 179
Rathfarnham, St. Colomba's Col-
lege, 148
Rathronan, 47, 48, 52
Ravensthorpe, 2, 8, 12*n*, 13 (*Map*),
14, 16, *Chapter Three*, 27–30,
223
Raymond Le Gros, 2, (*Plate iii*), 8,
23*n*, 115
Red Cross Society, 198
Reformation, 11, 17, 28, 152
Regency Culture and Dress, 137–139
Regensbogen *Mine*, 6 (*Plate iv*)
Reider Alp, 196
Republicans, 97, 105
retirement, 102, 182
Rhine (R), 187, 193
Rhodes, 18
Rhodesia, University of, 199
Richard I, King of England, 126,
142
Richardson Family, 74
Richardson, Anna, 70, 120
Richardson, Alexander, 148, 150
Richardson, Lt.-Col. E. H., 70
Richardson, Harriet (*d.* 1930), 148,
150
Richardson, Helena, 70, 129, 130*n*,
132, 139
Richardson, Helena, 129, 130
Richardson, James Nicholson, 70,
121*n*, 130*n*, 138
Richardson, John, 148
Richardson, John Grubb, 70, 120–
122, 130, 130*n*, 138–139
Richardson, Jonathan, 148
Richardson, Major T. B., 181
Richardson, Richard, H. S., 148,
150
Richmond *Mills*, 85
Ridgway, Eliza, 124, 132, 146

Ridgway Family, 74, 75, 83, 124*n*,
125
Ridgway, Henry, 123, 124*n*, 132
Ridgway, Richard Grubb, 124*n*
Ridgway, Sarah, 71, 75, 87, 124
Ridgway, Thomas, 124*n*
riding (*horseback*), 39, 48, 54, 58–59,
61–62, 110, 118, 137, 176–177,
193, 197, 199, 205
Riffel Alp, 186, 196
Rigi, 221
Riley Family, 151
Robinson, Lady Hercules, 221
Robinson, Mrs. 153, 154
Rochester, 15
Roland, Madame, 97
Rolls, Hon. C. S., 193
Rome, 90
Rooke, George, 88
Rose Green, 208
Ross, Mr. and Mrs. W., 184
Ross, W. Munro, 184, 187
Ross, Maud (*née* Bevan), 184
Ross-on-Wye, 101
Roundheads, 14*n*, 27, 32–34
Royal College of Aeronautics, 196
Royal Artillery, 165, 167, 170–171,
173, 176, 193, 221
Royal Engineers, 186, 193
Royal Geographical Society, 175*n*,
218*n*
Royal Irish Rifles, 148
Royal Military Academy, 170, 192–
193
Royal Military College, 194, 210,
216
Royal Navy, 12*n*, 188–189, 197
(*Plate xxxvi*)
Royal School for Officers
Daughters, 184, 194
Royal Scotch Foot, 207
Rugby football, 172, 181
Rugby, 13–14, 115, 133, 198
Russia, 11, 64, 90, 149, 162, 197
Russian Squadron, 189
Ryan the Highwayman, 125

S

ST. ALBANS, 12, 196
St. Andrew's University, 199
St. Anne of Russia, 197